Essays on the Quest

Essays on the Quest

Dr Paul Brunton

RIDER

London Melbourne Sydney Auckland Johannesburg

Rider & Company

An imprint of the Hutchinson Publishing Group

17–21 Conway Street, London W I P 6 J D

Hutchinson Publishing Group (Australia) Pty Ltd
PO Box 496, 16–22 Church Street, Hawthorne, Melbourne, Victoria 3122
PO Box 151, Broadway, New South Wales 2007

Hutchinson Group (N Z) Ltd
32–34 View Road, PO Box 40–086, Glenfield, Auckland 10

Hutchinson Group (S A) Pty Ltd
PO Box 337, Bergvlei 2012, South Africa

First published 1984
© Kenneth Thurston Hurst 1984

Set in 11/12 Compugraphic Bembo
by Colset Private Limited, Singapore

Printed and bound in Great Britain by Anchor Brendon Ltd,
Tiptree, Essex

British Library Cataloguing in Publication Data

Brunton, Paul
  Essays on the quest.
  1. Religion—Philosophy
  I. Title
  200′.1   BL51

ISBN 0 09 155 340 7

Contents

'There is a life which is higher than the measure of humanity: men will live it not by virtue of their humanity, but by virtue of something in them that is divine. We ought not to listen to those who exhort a man to keep to man's thoughts, but to live according to the highest thing that is in him, for small though it be, in power and worth it is far above the rest.'

Aristotle

Introduction

These essays are culled from the files of the late Dr Paul Brunton. They are as fresh today as when he wrote them, and they come to us glistening with inspiration from that divine source which so often moved his pen. Paul Brunton died on 27 July 1981 in Vevey, Switzerland. Born in London in 1898, he wrote thirteen books from *A Search in Secret India*, published in 1935, to *The Spiritual Crisis of Man* in 1952. He is generally recognized as having introduced yoga and meditation to the West and for presenting their philosophical background in non-technical language.

His mode of writing was to jot down paragraphs as inspiration occurred. Often these were penned on the backs of envelopes or along margins of newspapers as he strolled amid the flower gardens bordering Lake Geneva. Later they were typed and classified by subject, then he would edit and weld them into a coherent narrative.

Paul Brunton had lived in Switzerland for twenty years; he liked the mild climate and majestic mountain scenery. Visitors and correspondence arrived from all over the world and he played an important role in the lives of many people.

'P.B.', as he is known to his followers, was a gentle man from whom an aura of kindliness emanated. His scholarly learning was forged in the crucible of life and his spirituality shone forth like a beacon. But he discouraged attempts to form a cult around him: 'You must find your own P.B. within yourselves,' he used to say.

Kenneth Thurston Hurst

1

The Mystery of Evil

It is not the writer's custom to criticize the critics or to respond to their rejection of his work. Human opinions are so varied, intellectual standpoints so wide apart and emotional temperaments so different, that on these grounds alone an author may expect at some time or other to receive notices ranging all the way from undeserved praise to undeserved vilification. Moreover, he has no special desire to defend his work. No sooner is a book published than he becomes increasingly aware of its faults and errors, its deficiencies and shortcomings. He is, indeed, so emotionally conscious of them that he deliberately refrains from thinking about his past literary work because of the regret that invariably accompanies the thought. Only when other people raise the subject and he has to deal with it in order to answer or help them, does he submit to the ordeal.

This attitude is partly due to the shift of standpoint and the advance in knowledge which fate somehow brings him soon after each publication. The fact remains that he is dissatisfied with his books and depressed by their imperfections. So, like Emerson, he trembles whenever someone writes appreciatively about them and sighs with relief when someone does not! All of which is merely a preamble to the statement that he is his own worst critic!

England's leading literary journal, *The Times Literary Supplement*, usually takes notice of this writer's books and favourable notice, too. But *The Wisdom of the Overself* probably fell into the hands of a new reviewer, if one may judge from the internal evidence of approach and the external evidence of style. Most of his space was taken up with critique of a few unimportant statements in the prefatory chapter, the rest with a quotation from the middle of the book, dealing with the problem of evil, together with an expression of the reviewer's opinion that this quotation – which he asserts is the author's summing up of the problem – lacks 'finality' and treats the problem 'indifferently'. The great bulk of the book's teaching and its leading ideas were left undiscussed.

He is grateful to *The Times* reviewer for drawing his attention to what, he humbly agrees, is an unsatisfactory treatment of an important theme, although he deplores the uselessness of the other remarks to readers who want to know what the book contains. The treatment is unsatisfactory not because he would now withdraw any part of it, but only because as it stands it is unequal and incomplete, covering no more than a part of its field. It needs to be coupled with those paragraphs in the chapter entitled 'The War and the World' dealing with the existence of unseen evil forces, and with those paragraphs in the preliminary volume, *The Hidden Teaching Beyond Yoga*, dealing with the need for a double philosophic and practical standpoint. Such a combination would more correctly represent the higher teaching about this problem, but even then would not fully represent it. In the following pages, therefore, the writer of both books has tried to bring forward what was there neglected and to lay more stress on what was there too briefly stated.

Indeed, the author goes even further and asserts that not only are there the visible and ordinary instruments of evil which are so apparent all around us, but also unseen ones – evil spirits, in fact. The fall into black magic or evil occultism in mystical malpractice is the attempt to control or injure others by psychic or mental means.

The Two Viewpoints

What is the true place of evil in a universe whose informing soul is itself a benevolent one? We cannot arrive at the truth about this if we consider it in artificial isolation, but only if we consider it as part of the divine order of the universe. Whatever happens today in the world, or shall happen tomorrow, it will not happen outside of the divine knowledge and therefore will not escape the power of the divine laws.

Although the presence of evil was traditionally justified to blind faith as being the will of God, the modern religionist is developing his thinking power. He is ready to accept the will of God, but at least he wants a more rational answer as to why this thing exists at all. Two viewpoints present themselves to him: the popular and the profound.

This problem defies rational solution if treated from the first viewpoint alone, but begins to yield if treated from both in combination. There is, indeed, no popular explanation of evil which could escape being riddled with criticism by a sufficiently sharp intellect. He must not rest satisfied with what experience and common sense tell him; he must also hear what metaphysical reflection and mystical revelation have to tell. For practical purposes he can get along with the first, but for philosophic purposes it is needful to add the second. In a wide balanced mentality the two views are not mutually exclusive but can be readily mated; in a narrow mentality they cannot even meet.

The materialist, the egoist and the shallow-minded, when brought face to face with these two ways of viewing the world, find them opposite and incompatible, markedly conflicting and hopelessly irreconcilable. They are like a carriage whose wheels simultaneously turn in opposite directions. But the philosophic student, with his fuller and better-balanced cultivation of his psyche, is able to let them exist side by side without splitting himself into two disconnected personalities. It is quite possible for him to synthesize them without developing a divided mind. Thus, his rational comprehension of the world unites perfectly in the well-rounded personality with his sensual experience of it; his mystical apprehension of life balances itself agreeably with his emotional reactions to it. Nothing is subtracted and nothing denied.

The understanding of this matter is darkened to our mind through failing to give ourselves the trouble of defining our use of this word 'evil'. We should refuse to deny or to admit the existence of evil before we have discussed the question, 'What do you mean by the term 'evil'?' When that has been achieved, we shall find that the evil from which we are to be saved is largely – but not wholly – within ourselves. What do we mean when we say that an event, a thing or a person is 'evil'? In *The Hidden Teaching Beyond Yoga* it was explained how words are strongly interwoven with the very stuff of human understanding. When we investigate the language in which our concepts take shape, we are investigating the very concepts themselves. We may then discover, in startled surprise, how important are the psychological influences exerted by words and phrases which have become standardized clichés devoid of definite meaning. We may note how the whole character of obscure problems becomes illumined. The origin of evil will be easier to elicit after eliciting its nature.

We may watch in the tropics the 'evil' frogs hunt 'good' glowworms, and the 'evil' snakes hunt 'good' frogs in their turn. Whatever creates a state of conflict inside or outside a living creature, and thus disturbs or destroys its happiness, is 'evil' to that creature. It may originate from some animal obeying its appetites, some human behaving wickedly or some violence of Nature. It may result from an event, an action or the relation between them. Although this is quite true, it is true only in a limited and relative sense. The fact is that each creature 'thinks' the evil of a situation.

When we ask why wild beasts should exist in the Universe, we are thinking of their effects upon other creatures including ourselves. We never stop to think why these beasts should not exist for their sake and for their own selves. What they came to be as a result of the action and interaction, the development and degeneration of the bright side of things, just had to be. The one was not intended exclusively to serve any species, any more than the other was intended exclusively to harm that species.

In the case of men, whatever is unpleasing to their human point of view, uncomfortable to their human selfishness, contrary to their human desires and painful to their human bodies, is usually regarded as evil. The evil in the world is only relatively and partially such, never absolutely and eternally. It is evil at a particular time or in a particular place or in relation to a particular creature. This principle of the relativity of ideas leads to strange results. One of the first is that something may be evil from the standpoint of an individual placed in particular circumstances at a particular time, but may not be evil from a universal standpoint. Charlemagne cut a way through benighted Europe with his sword for Catholic culture. But when that same culture became too narrow and too intolerant, the Turkish hordes who broke into Constantinople dispersed the classic texts so long hoarded in the Byzantine libraries, drove their keepers to Italy and thus released upon Europe new forces which greatly stimulated the Renaissance movement already in being. In both these cases 'evil' warfare produced 'good' cultural results. In our own lifetime we have seen atheistic evil launch its work of destroying decadent religion. But in the hands of a higher Providence, we are also seeing in the end that it was indirectly used to purify and thus truly promote religion.

The Divine Idea works itself out through human frailties as well as human virtues. In this sense evil is at times our teacher. It would be valuable to count the number of cases where trouble led to our own good and sorrow proved to be peace in disguise. After experiencing the darker side of life, we are in a better position to pass up to the brighter side to which it directs us. Before the war some of us long looked for a Messiah, but we wanted him on our own selfish terms. We wanted him to be soft and gentle – even sentimentally flattering towards us. We never dreamed that a precursor like Hitler might come instead, one utterly hard and mercilessly harsh, to punish us for personal materialism and national selfishness. We looked for redemption, but never dreamed that we might have to be redeemed by the terrible power of suffering born out of evil. One compensation for wartime sufferings caused by other men is that they awaken the minds of a number of people and put them on the path to finding out the meaning of suffering and of life itself. But so long as they persist in ignoring the relativity of ideas and set up their personal opinions or individual perferences as truth, so long will they continue to mislead themselves and others; so long will they unnecessarily protract their sorrows. The evil which appears in the first sight of events, may disappear with the second sight. This is because there is an ultimate rightness in the ordering of universal life.

Who is Satan?

'Evil is ephemeral. In the end it defeats itself. It has only a negative life. It represents the not-seeing of what is, the not-doing in harmony, the not-understanding of truth. Evil is, in short, a lack of proper comprehension, a too-distant wandering from true being, an inadequate grasp of life. When insight is gained and these deficiencies are corrected, it ceases its activities and vanishes. The mystic who penetrates into the profound core of being finds no evil there.'

This quotation from *The Wisdom of the Overself*, which *The Times* reviewer claims to be and criticizes as the author's 'summing up' of evil, was never intended to be a 'summing up' even then. But an adequate comprehension of the teaching calls for knowledge of the fact that its attitude towards evil is not exhausted by this quotation but is really twofold in character. The belief (which the reviewer seems to hold) in a satanic opposition is also, but in a different way, included in the author's own attitude. He does not deny but, on the contrary, fully admits the existence of individual forces adverse to spiritual evolution.

He does not question the presence of malignant entities and satanic powers.

There are evil forces outside man as well as inside him. These superphysical agents operate in the invisible world and, under certain abnormal conditions, intermingle with living human personalities to influence their thoughts and actions or to oppose their spiritual progress. The spiritual aspirant inevitably encounters opposition from these adverse elements and the evil forces move against him in a cunning way. However well-meaning his intentions in the beginning and however noble his ideals, he may yet be unwillingly and subtly influenced by their malignant power. If he succumbs to them, some of those he trusts betray him, his judgements turn out to be wrong, his actions mistaken and circumstances work against him. They lead from deed to deed, first by internal temptation but later by external compulsion, each involving him more and more in their toils and menacing him with worse and worse consequences. To escape each consequence as it arises, he has to commit fresh acts which drag him farther downwards. In the end he is caught by tragedy and overwhelmed by disaster. If we could trace apparent effects to their hidden causes, we would trace many a trouble to such adverse psychical forces of the invisible world.

World War II was an outstanding example. It had a psychical content even before its physical, visible start. Whatever it was politically and militarily, it was also a dramatic struggle between the forces of good and the powers of darkness. We may be sure that whoever tries to arouse hatred of the good and inflames anger against the True has lent himself to the dark forces of Nature. The Nazi hierarchs were possessed by foul demons, animated by malignant powers from the occult regions. They attempted to cover their own guilt by the old trick of malicious fabrication. There were entities other than human at work behind Hitler. He tried to make men turn into the most dangerous of all beasts by seeking to turn them into cunning animals devoid of moral discernment and debarred from higher reflection. There were wicked agencies, human but disincarnate, inspiring the Nazi movement. All were devilish: all were powers of the lowest hells. Hence the lies, oppression, cruelty, materialism, greed and degradation which they spread everywhere. It was not so much by their arrogant aggressiveness and violent brutality that the Nazis sought to crucify mankind. Rather it was by their denial of justice, their opposition to spirituality and their contempt for truth that they sought to nail the human race to the cross of unexampled sufferings. At the innermost heart of Nazism lay a foulness indescribably black and immeasurably worse than any plague which ever beset humanity. For it sprang out of infernal diabolic regions, out of a gigantic mass attack of unseen sinister forces hoping to destroy the soul and enslave the body of man. This dangerous incursion of evil spirits into our world's affairs on such a vast scale had never happened before. It can be said that humanity barely escaped the most terrible setback in its history. Had the Nazis won, every spiritual ideal would have been strangled, every spiritual value stifled. The inner justice of things foiled them, and mankind emerged – sore and wounded but safe and alive – from its great peril, only to find itself facing a further attempt of the same dark forces to dominate the world again, but using a different channel.

But all this does not place these opposing powers on a level of equality with the force of good in the universal struggle; they play their necessary roles and we need not regard them as unforeseen lapses or evil accidents in the divine thought. The evil forces are always aggressive because they must always try to destroy that which in the end will destroy them. The good alone will endure. It is in the very nature of evil beings, as of evil thoughts, to attack each other and, in the end, to destroy each other. Meanwhile, their powers are strictly limited and their opposition, when overcome, actually helps to develop the good in us. We need not hesitate to believe that the good will always triumph ultimately and *always outlive the bad*, that no kind of evil has an independent existence but all kinds are only relative aspects of existence. But this struggle and this triumph can exist only in each individual entity. They do not and cannot exist in the cosmos as a whole, because this is itself a manifestation of God. God's will alone prevails here.

Evil men and evil spirits do exist, but whether there is an independent principle of evil is another matter. Whoever believes in the eternal existence of God and admits the eternal reality of evil, will have to trace the latter to its source. If that source is a personality or a principle coeval and co-enduring with the universe, then it works its fiendish will in spite of God; then there are really two supreme beings. The logical demands of unity do not permit such an impossible conclusion. It deprives God of his much-vaunted omnipotence and represents a dualism which puts its thoughtful believers in a profound dilemma. If, on the other hand, he traces the source of evil to a lesser principle or

17

personality, he again puts them in a dilemma. For such conclusion leaves unexplained the question why God tolerates the existence of this dreadful entity instead of extinguishing every trace of evil from His Universe. If this were true, then God must share Satan's guilt! If, finally, he traces evil to man himself, then God, in letting him fall to his doom, is either ignorant of His creatures' misdeeds or else indifferent to them.

Just as philosophy says that the man-like conception of God is suitable only for immature intelligences, so it says that the man-like conception of evil personified under the figure of Satan is also only for immature intelligences. There are individual evil influences, individual evil spirits even, and they constitute at times an opposition to the aspirant. But the greatest opposition comes not from a creature called Satan; it comes from the aspirant's own heart, his own weaknesses, his own evil thoughts. The recognition of those unseen forces must not be allowed to occlude the recognition of his own primary responsibility.

It is not pertinent to take up the question of the nature of God's existence here, except to note that philosophy combines both the transcendental and immanental views. But any dualistic thought which admits both good and evil as separate, real and eternal forces in the universe, will always involve itself in these contradictions. And every doctrine is a dualistic doctrine which teaches that the primal forces in the world are two and not one. The orthodox and popular view, which holds that the divine power is forever fighting desperately against a satanic power, and that the latter is entirely independent of and eternally opposed to it, is dualistic. Therefore it is caught in these contradictions, too, yet it represents the most tenable immediate point of view. Philosophy, however, goes further and deeper than mere appearances and hence represents the ultimate viewpoint.

We are entitled to ask those who have banished spiritual values from their world view, what they have gained. No answer can hide the ugly fact of a world in the grip of evil and distress. Their failure to integrate spiritual reality into our view of life has produced the most unfortunate inner and outer consequences. It has produced a decade when the unheard-of crimes of unprincipled tyrants and the misfortunes of helpless masses dismayed and distressed all thoughtful, good-hearted people. This gloomy derogation of human dignity is the logical end of materialism, and it is for such reasons that those who can comprehend the momentous issues of the human race's destiny which confront it today must engage in the hard struggle against materialism as in a holy war. The war and the crisis constitute a tragic judgement on a society which was falling headlong into the abyss of such a wrong world view. Its present anguish and bewildered state show, to their shame, how little wisdom and how much frailty there still is in human beings. It demonstrates, too, that materialism has no future, for it cannot provide a sound moral basis for living or a hopeful metaphysical basis for thinking about humanity.

Because our generation has been violently confronted with and shaken by those shaded aspects of life, such as death and suffering, which most generations habitually ignore, it has either to consider them or to flee from them. The first course brings it to a vital religious feeling or a rebellious atheistic one. The second course plunges it into sensualism. This is the century of challenge. Humanity must choose between continuing in the old materialistic way of life or starting a more spiritual one. And unless the suffering of the war and crisis awakens a sufficient number of people spiritually, the outlook will be dark. The situation is still grave. We shall shortly learn exactly how far this awakening has gone. Events will not let humanity alone; they are forcing it against a blank wall from whence there is no escape. It must find a new and better way of life – or sink down and perish. It was written in *The Wisdom of the Overself* that humanity was walking on the edge of a precipice. The warning must be reiterated here that if it does not respond to the new call while there is yet time, its days of safety are numbered. The alternatives are clear. Humanity must either penitently enlarge its outlook to include the spiritual basis of life or continue to restrict itself to a sometimes open, sometimes camouflaged materialism. In the first case, it will save itself and its civilization; in the second, it will succumb to the evils bred by such materialism.

When we interpret these events in the light of philosophy, we observe that while men sought only a personal, a partisan or a group triumph over other men, instead of seeking for the triumph of good over evil and truth over falsehood, their affairs continued to move from one blunder and one misery to another. Such people naturally, but quite wrongly, apportion censure to other men or to untoward events or things. The political and social problems covered a still deeper problem. Those who made quick judgement on limited data, or those who believed that mind is a mere by-product of matter, could not perceive this truth. Amid all this clamour of tongues and systems,

19

individuals and interests, the fundamental issues became obscured and their essentially mental and ethical character remained unseen. The spiritual failure and political crisis of this epoch went deep before the war; neither its mind nor heart was capable of retrieving the one or solving the other. Its boasted progress was found to be surface-deep.

Philosophy rejects the esoteric Hindu views that the Universe is nothing more than an illusion, that its struggles are God's jesting sport or its birth God's blunder.

Yet it is wrong to say the Supreme creates evil. Man creates it; the Supreme merely permits it. If this were not so, man could claim freedom from personal responsibility for his wrong-doing. If man's individual will is included in, and subject to, the more powerful will of Nature (God), it still has the independence to choose the power to create and the freedom to act within set limits.

It is not inconsistent to grant that, in its immediate character, evil does exist and does have widespread range and formidable power, whereas in its ultimate character it is rather the absence of good. Experience testifies to that. But it exists as our human *idea* and in a relative sense. It has neither more nor less reality than any of our other ideas. Philosophy enunciates no new doctrine here. In the Middle Ages, Thomas Aquinas argued that sin is a privation of good. In earlier times, Plotinus argued that the very infinitude of God must therefore involve imperfections like moral and physical evils and that instead of infringing on the omnipotence of God, these imperfections really point to His infinitude. In the pre-Christian age, Plato transmitted a tradition which explained evil as the negation of God's positive and beneficent activity.

It is a long way and a trying one, but it is a fact that until men reach an advanced stage of development, they will not learn except by taking to themselves the teaching of suffering and the lessons of trouble by noting the miseries which follow in the wake of mistaken action and evil-doing. The results of past evil or foolish actions sooner or later confront them.

The terrible spectacle of organized hatred would alone be enough to make anyone cynically pessimistic about human nature. But when he realizes the monstrous extent of the evil in human character all over the world, and especially when he discovers its deep penetration in so-called spiritual circles, he must draw back appalled and affrighted for himself, despairing and hopeless for humanity. He must feel that the

Roman Catholic dogma of original sin is not far from practical truth, however distant from ultimate truth. Such a position as humanity's present one is filled with the gravest dangers and cannot continue much longer than a decade or so. If it is not soon brought to an end, the evolutionary forces will bring our pretentious human civilization to an end.

They took a man possessed by devils – Hitler – as a new Messiah, as a prophet of God. That Hitler did more in less time to shape the thought and life of millions for evil than any other man has ever been able to do for good, is sad proof that morality will fall sooner than rise and that spirituality is harder to come by than materiality. The Germans followed this Anti-Christ with a devotion and faith greater than they had shown to Christ.

Anti-Christ always takes the field before, during or after the hour destined for the appearance of the true Christ. But in our time this is not only true of spiritual – that is, religious, mystical, moral and metaphysical – issues, it is also true of the social images reflected from them. Because the swift movement of modern technique is compelling a parallel movement of modern nations towards a supranational world association, Nazism offered in advance its own selfish caricatured version of what such an association should be and tried forcibly to materialize it. Success would have prevented the establishment of a true world association. The Nazi version was quite simple. It consisted in the German python's swallowing up all the other animals and thus creating a union of them all! The Nazis had sufficient intelligence and willingness to appropriate some spiritual values by offering their materialist counterfeits. The startling fact is that they created a hideous travesty of leading ideas which have become timely for incorporation in the modern man's outlook on life. It is thus that they hoped to take advantage of the time-spirit to deceive him.

It may be asked, if evil is a relative and not an absolute thing, why do we call the forces which inspired the Nazis 'evil' forces? The first answer is that at the stage of ethical culture which the German masses had generally reached, that which should have been right to them was represented by the Nazis as wrong, while what should have been wrong to them was represented as right. The second is that malignant lying spirits did direct the Nazi movement from within . . . Why not work for self-aggrandizement alone if self be nothing more than the physical and egoistic person? Why not let war destroy a million men, women and children when they stand in the path to such personal triumph – if, sooner or later, they are doomed to perish forever anyway? Why not set up the acquisition of more and still more possessions by the most frightful means if successful acquisition of material things be the only sensible aim in a man's life? Why not bludgeon the brains out of every minister of religion, every student of literature, every preacher of ethics, every philosopher of spirit, every artist of exalted mood whose influence gives his followers the weakening idea that there can be a reality beyond this lump of flesh and its earthly environment? These were reasonable questions to the Nazi mind because it was filled with hostility to the divine in itself and with hatred of the divine in others. Hence, its worst postwar legacy to the world is prejudice, malice, suspicion, intolerance, envy, wrath, unbalance, greed, cruelty, violence and hatred – evils that are corroding the hearts of millions with terrible intensity. This is the dangerous emotional situation which Nazism has left to humanity. Never in history was there so much hatred and malice in the world. Never in history was there so much need for goodwill and mutuality among human beings. The situation shocks and dismays every true well-wisher of mankind. What lesson, therefore, does humanity now need to learn most? The lesson of pity, compassion. The need for more love and less hate in the world is obvious. Yet the external events and emotional movements of our time show more hate and less love. Where is our vaunted progress? The ultimate issue of all this trend in the pre-1939 world was the desolation and violence of war. The ultimate issue of it in the peacetime world may be disastrous in its own way. The younger generation has grown up in an explosive, selfish and materialist atmosphere. If the public tragedy and private emptiness of our time cannot turn them and enough of their elders towards a spiritual way of life, nothing can do so quickly enough. In that case, utter destruction will before long end our failing civilization.

For those who had eyes to see it was clear, even during the very zenith of Nazism, that one of its main historic tasks would be to quicken this process in Germany itself where Nazi forms collapsed altogether after a briefer existence still. This is because those forms were essentially too retrograde in such an age. They provided their adherents with all the illusion but little of the reality of progress. In this way they were poisoned offshoots from the true line of progress. Part of Hitler's half-conscious mission was to liquidate the old order of things and destroy world views which had lost their timeliness and serviceability. But although in this way far ahead of his times, in others Hitler was, of course, far behind it. He did not understand that the age of moral dinosaurs and mental pterodactyls was long past.

The prevalant state of materialism in the world and its consequent influence on human character may lead to something even more devastating than war. Nature might take a hand in the game. Within a couple of months, there were slain by the influenza epidemic just after the First World War many times more people than were slain during the four years of that war itself. The science and civilization, the culture and cities of Atlantis were erased from the earth's surface, engulfed by a vast mass of water which has since, during thousands of years' ceaseless rolling, washed its site clean of the ancient foulness. Through such cataclysms does Nature free herself from the obnoxious presence of evil men, purify her body from nests of corruption and defend herself against the vices which her own spawn seeks to plant upon her. Thus she returns to mankind the penalties of their own iniquities. When Nature's violence, as in earthquakes and cyclones, is so great or when fate's blows are so hard as to make men feel their littleness and helplessness, the instinct to turn to some higher power in resignation or petition arises spontaneously. Many in our age have been so stupefied by a hard materialism as to deny the reality of this instinct, but they have only covered it over. They cannot destroy it.

But the challenge has been dramatically made final, urgent and pointed by a new force which has been let loose in the world – the atomic and hydrogen bombs! The energy released by atomic disintegration is now in our hands. What was once the fantastic dream of a few scientists has become the awful reality of contemporary history. The new type of bomb has unparalleled effects. It can blast and burn a vast area with a thoroughness previously unknown; it can obliterate whole cities in a single raid by its tremendous concentration of incendiary and explosive power. It has outmoded all known military weapons and outdated many security problems. Its possibilities for mass slaughter constitute the major revelation of our times. It is significant that the atomic bomb did not appear until the end of the war against Japan and did not appear at all in the war against Germany. This points to the fact that if another war develops, this new kind of warfare has been reserved for it alone in fate's design and history's record. War must now either slay most of the human race altogether or slay itself through its own perfection. It is perhaps the most dramatic and the most visible form of evil in the whole history of mankind.

The order which humanity constructs itself for is, after all, the expression of its own spiritual perception or spiritual blindness. The new order will be no better if understanding is not better. All will fall into false hopes who fail to perceive the direct causal relation between the inner and the outer life, and who ignore the precise unfailing operation of the moral law. The widespread crises and calamities which have struck the world have aroused millions of people to lively expectations of an impending social change and universal renovation in the spiritual and material forms of society. These terrible distresses have caused a number of sufferers to engage in the quest of self-redemption. How large this number is nobody can yet accurately determine, but how small it must be in proportion to the total population anybody can begin to perceive.

Because fate permitted the tremendous consequences of nuclear power to be placed at the disposal of mankind at this precise juncture of history, we may be sure that there is a tremendous reason for it. That everything in this generation has been thrown into a state of crisis is therefore no accident. A higher will is guiding world affairs. This state could not have developed earlier, for then it would have been quite premature. It is karmically synchronized and inwardly connected with the grand turning-point in the human entity's evolution, with the shift away from the unbalanced immersion in physical externals and excessive attachment to the personality. How much human evil would vanish when men enlarge their outlook and belittle their self-centredness! The outer effects of this inner evolutionary movement are being everywhere greatly felt but nowhere clearly understood. The statement in *The Hidden Teaching Beyond Yoga* that humanity is approaching the threshold of adulthood means that, from the moment that the new evolutionary twist began, the human entity's ignorant, childlike development also began to come to an end. Hitherto, it had blundered about half-blindly in its adolescence and youth. Henceforth, it will receive knowledge and be able to move more consciously; it will also have to assume more and more of the responsibilities of spiritual maturity. When the present crisis eventually draws to a close, there will interiorly be released a divine influx and there will exteriorly manifest various high-grade spiritual teachers. The twentieth century will indeed be 'the century of enlightenment'. Thus, at first involuntarily and later voluntarily, man obeys the higher purpose for him of the divine plan. This purpose cannot but be fulfilled, for every thing in this universe works to that end. It does not depend for such fulfilment on his conscious co-operation, nor will it be thwarted by his blind opposition. He may work with it or oppose it. The first course will lead in the end to rejoicing, the second to suffering. It is not easy for him, constituted as he is, to take the wiser course. Yet evolution will force him into it by degrees, easy or not, for the world is a rightly ordered one.

The movement of mankind is cyclic and in this moment when the wheel must take a fresh turn, the two universal forces which forever struggle with each other – the force which elevates man and the force which degrades him, the evolutionary and the adverse elements in Nature – are meeting in a tremendous grapple whose tension was unheard-of before. Whoever fails to perceive that this is the fundamental problem or whoever, perceiving, seeks to evade it, contributes to the responsibility for the sequence of events. If we do not understand the human and superhuman forces which are at work in the world, we shall not understand how rightly to deal with the world crisis itself. We must arrive at a consciousness of what direction inevitable historic forces are taking beneath visible events; and we must learn to interpret aright the various currents and cross-currents which have been started by the post-war period.

The nuclear discoveries force humanity to choose between the two alternatives: real acceptance of the moral law or virtual self-destruction. This is the divine working. Today is indeed a fateful time. Today we all live with such terrible bombs invisibly suspended over our heads! Only a drastic change in moral attitudes can effectively meet their dangerous challenge. And what else is this except a choice between cultivating a greater self-discipline or clinging to an outmoded selfishness; a decision between an alliance with the sacred presence or a continuance of indifference to it? If we fail to make a right choice, then it will not be long before civilized life on this planet comes to an end.

The course of events after the Second World War cannot resemble the course of events after the First World War. Everything is against it. For this time an ultimatum confronts humanity, a final challenge to inaugurate a new and nobler epoch or else largely perish from the earth. The alternatives have been clearly presented for us to choose between. There is no middle way.

2
The Adventure of Meditation

It has been customary for learned professors of the metaphysics of psychology to teach that consciousness always implies a relation to an object because it is always directed towards something. While this is true, it is true only of the level of ordinary experience. It is no longer true on the level of the highest type of mystical experience. Here consciousness can exist without any relation at all for it can be directed towards its own self. This is the one experience which occurs in the mind and which possesses absolutely no correlation with, nor determination by, what is happening in, to, or outside the body at the same time. Therefore, it is itself a demonstration of the falsity of the materialistic view of man. The world of ordinary experience is not the last possible one. There is a deeper and diviner world, or in Wordsworth's good phrase, an 'unknown mode of being', open to man's adventuring. He has not yet attained true self-consciousness; he lives too completely on the lower level of his existence for that. It is indeed time he took full possession of himself.

But the external encounter with mystical statements is one thing, the personal experience of mystical states is quite another. Mystical theory has to justify itself in mystical experience. This it is quite able to do. Indeed, its practicality can best be proved by such experience. It will then be found that it cannot be easily disposed of as chimerical. For the experience of thousands of men throughout history, situated in every station of life, has confirmed the reality and attainability of the transcendental state. However, by contrast with the total number of people in the world, it is relatively only a few sensitive persons who have heard these mystical overtones of human existence. Yet we should not regard the mystic as a highly specialized type of human being. He is like ourselves but has had the vision and patience to follow up an act of faith with a long-drawn series of active experiments to test the truth of that faith. If one man has touched this higher consciousness, all men may touch it. The prerogative is not exclusive but inclusive, not personal but common.

There is something in us of which we are not normally conscious. It is only at rare moments that we become aware – and that dimly – of a second self, as it were, of a nobler and serener self. We may have experienced such an uplift for only a few minutes but we will be haunted for ever afterwards by a sense of its tremendous importance. For we sense that we have then been in contact with something other than our ordinary self, sublimer than our ordinary self, yet despite that somehow related to it. Those of us who have passed through such an inspired mood, who have felt its serenity, tasted its power and obeyed its monitions, know well enough that only then have we been fully alive. Against the adamantine fact of our own overwhelming experience, the barbed arguments of others' scepticism avail nothing. There is no substitute for it. It is beyond all intellectual scholarship, above all religious rites.

This is indeed nothing else than the recognition of the 'soul'. The soul is most certainly there but if men do not turn inwards and attend to it, then for them it is not there. But really it is always there and the failure to recognize its existence is really the failure to turn attention away from the endless multitude of things which continuously extrovert it. This is why meditation, which is the art of introverting attention, is so needful. By means of our own mind, we can discover the soul. The introverted consciousness, turned away from five-sense activity to contemplate itself, first feels the presence and later becomes aware of the divine mind behind it. Therefore, the practice of mental introversion, or meditation, is quite essential on this quest.

We cannot recapture those glorious moments of recognition, yet we cannot forget them. This tantalizing situation imposes a restlessness and disquiet upon our feelings, which will never be assuaged unless and until we take to the quest. If we would be inspired by the Spirit at all times and in all places, we must first let it inspire us at set times and in set places. This is one justification of meditation. For all inspiration rises out of the inward deeps of our nature. We cannot compel it, but we can invite it. We cannot command it, for it commands us. The best way, therefore, to become inspired is to trace it out intuitively to its source, that is, to the divine self within us. Meditation will help this unfolding of latent intuition for it is itself an intuitive process.

27

Mysticism is a territory with which the average man is quite unfamiliar. He enters it, if he does so at all, with a certain uneasiness and
a certain hesitancy. Consequently it is a common habit for ignorant
critics to sneer at the mystic, who cultivates the power of introspection, as being morbid. But the fact is that if he is a philosophic mystic,
he will become a victorious master of introspection rather than its
morbid victim. Whoever, by steady practice, has succeeded with the
processes of meditation, becomes a living testimony to its indubitable
worth. He gives in himself a demonstration that its promised results
can be realized, that it is not a wild dream or fanciful abstraction. If we
have never before practised the art of meditation, surely we cannot use
our time to better purpose than to begin doing so now. Thus, we will
introduce a new rhythm into our life which will eventually assist us in
every imaginable way, which will make possible the improvement of
our character and capacity, our ethics and consciousness, our understanding and peace, our intuition and sometimes even our fortune.
Faithfully practised and over a sufficient period of time, it will amply
repay the effort given and will confer benefits for which many are
longing but few are finding. There is also the testimony of history,
though because of its confused character our iconoclastic age may deem
this of little account. The yoga system was being taught and practised
beside the Ganges long before Rome had reached its heyday. The
Quaker method of silent 'waiting on the Lord' has been practised
during the modern era in English villages and American cities. A
hundred different forms of mystical technique may be gathered from
mysticism's archives by the student who has the time to do so. Out of
this confused collection of ideas it is still possible to extricate some
praxis, definitely common to all of them, for a methodical cultivation
of the inner life.

A more precise and less poetic description of the art of meditation
than is usually given would better assist the Western novice. Why
should there not be a science of its technical side as already there are
sciences of the technical aspects of so many other arts? The following
pages are one contribution towards the attempt to formulate such a
scientific statement.

The need for solitude and time to cultivate the inner life, in both its
metaphysical and mystical phases, is the first imperative. Solitude is
needed because the presence of others definitely disturbs the emptying
process. Time is needed because the mind is habitually filled with

thoughts of the outer world; it is essential totally to empty it of them for a while – regularly, habitually and deliberately. Without a determined use of willpower it is, however, hard for most persons to get solitude or find time.

If the one requirement develops partly out of the aspirant's need to be able to concentrate thought without interruption, it also develops partly from the restless mental auras which most people carry about with them. They themselves shrink from being alone and naturally introduce an antipathetic influence wherever solitary meditation is being practised. Perhaps their terror of solitude arises because it makes them conscious of the spiritual aimlessness and intellectual vacuity of their sojourn on earth. The fear of being alone simply means that a man has no inner life at all. The scale of values which lists solitude as a frightful evil to be avoided, or considers the desire for it as an eccentric or even antisocial trait, is materialistic and stupid. The mystic who has learnt the art of creative solitude can hear a mental voice in its inner silence. Thus for him the loneliness which is maddening for some is enlightening.

For the other requirement, for a certain period each day there must be a separation from all usual physical labours and intellectual activities, a period wherein the aspirant can become and remain bodily still and mentally quiet. He must set apart a little time once or twice a day for meditation, just as he sets apart some time for eating food. This is indispensable to achieving spiritual progress. It is quite practicable for most people to create a routine which, whilst satisfying the need of withdrawal for meditation, nevertheless would not interfere with worldly activities and responsibilities.

It is needful periodically to put aside the things of time so as to seek the timeless, to isolate oneself from the outward world so as to seek an inward one. The psychological purpose of such isolation is to create a new habit and a new attitude. The habit is meditation. The attitude is introversion. The aspirant is led to the hard task of re-educating his powers of perception, understanding and attention. These powers have to be cultivated through a series of regular exercises. This involves self-training in definite work and a long progressive apprenticeship. Meditation is an art which has to be learnt by repeated practice like the art of playing a piano. It comes naturally to virtually no one. Its technique requires a skill which has to be learnt like that of any other art.

Here the habit-forming tendency of the mind can be an excellent aid. He will gain more by exercises regularly practised over a period of, say, six months than by the same exercises done in fits and starts over the same period. Consequently, a fixed time of the day should be appointed for them. The ideal rhythm would be to meditate three times a day in coordination with the rhythm of the sun's movements – at dawn, noon and dusk. But he could not arrive at this all at once. He could best start with a single period and continue with that for months, or even years, until he feels ready to advance and add a second period to it. He will have to work at these two periods, be they dawn and dusk or noon and dusk, for a considerable time before the inner prompting is likely to tell him to take the further step and add the third period. Even then it may not be possible for him always to adhere faithfully to the programme thus laid down. Social necessities, for instance, may compel him to leave out some period or other almost every week. Hence, he must do his best within the limits of his personal circumstances.

Situated as the average Western man usually is, however, a single meditation is as much as he can conveniently practise each day. This will be enough and satisfactory progress can be made on such a basis. If sunrise or sunset hours are not available for mystical practice, then he may adjust its timing to suit his own convenience. Although the general rule is that meditation is much easier and more effective immediately before a meal, this rule need not always be rigidly followed. If, for example, it is more convenient to practise after partaking of the first meal of the day and if this breakfast be a light one, that will not be a hindrance; or if at any time of the day there is a genuine feeling of hunger, it would be better to satisy this feeling first and then try to meditate, rather than to be disturbed by it during the practice period. The rule about selecting a time before meals for meditation does not apply to advanced students. In their case, if a contact with the higher element is made during practice, and the latter is then stopped to partake of food where domestic convenience, social necessity or other circumstances place the time outside their control, they may if they wish resume meditation after the meal and will usually find that the contact is quickly and easily regained.

It will take some time for the mental agitation created by getting immersed in worldly business or personal affairs to subside. Until this happens, the aspirant cannot proceed with the positive work of meditation but rather must engage in the merely negative task of clearing out those distracting memories. This is one reason why in the Orient the morning period is recommended for such practice. At the beginning of his day the thoughts and emotions are still undisturbed, hence withdrawal into their centre is then easier. Some, however, may find the morning – with its anticipation of activities yet to be started – unattractive for this purpose and may regard the very fatigue of a hard day's work as an inducement to relax in the evening and seek inner peace. The writer's own rhythm, which developed to accommodate his circumstances as a busy, hard-working man, is as follows: every morning he remembers the higher purpose of his life in prayer, be it only for two or three minutes. Every evening he withdraws, if he can, in an hour-long meditation.

If the regular hour for meditation occasionally proves inconvenient, it may be postponed to a later time. Should this be impossible, the practice may be abandoned for that day. If it is possible to hold enduringly to the full period previously laid down as desirable and available for such exercise, this will help to create an advantageous habit. But if on any particular day the fatigue becomes intolerable, then also it will be better to abandon practice for that day. Aside from these fixed times, or perhaps in displacement of them, the intuitive call to abandon every physical labour and every intellectual activity will recur again and again. He should obey it. In the very midst of business affairs or daily work, he may have sudden lapses into inward abstraction. These will ordinarily be quite brief and definitely should be kept so. But they are worth cultivating wherever and whenever they happen to come. If this is done frequently and faithfully, the power to meditate increases.

Although no universally tenable duration may wisely be fixed, for it will always depend on individual circumstances and personal aptitudes, nevertheless it may be said that in most cases full and perfect concentration for two-and-a-half minutes, or full and perfect meditation for forty-two minutes, is quite enough. The preliminaries of clearing all distracting thoughts out of the mind are not included in these figures. The advanced practitioner who is able to enter the third degree, contemplation, is by the tradition of the hidden teaching – both in his own and in society's interests – advised to limit this delightful experience to twenty-six minutes. But as already stated, a rule for all men at all times and in all places would be unwise. The apprentice meditator is easily fatigued and will best proceed by setting himself easy tasks and short periods. These can be increased gradually as and when the inner prompting bids him do so. Whenever the aspirant has advanced to the point where he intuitively feels that a little more time devoted to these exercises would yield great results, he should follow the leading and seek out ways and means to add a quarter-hour, twenty minutes and so on. This usually happens only at a certain stage of his progress and should be linked to that stage.

'I often think how tenuous is the thread that holds our thoughts together. Hunger, thirst, heat, cold – a touch of any of them and all the aesthetics . . . vanish as by a wand.' So writes Robert Gibbing in his travel book, *Coming Down the Wye* . It is precisely this dependence on externals which makes it necessary for the aspirant to shape them into a cooperative rather than let them remain in an obstructive form. He must not be hampered by the physical apparatus of meditation, but neither must he neglect it. Too much light, for instance, is disturbing to meditation. In the daytime, the window curtains should be drawn. In the evening, city dwellers will find that indirect or shaded electric lighting is best.

The first point to be attended to is the place where he proposes to practise. It should be one where he can remain undisturbed for the chosen period. Wherever this is possible, the place should also be rural rather than urban, but freedom of choice is seldom available here. We have only to contrast the soothing tranquility of country life with the jarring bustle of city life to realize where the mystic can best attain his purpose. Life in a large city, with traffic constantly passing, is not conducive to meditation. Forests are particularly friendly to the aspirant seeking the right atmosphere for deep, peaceful meditations; gardens to the aspirant seeking happy mystical ecstasies.

The next point concerns the body. A straight, upright spine with the head erect and in line with it often helps to keep the meditator's attention alert and gives more force to the concentration. He should try to cultivate the habit of sitting during the period as steadily as a figure in a tableau. At first he will find it hard even to keep physically still for the period of practice, harder yet to keep mentally still; but the old habits of being fidgety or restless do yield eventually to such endeavours. However, it is absurd to elevate this particular suggestion into a rigid universal dogma, as many yogis do. The importance which they attach to a particular bodily posture during meditation is an exaggerated one. They insist on a perfectly erect spine as the prerequisite to success. Yet the Sufi mystics in the Near East and Iran have meditated for a thousand years with head bent towards the chest or with spine so curved as to bring the face close to the knees, or even with a swaying rhythmic forward-and-backward movement. They have not found this a bar to success and have produced attainments fully equal to those of the yogis. Ralph Waldo Emerson, who was the equal of most Oriental mystics and yogis in mystical apprehension and moral reach – and unquestionably the superior of many in intellectual attainments and psychical balance – used a rocking-chair at his writing table. Its rhythmic rise and fall helped his work. Now it could have done so not during the physical act of writing – for that would have been interfered with – but only during the intervals of contemplation between such acts. Therefore he was helped and not hindered by its movement. Thirty years ago the writer personally could not obtain the mystical trance except by lying on his back in bed. Ten years later, that was the one posture which effectively prevented him from obtaining it! Today it makes no difference whether he sits erect, lies recumbent or droops the head – the concentrated thought of the Beloved is enough to bring the mind unhindered into quick union with the Beloved.

What is the moral of this? The first is that the *thought* is what matters most, and what happens inwardly in mind and heart is more important than mere outward activity. Why do the great Oriental religions like Islam, Zoroastrianism and Hinduism prescribe ablutions before prayer? The real intention is to ensure freedom from the mental disturbance resulting from an unclean and hence uneasy body. There is no mystical virtue in cleanliness. Some of the most reputed saints in the West and fakirs in the East have been physically dirty. Many lamas in Tibet do not bathe for months at a time. The real value of cleanliness lies in removing a possible hindrance from mental concentration during prayer. Therefore, all rules relating to the body in relation to prayer or meditation, including those concerning its posture, should not be overrated, idolized or made coercive.

The second moral is that each individual should choose the bodily posture which best suits him at the time, or which he receives an inner prompting to adopt, and not torment himself trying to conform rigidly to some system when he finds that system uncomfortable or impossible. The more he can quieten his body and keep it from fidgeting, the better his concentration will become and the sooner its development will proceed. Comfortably seated, adequately relaxed, with nerves and muscles tension-free, his fleshy house must be kept as still as its mental tenant will, in the highest stage, one day likewise be.

He has accomplished his side of the task when he can sit motionless for the prescribed period without moving a limb and without any other signs of bodily fidgeting or mental distraction.

It is now necessary to inquire into the nature and object of the concentration here required. Those who equate the word with what ordinarily passes under its name are both wrong and right. It is true that many people who have never even heard of yoga, such as business executives for example, show a well-developed quality of concentration in their work. But this does not bring them any nearer to the knowledge of the inner self. On the contrary, they use their concentrative power to bind themselves closer to spiritual ignorance, because they use it to sink more strongly into attachment to external things and, quite often, into the belief that matter is a reality. The kind of concentration inevitably practised by a business executive is the same in some ways, but vitally different in others, from that deliberately practised by a mystic. The one is usually animated by a desire to retain or increase his earthly possessions; the other by a desire for his higher self to take possession of him. The one clings throughout to the intellect's working; the other is glad to let it lapse entirely into stillness at a certain point. The one is concentrating on external things of which he can form concrete images in his mind; the other is concentrating on abstract concepts which eventually rise to the imageless plane. That is, the one often extroverts his mind and the other always introverts it – an entirely opposite process. The mystic's effort should be to penetrate more and more into his own conscious being. During the earlier phase of this meditation there is a double endeavour, paradoxically one to forget and the other to remember. On the one hand, he has to strain continually to let go of his earthly self and forget it. On the other hand, he has to strain equally hard to take hold of his higher self and rediscover its existence, that is remember his origin.

All ordinary concentration concerns the *form* side of life, not its *essence*. The mystic may not indeed possess a greater concentration than the other is able to show at his best, but by giving it *inward* direction he uses it to detach himself from externals, to weaken his belief in matter's reality and to become spiritually self-aware. The antennae of his mind must reach out towards that which as yet he can neither feel nor see. This first movement in the mystical exploration of the human consciousness is the sense in which philosophy uses the word concentration.

34

When the mind stops working, the senses automatically follow into inactivity. When the mind's power is completely stilled, as in sleep, we cannot see, hear, feel, taste or smell. Hence, mentalism says that the mind is the real experiencing agent. Mysticism takes advantage of this scientific fact to evolve a technique whereby thoughts may be brought under full control or even suspended, the sense-reports dimmed or even banished, but yet the mind's power of self-consciousness may be kept alive. The outgoing tendencies of the self are called in through a deliberate effort of will, the attention is gathered up and its habitual direction reversed through introversion, so that the senses' reports become somewhat blurred. Hence, the first working principle of yoga is the diversion of attention and interest from outward things to an idea, a feeling, a series of thoughts or a mental image which fill the void thus created. When thoughts are continually fastened to the senses, they keep up a restless rhythm of attraction and repulsion, of pleasure and pain, which imposes itself between us and stable peace. These minutes of mental quiet must be consecrated to suppressing the outgoing direction of thoughts, to turning them inwards and finally to interning them in their ineffable source.

In your innermost being you are already as divine as you are ever likely to be. Hence, no interior training can give you what you already possess, but a suitable training can help to give you the *consciousness* of what you possess. No practical system can develop a soul for you, for it is already there; but an adequate system can lead you into the awareness of it. And among the meditation exercises which must necessarily stand foremost in such a system, no single one is absolute and indispensable. There is no universal formula for the practice of meditation suited to all men at all times. It is not advantageous to the aspirant to repose in the bed of one formula during his whole lifetime. The philosophic ideals of a balanced development and an equilibrated personality would alone forbid it. On the contrary, he will find it necessary to use different exercises at different periods of his mystical career.

The mystical course passes through a spiral-like ascending rhythm so that if, for instance, he began by meditating on defects of character and later dropped that for a more abstract topic, he will one day return to his former practice again; but this time it will be from a higher standpoint which will yield correspondingly more important gains. He may fix his attention on mental pictures or on abstract ideas, on specific themes or on vague feelings, on keen rational thinking or on the rejection of all thinking whatsoever. All these exercises have one and the same objective. All are approaches to one and the same psychological state. If the approaches differ, this is only because their points of departure are different. We must smile indulgently at those who insist that their particular method is the only effective one, as we must smile tolerantly also at those who limit truth to their small conception of it. Philosophy does not say that the aspirant should not follow such a method, but that he should not follow it to the exclusion of all others. A method or technique which is good for one person may not be good for another. And the methods which well suited the ancient mind may be ill-suited to the modern one, while the conditions laid down in former times may be inadequate to the present time.

But whatever exercise he adopts, let him remember four indispensable points. First, his labour must seek to eliminate all thoughts except the thought of its own theme. Second, the more interested he becomes in what he is thinking of – yes, even the more excited he becomes about it – the more successful his concentration becomes. The converse of this is also true. Third, the concentration must pass from thinking about its chosen object in a logical way to entering into the object in a fixed, settled way. Fourth, if the first step is to get a thorough grip on his thoughts and feelings, that is to achieve concentration, then the second step is to elevate them above all worldly activities and desires, that is to achieve meditation. That meditation begins well which begins by fervent prayer or ardent worship. Man must approach the divine withinness of his own self with all possible reverence, putting away the soiled shoes of worldly cynicism at its threshold.

Real meditation is an intuitive process. But the tensions that prevail in the mind usually prevent this intuition from being felt, and still more, from being followed even if felt. If he is going to carry on with the same thoughts, the same cares and the same hopes which preoccupied his busy hours, he might as well continue with what he was doing before the meditation hour. The first advantage – as it is the first necessity – of meditation is that it shall concern itself with something entirely different. It must lift him out of the stream of personal life. It must, in short, start and end with one theme: the Overself. Hence, he must begin to meditate by withdrawing his thoughts from his own affairs and those of the world, fixing them instead on the object of his quest – the Overself. During these intervals he should cultivate the capacity to place his worldly business at a distance and to calm the outward-rushing emotions. When he 'goes into silence', when he sits down to meditate, he should first clear all the day's business or occupations out of his mind. When he enters the meditation chamber, he should let the door shut completely not only on the outside world but also on that inside world where trivialities, routine, business affairs, angers, resentments, irritations and passions are native inhabitants. Equally so, he should let the past go and disdain the future. He is there to engage himself in a holier business than that in which the world usually engages, to follow a diviner occupation than the personality's fated round and to lift his thoughts to higher levels than the wonted one. The renunciation required of him during this period is both external and internal: it must indeed be total. The mother must put away her children as though they had never been born. The scholar must forget his books as though they had never rested on his shelves. The manufacturer must travel far from his factory as though it belonged to a dead past. The worker must join the ranks of the unemployed as though he had never been elsewhere. It often happens that failure in meditation is caused by this failure to detach thoughts from the personal affairs of everyday routine. The first remedy is to choose a theme which in itself holds sufficient interest to keep his thoughts tethered to it. The second remedy is rigidly to transfer attention back to this theme every time he becomes aware of having strayed.

In theory, the attention ought not to deviate for a single second from the thought upon which it is being held. In practice it will certainly do so, for ancient habit has made it restless, intractable and dissipated. How weak man has become is shown by his widespread incapacity to pass even a half hour in uninterrupted withdrawal from the affairs of his personal individuality and in unremitting communion with his higher individuality. Concentration inexorably demands that the mind shall not think of twenty different things and people in as many minutes. Yet as soon as anyone sits down to meditate, a motley crowd of thoughts will batter at the gates of his consciousness. No one except the experienced person, who has practised for some years and practised with regularity, determination and understanding, is likely to be free of this nuisance. These distractions are so persistent and so troublesome that they drive many, if not most, beginners into hopeless despair or utter boredom and so ultimately drive them away from meditation exercises altogether. How many people have had this time-wasting experience in meditation: they think for a moment or two about the spiritual theme they have assigned themselves, but it is soon dropped or crowded out by a host of irrelevant thoughts, memories and anticipations – mostly of a worldly nature. They finally rise with relief from this irksome effort as soon as the allotted period ends. How often must they wait for the feeling of divine contact only to find at the end of the meditation period that it has again failed to manifest itself! How often have they begun with expectancy only to end with despondency as this tantalizing elusiveness recurs yet again! If others have found the divine self by turning inwards, they themselves have been unluckier and found only irresponsive emptiness.

The aspirant must be willing to go through these boring preliminaries and endure the depressing unease of his early experiments. There is no escape from them at his present stage. During the meditation, most of his time is frittered away in fighting his mental restlessness and emotional distraction. As thought after thought encroaches upon his attention, he must try to brush each one away as it appears and keep himself vigilant in this matter. It will require a kind of grip upon himself, an inner reserve which says, 'Thus far but no farther.' It is a strenuous exercise to keep the mind in undistracted and undisturbed concentration upon the quest of the free self. He is habitually so active, so restless and so extroverted that the reversal of his ways inevitably meets with stiff and stubborn resistance. Even for the many persons of moderately successful advancement in the art, meditation is not outright smooth sailing. Alas! There are times for them, too, when the meditation period is filled with desert-like aridity, leaving thoughts restless and emotions bored. However, even such periods are not really wasted but teach them humility and patience. Although each practice period has no longer to surmount the natural inertia of the extroverted mentality, it still has to overcome anew not only the inner resistance of a turbulent mentality – although this will be far less than with the unpractised person – but also the added resistance of alien thought-conditions and emotional strains temporarily 'picked up' during the day's contacts and meetings with others. This, indeed, is one of the added reasons why students of yoga in the East take to solitude and avoid society. All these resistances evoke shadows of depression, even despair, but they can be overcome by using the sword of *patience* to pierce them. So, unless they can bear the fatigue no longer, they should not impatiently abandon the practice on that occasion as being useless, but should persist – trying the effect of a prayer to the higher self to come to their help. After some minutes, or perhaps a longer time, the resistance may melt away of its own accord.

Few of those who sit down to unroll the coloured carpet of meditation really succeed in entering the state of mental quiet. That is a positive and later result, whereas the earlier one is negative. The struggle to keep the attention fixed during the preliminary part of a meditation period is intense. Many become disheartened by its difficulty. Yet the more they attempt it, the easier it certainly will become in time. The disciple should recognize that, just as it often takes a certain period of time satisfactorily to embark on some intellectual work, so it takes a certain time to get started with this spiritual work. Only the adept in meditation can obtain immediate results; all others need to work their way gradually towards this goal. The aspirant must accept the fact that these negative preliminaries, which yield no immediate fruit, must needs take up the greater part of his allotted time, and that he should not look for quick results. This cannot be helped. He must cheer himself with the thought that the reward of perseverance is expertness, but until then he must learn to wait and work for the agitated mentality to collect and calm itself and stop its whirl of themes and thoughts. He must remind himself that if the practice of meditation is most difficult, it is also most essential; that without this unremitting practice being incorporated into his everyday life, it is not possible to succeed in either detaching himself from earthly desires or attaching himself to the Overself. Here impatience is a sign that the lower self naturally resists the inward drawing towards meditation, for it sees in such a course the ultimate loss of its own sovereignty. If the commonplace qualities of patience and perseverance have any value anywhere, it is here. With their help and with devotion to the practice, he may after a protracted period of trial and error become possessed of a good technique. It was no less a master of the art than the renowned Indian sage, Shankara, who said that if meditation is carried on with perseverance and fervour, it will attain its goal in not too long a time.

All the powerful and predominant tendencies which make both the movement of thoughts and the externalization of attention the ingrained habits which they really are, assail the student and draw him back to the common enslaved condition in which he and all mankind have hitherto dwelt. His duty is to summon his inner strength to resist the return of these thoughts and to repel the intrusion of objects upon his attention. The effort to maintain the introverted state must be sustained, not in a violent nor self-conscious way but in an easy and gentle fashion. And it must be repeated day after day without remission until success is complete and permanent. Many beginners make the error of believing that the result, if any, of each individual meditation must necessarily show itself at the time of practice, and of assuming that because the end of a meditation leaves them as they were at the beginning, because it seems barren, dry and without result, that therefore it is a disappointing failure. This is not so, for the result may show itself a little later and the effort is not wasted; it is only that the profit has not appeared above the threshold of consciousness. These exercises may make the going seem slow and laborious; they must look upon them as a kind of gymnastic discipline, a self-training whose results in self-development will surely show themselves, although at an unspecifiable date.

Just as we do not discard a mirror because we cannot see our face in it the first time, but rub and polish it again and again until we do, so should we not discard the regular practice of meditation because we do not see our spiritual self in it the first year, but should persevere until we do. To hush the outgoing energies of the body, to stand aside from the active functioning of the senses and to bid the waves of thought be still, is a task which naturally calls for a great concentration of all our forces. Therefore it is not an easy one; but nevertheless it is not impossible. Hundreds of men and women have successfully accomplished it during the past centuries and in different lands. The secret of this achievement is not to give up the quest because results remain monotonously absent, not to cease efforts through impatience, irritation or despair. In the early stages, meditation feels arduous and profitless. In the intermediate stages, there are periods of conscious progress with intervals of staleness. For it is then that the mind works on the pneumatic drill principle. Persevering endeavour will bring proficiency, irregularly no doubt but to an ever increasing extent. If the thinking consciousness resents these daily attacks upon its restless wandering character and stubbornly clings to its old habits, one day its resistance will be worn out and it will quietly yield.

For months and perhaps years, the practitioner will have to draw attention forcibly back from these wanderings, but if he persists the day will surely come when it will stop them of its own accord and willingly seek the rest which meditation offers. The hour will eventually arrive when he will no longer have to try to meditate; meditation will come to him of itself, facilely and smoothly. Expertness in the art of meditation comes, as in all other arts, through this untiring practice. The concentration becomes easy and pleasant. The proficient's internal tension disappears and his whole being becomes well-poised, harmoniously relaxed.

In this development there are three stages: first, the long, monotonous, tiring fight against the wandering tendencies of the intellect; second, the shorter and easier struggle to maintain and prolong concentrative power once it is developed; third, the effortless triumph of habitual practice finally making expertness a natural phenomenon. The firmness with which he holds the single idea of finding the divine self within and the immediacy with which he returns to its quest when he becomes aware of having deviated from it, will mark the end of the first stage with any exercise. If the first stage of concentrated attention inwardly directed upon the mind itself is successfully achieved, the second stage will then be to prolong it. The second stage has been satisfactorily achieved when the practice is resumed with pleasure and discontinued with reluctance, when the mind is able to concentrate and withdraw inwards within a minute or two of sitting down. He may arrive at such an expertness that he will be able to pass at once with ease, and at will, into the first and then the second stages of meditation.

As the effects of meditation become more and more familiar, understanding of its mechanism and facility in its practice grow with them. With the increase of facility which time thus brings to him, the decrease of distraction will correspondingly delight him. Shorter and shorter will become the waiting preliminary period during which thoughts, memories, anticipations, emotions and agitations aroused by his external life manifest themselves and prevent perfect concentration or delay inward self-absorption. Anyone who is already well-advanced on the quest always finds the meditation time a joyous tryst with the beloved, whereas he who is taking his first steps often finds it an irksome meeting with boredom. The novice moves reluctantly and unwillingly to his self-commanded duty of daily meditation on his higher self. The proficient, who has conquered the technique, moves joyfully and eagerly to his God-blessed gift of daily communion with his higher self. It has passed from the stage of being a drudgery to that

41

of being a privilege. In the fully developed meditative life there is ease, naturalness and stability. It will demonstrate poise and show balance. The difference between a restless mind and a disciplined one is like the difference between mere chatter and good conversation.

The inner search for the spiritual self must go on steadily and uninterruptedly. If at first the seeker finds nothing and feels nothing, he is not to be discouraged. He is digging a well. Some have to dig far and long before water appears, therefore he should push his search deeper down. The water of life is there; he need not doubt that. Every ancient seer, every medieval saint, every contemporary mystic testifies to this fact. His mystical progress will be characterized by an increasing withdrawal into himself, by a drawing back from the physical senses and an interiorizing and immobilizing of attention. Deeper and deeper will his consciousness sink away from environment and into itself. During the mind's movement back upon itself, he will quite definitely experience the sensation of going inside. It will be like trying to penetrate through layer after layer of the mind. He has to shut out not only all sensations of external objects but also of his own body's existence.

However, it is one thing to introvert attention to this deep point and another to be able to sustain the introversion itself. He must not only achieve it fully and completely, but also remain immersed in it for some time to develop its strength and effectiveness, to enable the daily renewals to become almost instantaneous. The troublesome temptation to get up and stop the effort before the full time allotted for meditation is over, occasionally becomes overpowering. But to yield to it is to accept defeat. To resist it is to cut a further length of the road to victory. Or, the temptation to get up and do this or that, to think about some other matter – even a spiritual concern – will also come insistently. He must remain firm and not yield to it. This is hard to do, but only because he has for so long – for a whole lifetime probably – allowed his attention to become absorbed by the outer world that it now tends naturally to fly back there the instant his vigilance ceases. Through insistent practice and patient cultivation, he can definitely make this turning to the inner world, this silencing of body and mind, just as easy to do eventually as it is hard to do now.

He has now reached the most critical and most important part of his adventure in meditation. It is the borderline where his own effort must gradually cease and the soul's effort must commence. He has to keep

42

perfectly still, in body and in thought, so as to let this other presence overshadow him in a beatific quiescence. It cannot do this while he is physically busy, mentally preoccupied, emotionally attracted or repelled by something or someone. He must keep still in every way. Thus, he will introduce nothing to impede the holy presence's movement stealing over his body and taking hold of his mind. All this can be literally felt. But the slightest obstruction causes its instant withdrawal. From being positive, he must now become passive. The profound mystery of Grace is involved here.

The psychological condition of this degree is quite involuntarily induced, whereas those of the earlier degrees cannot arise without willed endeavour. If the meditator does not brush aside its early beginnings or otherwise obstruct it, it often grows so rapidly into mesmeric strength as to become wholly irresistible. Although it is a power outside of his ordinary self, somehow it is also a power not separate from that self. The effect of this grace is a mighty one. With every influx of it he feels a change coming over him, although this change may take a variety of forms. But whatever the form, the strain which accompanied his earlier essays in concentration comes to an end and the struggles through which he then laboured will no more vex him. The aspirant has to feel his way into this higher mood much as the artist has to feel his own way into a creative mood. Attention must here move as vigilantly as a man walking along the narrow parapet of an embankment which overtops a river. When the central consciousness lies effortlessly fastened to this central point, its attention now wholly held, the period of novitiate with its disheartening failures is definitely at an end. His vague feelings will now begin to assume concrete form.

If the student faithfully follows these instructions and diligently performs these exercises, he will sooner or later become conscious of this subtle presence within his own mental atmosphere. It will be something exalted, noble, serene and transcendental, but it will also be something which he cannot keep and quickly loses. Nevertheless, it will return again and again. As soon as he sits down to meditate, its spell will seem to be magically thrown over him like the fabled enchantment of fairy tales. He should unhesitatingly surrender to its mysterious but delightful influence. The process of bringing this new life to birth within himself, which was hitherto naturally a painful and prolonged one, will henceforth be a source of growing joy. Little by little he will forget his worldly affairs as he sits in meditation and more and more remember his spiritual affairs. He will come to love the calmness and contentment which these periods of fruitful contemplation bring him and which are unknown to those who despise such exercises. The sense of satisfying rest which comes over him in this state will always be noticeable. He will enter it each time feeling like a weary traveller who has reached the end of a long exile, like a fatigued wandered who has returned home. During these brief periods, his consciousness will become invested with a ripeness of understanding that it does not possess outside them.

What he has most to learn at this stage is, in one sense, easy and simple. Yet in practice, it turns out to be hard and elusive. It is to 'let go', to cease from striving, to let his will relax, to stop thinking that the Overself is something he must grasp and to let himself be grasped by it. Moreover, he is not to limit this attitude to the meditation period only, but to bring it into his ordinary life briefly several times a day. He is, indeed, to be like the swimmer who now and again turns over on his back and floats quietly with a few gentle foot–strokes, where before he rushed noisily forward with vigorous arm–strokes; or like the archer whose task is to concentrate on drawing the arrow as far backward as he can attain but not to supply the actual propulsive force. So the yogi's task is to concentrate his attention inwardly as much as he can, but the actual entry into mystical consciousness is entirely beyond his own determining. This inner quest during meditation is something like the outer quest of a radio listener who is twirling the tuning dial at random in an effort to establish contact with a satisfying broadcast. For the meditator who has succeeded in turning his attention well inwards must then use it to explore his inner being in an effort to establish contact with its profoundest point, with the mystical centre where everyday consciousness emerges from the Overself. Until he has trained himself in this mysterious art through long practice, his earlier explorings will naturally be slow, blind and groping. But just as naturally they will be transformed with time into well-directed movements which will quickly bring him to the sought-after point. Once he touches it and faithfully holds fast to it, he will have to cease being active and instead become quiescent and open to the diviner influence which will now play upon him – just as the radio listener when he has found the desired station must remain passive and open himself to the sounds which will now play upon his eardrums. (We do not offer these comparisons for their exactness but for their instructiveness. They are only analogies and should not be pushed beyond their usefulness or they will land us in difficulties.) One reason for this insistence on meditation as a part of the fourfold quest may now become clear. In all worldly affairs he is ordinarily using his personal will, whereas the philosophic ideal calls for its surrender to a higher will. The advanced phase of meditation enables him to practise this surrender in the deepest way. Hence, meditation is vastly important and imperatively necessary to the seeker for this reason alone. What he achieves temporarily in displacing the ego and stilling the mind during its short practice, will become a root from which the possibility of a more durable result can grow through the earth of his whole character.

A return to the attitude of prayer is helpful here to attract the onset of the state of quiescence. This is the way of utter humility, for it merely sets up a quest and then waits for the divinity in him to rise up and end the quest by its own self-revelation. It is a way consonant with the words of Christ, satisfying the condition which He laid down when He said, 'Except ye become as little children, ye cannot enter the kingdom of heaven.' The keynote of this new stage is surrender, utter and complete. He must let the divine current flow unhindered and unregulated, not attempt arbitrarily to divert it into ego-chosen channels, or it will disappear. The moment when he feels the 'Overself's spell' laid upon him is a crucial one. He must submit to it without resistance and without delay. Otherwise, it may be 'gone with the wind' for that day. All he has to do is to receive humbly rather than to strive egoistically. His work is to yield himself up; the Overself's is to take possession of him.

If the first stage of this adventure involves an eager, willed endeavour of the mind, the final one involves a quiet, passive surrender of it. If the one depends wholly on the aspirant's own exertions, the other depends wholly on the Overself's bestowal of grace. In both the first and second stages, that is, in concentration and meditation, the will is eager and active so that the results are its own productions; but the very contrary is the case in contemplation, which is the third stage. He has absolutely nothing to do except be content and receive what the higher self graciously bestows upon him.

The state of attentive absorption is not a passive one. How could it be when the mind must be made strong enough to endure the strain and steady enough to hold the stillness perfectly when the thoughts are dropped? It is definitely and energetically positive to the external world, although necessarily plastic and sensitive to the influx from the deeper mind. Indeed, he must beware of making his meditation merely negative and nothing more. He must disdain the glib easy assurance so often made by half-baked mystics or incompetent teachers that all he needs to do is sit down and wait passively for the 'spirit' to enter into him. For this is a way which may not bring the 'spirit' at all, but instead may lead either to waste of time or to psychic danger. He must not be vague, hazy or purposeless when he sits down, should not seek a mere blankness. On the contrary, he must be fully alert and wholly attentive, positive in attitude and definite in understanding of what he is trying to do. There must be a definite subject for his thoughts to start with and only afterwards an object in repressing those thoughts. Only then may he become receptive and expectant; but such relaxation should be like that of an eagle vigilantly poised in mid-air over a possible prey below. The dangers of faulty meditation – the lack of personal instructions and common experience to draw on which confronts the modern western man who attempts it, the excesses, extravagances, absurdities and aberrations into which neurotic meditators may easily fall – all this constitutes a case for informed vigilance and commonsense controls, not at all for dispensing with meditation altogether.

What will be the physical condition of the meditator when he reaches this degree?

It may be said in a real and definite sense that during the advanced stages of this endeavour, when he begins to sink in the heart and stop thinking on the way, he quite literally goes inside himself. As attention deepens, meditation passes into contemplation and the world of the five senses recedes. He will sit like a rooted tree. For as this great stillness settles on the mind, a corresponding motionlessness settles on the body. The whole muscular system becomes unresistingly inert, every limb gently rigid. Some power other than his own captures his body and its limbs, his mind and its thoughts. He can neither stir the one nor direct the other. He is its helpless victim. For a short time the body will be powerless to move, the mouth unable to speak and the will unable to assert itself. He will naturally fear the unfamiliar; he will instinctively recoil from entering this stage, with its apparent menace of losing consciousness or of becoming the helpless victim of unknown forces. But this condition will be a perfectly harmless one, the rigidity purely fleeting, the captivity utterly delightful. Ah! what a heavenly rapture permeates his feelings! No earthly counterpart could ever parallel it. He may even slide unwittingly into the deepest state of self-absorption, when the skin on the face quite often becomes pale and tightly stretched, thus producing the ethereal appearance associated with the saints.

Whether or not his eyes will be shut depends partly on the nature of his preceding meditation exercise and partly on the special kind of grace that is being vouchsafed him for the time being. Generally speaking, the indrawing process is helped by their closure, the stabilizing process by their opening. This point will not be for him to settle, however, but for the higher self. If they remain open, the eyes merely look unseeingly at their surroundings or into space. For the meditator's attention will be elsewhere, forgetting this world to remember a better one. During this semi-conscious and automatic fixation of the gaze, the lids may gently open a little wider than normal so that both pupil and iris are fully exposed, or else they may narrow down into almond-shaped slits. The environmental thought-form may vanish altogether if his eyes are closed, or it may continue to exist in a vague blurred little-noticed image if they are slightly open. If the first condition arises, then there are no perceptions of the world as a field of experience and no willing of acts. In this full self-absorption, the senses cease all activity and are quite unable to take any impressions from outside the body.

But absolute withdrawal from all sense-impressions of the outward world is rarely attained nowadays by the average meditator. Nor is this really necessary. The meditator need not lose his awareness of the things around him and need not utterly forget his personal identity, that is, he need not fall into a trance of utter insensibility. Such an expectation pertains only to the ancient yoga methods, not to the philosophic path which is here expounded. The disadvantages of those old ways is that they lead to the loss of all sense-perceptions, hence to unconsciousness of the external surroundings. Indeed, pushed to their farthest point as in the yoga of body control, they lead to total unconsciousness. The advantage of the methods here advocated is that the consciousness of the world, sensations of sight, touch, hearing etc., may be retained to some extent without disruption of the higher condition. The trance condition is not at all indispensable to this path. It is a physical repercussion which manifests itself in some individuals but not in all. If the consciousness is able to become perfectly concentrated and perfectly introverted, then the presence or absence of trance is unimportant. He whose meditation attains utter self-absorption may or may not experience an entire loss of external consciousness and of the capacity to observe what is happening around him. It is not an essential condition. Indeed, modern man in a Western milieu is unlikely to experience it. For him, the world does not become utterly absent and he keeps throughout a hazy notion of what is going on around him. But it does become faint and far-off. He enters a profound absorption into himself.

It happens in some cases, but not in all, that on reaching what is called the 'neutral' point of his meditation, which is the point where his consciousness of outside things suddenly transforms itself into his consciousness of the fundamental self, he will slip insensibly into a total lapse of consciousness which will be exactly like a refreshing deep sleep. But this is not likely to last longer than a few moments or minutes.

Whatever physical end is the outcome of his successful adventure in meditation, the aspirant will invariably find that, for a brief while, he will seem to be without a body – a fleshless entity of pure thought, an invisible spirit of passive calm. It is after such an experience that he may come to feel that the body is an alien self.

If physical sensations and environmental images are more or less banished from the mind by this interiorizing of attention, abstract ideas, felt emotions or pictured forms, which have been deliberately set up as an object of concentration, become substituted for them. Now these, too, must be banished from the mind. Just as the attention has already emptied itself of sense-reports, so the intellect now slowly empties itself of thoughts and the imagination of pictures. This is the last important sign to occur when the second stage ends. The passage to the third degree is almost unwittingly and insensibly effected. The reasoning process is silenced, the memory fades, the image-making faculty ceases to operate as this mystical quietude descends on the soul. When the state of reverie can be induced without being a reverie on anything in particular, when the student is able to stop all movements of the mind, when he is able to hold his attention steady without fixing it on any object or thought in particular except his own spiritual being, when he has learnt the art of being still, when he can cease running after his thoughts and when he stops trying to keep step with time, he has learnt this part of the exercise. First, thinking must dismiss its objects; next, it must dismiss its own activity. For in this final stage, intellect impedes contemplation. The aspirant must initiate this process but he cannot consummate it; this will be brought about by a force outside his own volition. He may try forcibly to repress all thoughts, to arrest all intellectual operations and all emotional movements, but success will come only when and if the higher self takes a hand in the game. He may, however, greatly assist the process by understanding what is required of him in the various stages by the light of knowledge which has here been furnished him, and by offering no resistance through fear or ignorance to the unfamiliar and mysterious changes within his psyche which the higher self seeks to bring him.

The power which grips his mind will not let it form any thoughts, or, if it succeeds in doing so, will not let it hold them. That which clears all thoughts out of his consciousness is nothing less than grace. He reaches a point in his inward-bound journey when he is inhibited, and the faculty of reasoning ceases to function. Although there is a complete silencing of his thoughts, there yet remains the thought of the concept or symbol which represents the higher power for him and which receives his devotion and aspiration. But it is a thought held, fixed, immovable, not leading off into a train of succeeding ones. His attention must be so finely concentrated on that 'other' – whether it be his higher self, his idea of God, a revered scriptural personage or a living spiritual guide – that in the end he becomes absorbed in it and passes away from the knowledge of his own personal existence. Now he must let even this last thought go altogether and then hold fast to the sacred emptiness, sacred because an indescribable sense of divine beatitude overwhelms him. When this final thought-activity gently, almost insensibly, comes to an end, with it the centring of his consciousness in the personal individuality also necessarily ceases. But this does not mean that all consciousness ceases. Instead, it shifts over to his higher individuality, his soul. Consciousness in the ordinary form which it takes with present-day man will go; but it will not be lost.

This is the psychological condition of 'giving up self' to which every spiritual teacher has pointed as being of climacteric importance. There will be an overwhelming sense of release and then the ego will be taken up into and absorbed by the Overself. He feels that another self has emerged from the mysterious deeps of his own being and taken hold of him. What takes place is a veritable displacement of the lower consciousness by the higher one, just as the volume of the water in a vessel is displaced by an object which is placed inside it. He has effected a passage from the lower self to the higher, from the lower will to the higher will. It is the sacred moment when a man actualizes his higher potentiality, that is, when he becomes conscious of his divine part. 'By not thinking nor desiring, she arrives at the mystical silence wherein God speaks with the soul, teaches it wisdom,' explained Miguel de Molinos, Spanish adept who was martyred for his services to mystical seekers throughout Europe. Only now can he understand why, although it is said that the Overself sits waiting in the heart, it would be a mistake to consider it as a merely passive entity and the way to it as a one-sided endeavour. On the contrary, it has guided his search and draws him inwards to itself and sheds its quickening grace at various times. Only now can he perceive that what he believed would be his own final discovery is, in reality, a veritable act of self-revelation on its part, just as the final act of union is a self-absorption by it. If in the first stage the mind must leave outward distractions and in the second leave inward ones, in this third stage it must leave its own egoism. His search for the inner reality of his own selfhood, the quintessence of his own consciousness, has come to an end.

Although he feels himself drawn into another world of being, he also feels such life-giving self-completion in this experience that he knows with absolute conviction that it is what he has always most sought and most valued. Indeed, whilst he is in this state and wholly gathered in it, he experiences the extraordinary feeling that he is no stranger, that he has always been here and that it is his natural condition. In this deep slumber of the body's senses and the person's thoughts, the primal mode of man's real being is found. He knows then that this is the infinite source of his finite existence. Here the tired wanderer rejoices at last in return to his true native land. The conviction that this, indeed, is the Real will be more intense than he has ever felt before with other kinds of experience. That there, in this mysterious region, the higher self has through long ages awaited him and that this meeting with it is the most momentous of his whole life, is an intuition that flashes poignantly through him.

At such times, it is the soul that takes control of his everyday self. A definite feeling that he is mounting up to a higher level of his being, a joyous sense of liberation from the ordinary vibrations and customary agitations of the ego, naturally accompanies this psychological state. This makes him feel complete in himself and satisfied in himself, a wonderful feeling which he will never better. For the self he now realizes is as superior to the ordinary ever-frustrated ego as are real flowers to the artificial variety. In this moment when the contemplative mood fully matures, the man feels that he has passed over from a lesser into a new and higher dimension of being, that it is a state whose reality and authority certify themselves, that it is mentally illuminative, that it throws his personal will into abeyance and that nothing which he has previously desired can be so satisfying as this desireless consciousness. In the happy iridescence, the majestic silence and the dynamic awakening of this experience, what has heretofore been a mere mental concept, an ineffectual bloodless notion, the Soul, now becomes filled with life and power. The personal ego's normal control vanishes, but its own consciousness is not suspended while the Overself's pervades him. The two exist side by side, like two concentric circles one inside the other, but with this difference: that all the evil in the ego is for the time of this overshadowing entirely neutralized, all worldly attitudes and earthly desires are utterly transcended. The whole moral nature of the man is sublimely elevated. The current which has entered into him acts as a solvent upon the last remnants of his lower nature. It seeks especially and stills immediately the animal desires, the intellectual doubts, ill-will, pride, inertia and restlessness.

With the fading out of sensations, thoughts, desires, emotions and volitions in the deepest stage, the ego and its earthly interests fade out altogether. When all the faculties have gathered themselves into the mystical quiet, when will and thought lie passive in its still embrace, when no thoughts enter to disturb it, the mind is naturally even and serene to an extraordinary extent. The stream of ideas comes to an end. He sinks in a blessed quietude – wide, deep, and complete – never before known. As he approaches nearer and nearer to the Overself, he becomes more and more conscious of the stillness which appears to surround it like an aura. The passage in meditation from ordinary consciousness to mystical awareness is a passage from corrosive turmoil to healing tranquility. He seems to enter a land of eternal rest and silence, whose mysterious peace spins an incredible enchantment around his soul. A curious feeling of being laid under a benign spell comes over him. It is as though a little circle of impassive stillness has been drawn around his seated figure.

There is a dead silence which is merely the absence of words and there is a living silence which is really the presence of divinity. It is about this condition that St Augustine in Europe counselled, 'When thou inwardly hearest the affirmation "Truth", there remain if thou canst.' And it is about this same condition that Gaudapada in the Himalayas advised, 'Touch it [the mind] not when it has found the condition of evenness.'

But if the meditator must not let himself fall away too soon from this inner stillness, on the other hand he must not allow the habit of remaining overlong in it to grow. It has already been mentioned that for this practice at the contemplative degree twenty-six minutes will suffice. Such counsel is given only to students of philosophical mysticism, however, for it is only they who seek a balanced integral attainment. It will be rejected by all others, so it is not tendered to them.

Sometimes the shedding of the grace, which draws the consciousness 'inside', is so swift in its operation that it has forcibly to overcome the ego's resistance. When this happens, there is an abrupt but intense focusing of emotion upon the heart, a sudden but overwhelming yearning for the soul that dwells within it and a tremendous agitation of the thoughts generally. The eyes may close involuntarily, the better to concentrate, with muscles around and behind them drawing tensely together around a common centre – the gap between the eyebrows. After a while the nervous excitement subsides and a beautiful calm replaces it. Then there will arise the loving, joyous perception of the soul already described.

The meditator who reaches this state – and it is only a determined few who do so – enjoys its enthralling condition for a limited time only. There is a repeated experience of being possessed by the Overself for a brief while, coinciding with an occultation of the ego, and then the reappearance of the ego coinciding with an occultation of the Overself. This sense of being over-shadowed by another being, enclosed and held within its divine aura, presently stops. Unheedful of his desire, the visitation comes to an end. Neither by power of will nor by cunning of thought can he prevent this loss from happening. Such a profound self-absorption is not attainable for more than a short time. To be granted this blessed period is one thing; to be able to sustain it is quite another. Nevertheless, if the beautiful experience passes, its beautiful memory remains. A hallowed light rests upon these shining hours.

If it be asked why these states are not sustained outside the peak hours of meditation, the answer lies concealed with the question itself. *Meditation alone is not enough.* The fulfilment of all the conditions regarding meditation exercise will advance him in his vocation as a mystic, but will not be sufficient by itself. What is still required of him is that he should become a *philosophical* mystic, should unfold the possibilities of his whole psyche and not only his intuitive ones. The effort to attain spiritual awareness is not only a matter of the acquisition of concentration; it is also a matter affecting every side of the life of man. If the quest were only a technical process and its problems only problems in meditational technique, it would be easy enough. But it is much more than that. For it also involves the emotions, the desires, the will, and even an unknown factor – the Overself's grace. An integral and total quest must be followed. If, for instance, the aspirant meets with blockages in his attempts to go inside himself in inward-pressing concentration, it is certain that some of those blockages arise from earthly attachments and extroverting desires. Hence, an analytic purification of the heart, an emotional pruning of it, is indispensable side-by-side with his efforts to achieve the one-pointed, stilled mind.

He can make a success of meditation only if he has veneration and sensitivity, only if he gives it the character of an act of tender devotion and makes it bear the quality of heartfelt reverence. The failure to obtain successful results is, in a number of cases, due entirely to neglect of this rule. It is an indispensable condition of progress in this quest that love of the divine soul should become ardent and fervent. Only the complete fourfold path can lead to a durable realization. Therefore, his further efforts are to be directed towards this end. It is this joint effort of will and intuition, of thought and feeling, which constitutes the integral path. By steadfast practice of meditation and by assiduous efforts along these other lines, he becomes able in time to transfer himself at will to this deeper state and to sustain his consciousness therein. When, through the united and elevated efforts of thinking, feeling, willing, intuiting and aspiring, this meditation upon the Overself as being his own self becomes serenely uninterrupted and permanently stabilized, the man is said to have attained life's highest goal.

3
Karma: The Law of Consequences

The literal meaning of karma is 'doing' and the applied meaning is simply that a man's karma is his own doing. He has made himself what he is now by his own actions – the term karma in its original reference includes mental actions. Karma is simply a power of the Universal Mind to effect adjustment, to restore equilibrium and to bring about compensatory balance. In the sphere of human conduct the result is that somehow, somewhere and somewhen, whatever a man does is ultimately reflected back to him. No deed is exhausted in the doing of it; eventually it will bear fruit which will return inexorably to the doer. Karma is a self-moving force. Nobody, human or superhuman, has to operate it.

Writing practically and not academically, as a philosopher and not as a philologist, we would say that karma means result, the result of what is thought and done. Such result may happen instantaneously or it may be deferred; it may be achieved partially so far as we can observe, but it will be achieved completely beyond our conscious knowledge. The belief which ties it up wholly with remote reincarnations, whether of the past or of the future, is greatly exaggerated. The principal sphere of its operations is always the same life within which those thoughts and actions originated.

The word karma need not frighten anyone by its exotic sound. It means that which a man receives as the consequence of his own thoughts and actions, and the power or law which brings him those consequences. It also signifies the working out of a man's past in his present life. Destiny signifies the manner of such working.

With this key of karma in our hands, we can see how a clear inevitability rules life, how the effects of past actions are brought to us all too often in the same birth, and how so much that happens to us is the linked result of what we did before. We do not have to wait for a remote future incarnation always for the effects of karma. Quite often they may be observed in the present one. How many actions in a man's life, how many of his emotional tendencies and mental habits can be seen to lead directly towards the events which have happened to him in his present life?

We do not carry around with us the accumulated memories of all the incidents of all past lives. What a burden they would be if we did! But what is most valuable in them reappears as our conscience, what is most profitable reappears as our wisdom and all our experience reappears as our present characteristics and tendencies.

Intelligence acquiesces in and conscience accepts such a reasonable, noble doctrine.

The existence of karma as a principle in nature can only be inferred; it cannot be proved in any other way. But the kind of inference is of the same order as that by which I accept the existence of Antarctica. I have never visited Antarctica, but I am compelled to infer the fact of its existence from many other facts. Similarly I am compelled to infer the fact of karma from many others.

We can better grasp the nature of karma by considering the analogy of electricity whose transmission, conduction and motion offer good parallels to karmic operation.

Just as the falling of an avalanche down a mountainside is not a moral process but a natural one, so the falling of suffering upon a man who has injured others is only a causal consequence and not really a moral punishment. It is a rectification of equilibrium rather than a deliberate rectification of injustice on the part of the deity.

Is the poetical notion of nemesis unfounded or may we indeed adopt it as fact, independent of personal opinion or individual experience but dependent as all scientific facts are upon the tests of reason and verification? The answer is 'yes'; rebirth may be held to be true because like all scientific laws it conforms with all the known evidence. Yet it is incorrect and unscientific to speak of a 'law' of karma. Karma is not a law to obey or disobey, nor is it a penal code for wrong-doers. It is simply the principle of inevitable consequences.

Karma and Freewill

Whoever declares that karma rules out all accidents preaches predestination, and thereby proves that he has not understood karma. For the difference between these two doctrines is the difference between a fixed structure and a flexible process.

Is the human will free or not? It cannot be said with full truth that our destiny is in our own hands; it is more accurate to say it is partially in our own hands. Limits have been set for us within which we have to carry on our lives. This is not at all the same condition as one where we cannot influence our future. There is no completely fatalistic mold into which our lives must run; we have a certain amount of freedom, even though we have not total freedom.

It is true that so long as the element of inner freedom exists in man, his future will be unforseeable and incalculable. But this element does not exist in solitude. There is also an unbroken but hidden causal chain which connects his present life with what is rooted in the remote past of former lives. To say that he has a free will and stop with such a statement is to tell a half-truth. His will always coexists with his karma.

We tolerate the tyranny of the past because we are weak, because we have not yet entered into that knowledge of our inherent being which makes us strong and gives us the mastery. We inherit the body from our parents with the genes which are the germinal beginnings of it, but we inherit our mind from ourselves. What we were mentally in former lives is the heritage we receive and unfold in the present one. Both heredity and environment nurse the unfolding mind of man as it itself was born elsewhere, albeit that its attractions and affinities lead it to such heredity and environment.

In this struggle against fate-sent conditions, human will and personal endeavour can be effective within the circle of their own limitations.

We may ask if there is any point along our entire course where we really have a choice, really have a chance between two ways, to do what we actually want to do. Our freedom consists in this, that we are free to choose between one act and another but not between the consequences arising out of those acts. We may claim our inner freedom whatever our outer future may be. We may fix our own life aims, choose our own beliefs, form our own ideas, entertain desires and express aversions as we wish. Here, in this sphere of thought and feeling, action and reaction, freewill is largely ours.

We are the victims of our overshadowing past. It is not possible to wipe it out entirely and start writing the record of our life on a clean slate. We have to put up with the consequences of our own thoughts and acts until we learn wisdom from them. Then by changing present causes, we shall help to modify these effects of the past. Tears will not wipe them out.

Our life is circumscribed by destiny, but is not completely fore-ordained by it. A wholly fatalistic view of life is a half false one; worse, it is also dangerous for it banishes hope just when hope is most needed.

It is wise to submit to the inevitable, but first it is needful to be sure it is the inevitable. There are times when it is wiser to struggle against destiny like a captured tiger, and other times when it is wiser to sit as still in its presence as a cat by the hearth.

Our course of experience insofar as it brings us pleasure or pain is partly predetermined by our actions in past existences and partly the consequence of our freewill exertions during the present existence. The two factors of dynamic freedom and deterministic fate are always at work in our lives.

Each man is his own ancestor. His past thinking is the parent of his present tendencies and the contributor towards his present deeds.

That chance, coincidence and luck seem to play their role in man's life is a fact which nobody with wide experience could gainsay. But there is no justification for asserting that these happenings are quite blind. Although we may fail to understand the strange decisions of fate, we should never fail to believe that it is itself governed by inexorable law. There is an outside agency which plays a hand in the game of life, and behind human existence there is infinite wisdom.

Karma has a twofold character. There is the kind which nothing that the wit of man may devise can alter, and there is also the kind which he may alter by counter-thoughts and counter-actions, or by repentance and prayer. Evil karma cannot be extinguished without moral repentance, although it may be modified by astuteness.

In a chapter in *Living Philosophies*, Albert Einstein says, 'I do not believe we can have any freedom at all in the philosophical sense, for we act not only under external compulsion but also by inner necessity.' Schopenhauer's saying, 'A man can surely do what he wills to do, but he cannot determine what he wills,' impressed itself upon me in my youth and has always consoled me when I have witnessed or suffered life's hardships.

Freewill versus Fate is an ancient and useless controversy, which is purely artifical and therefore insoluble as it is ordinarily presented.

They are not antinomies but complementaries. They are not in opposition. The wise man combines both. In the absence of a knowledge of the factors of karma and evolution, all discussion of such a topic is unreal, superficial and illusory. As spiritual beings we possess freewill; as human beings we do not. This is the key to the whole matter.

If we analyse the meaning of words instead of using them carelessly, we shall find that in this case of 'freewill' the term often stands for the very opposite idea to that for which it is supposed to stand. Where is the real freedom of a man who is enslaved by his appetites and in bondage to his passions? When he expresses what he believes to be his own will he is in actuality expressing the will of those appetites and passions. So long as desires, passions, environments, heredity and external suggestions are the real sources of his actions, where is his real freewill? Without freedom from desires there is no freedom of will. Unless a man find his true self he cannot find his true will. The problem of fate versus freewill must first be understood before it can be solved. And this understanding cannot be had whilst we make the usual superficial approach instead of the rarer semantic approach. Our will is free but only relatively so.

Freewill is a fact in human existence, but destiny is a greater fact. To obtain an accurate picture of that existence we must put the two together, although we do not know the exact proportions to assign to them. But we do know that the greater emphasis is to be laid upon destiny. We have only a limited measure of freewill; we cannot exercise complete control over our lives.

The course of fortune is not swayed by blind chance nor determined by implacable fate. The human will is partially free, the human environment partially determined. What we never anticipated comes with a painful shock or a pleasant surprise into our lives. The freedom which we should like to possess, or which we feel we have, is always crisscrossed with an unpredictable element.

The time and place, the manner and conditions of any man's birth, as of his death, are entirely preordained by a power outside that man's individual will and freedom. Just as the leading events and characters in a man's past earth life will appear before him as in a cinema film after death, so will the new events and the new characters of his coming reincarnation appear before him when he takes up his new earthly abode. Just as in the after-death experience he sees the whole course of his past life from the higher standpoint of his higher self, and can therefore see the reasons and causes which led up to those situations and those actions – and thus recognize that wisdom, purpose, and justice govern human life – so in the same way he is able to view the coming earth life from the higher standpoint and understand the karmic causes of the coming events and actions which his previous tendencies will most likely bring about. These pictorializations of the past and the future are not without their value, even though it is a subconscious value. As a result of them, something registers deep within the mind and heart of the ego. Finally philosophy points out that destiny plays the larger part in man's life. This does not mean that events are unalterably predetermined, but partially predetermined. Life viewed in this static fatalistic manner is life with all initiative killed, all progress crushed. This blind apathy is based not on real spirituality but on fallacious thinking. 'Because the whole universe is an expression of God's will, and because every event happens within the universe, therefore every calamity must be accepted as expressing God's will.' So runs the logic.

The best way to expose the fallacy lurking in this contention is to place it by the side of a counter syllogism. 'Because the whole universe is an expression of God's will, and because every individual resistance to calamity happens within the universe, therefore such resistance is an expression of God's will.'

It must not be supposed that man is so helpless as he would seem. Much of his destiny was made by himself in the past. He made it, therefore he can help to change it. Destiny controls him, but his freewill has some control over destiny. This will be true, however, only to the extent that he learns the lessons of experience and creatively exercises that freewill.

Because the divine soul is present in man, there is laid upon him the duty of reflecting divine qualities in his thought and life. If he tries to evade this, he is forced to suffer this same will in pain. A real freedom of the will he never obtains.

Karma and Rebirth

How is it that karma can perpetuate itself in the absence of an ego that outlives the body? How is it possible for continuity of karmic existence to happen when there is a complete break in it? This is a question which

59

has never been adequately answered by those who like the Buddhist philosophers have risen above the crude animistic notions of transmigration held by the ordinary unphilosophic Hindu. Nor can it ever be adequately answered by any who do not lay hold of the rational key to such major problems – the key of Mentalism. For this alone can explain the contradictions involved in the assertion that karma can continue in the absence of an ego-entity to which it can cling. And it does this by positing the doctrine first that all things are mental things; second, that the mind has two phases, the conscious and the subconscious; third, that whatever disappears from the conscious disappears into the subconscious; fourth, that the latter is a wonderful repository of all ideas and forces which have ever existed, albeit that they repose in a purely latent state; fifth, that both ego and karma find their link from birth supplied by this subconscious latent storehouse. Karma as an equilibrating process resides in the subconscious and, unseen, ties the fruit of an act of its agent, the consequence of his deeds to the ego; and because time and space are non-existent in the subconscious, it can work unhindered and leap the chasm between rebirths. The ego, as Buddha pointed out, comes into temporary being as the compound of five things: namely body, sensations, precepts, characteristic tendencies and waking consciousness; but when these fall apart at death the ego perishes, too. It is not to be conceived as an individual entity binding these five elements together, but rather as the illusory consequence of their meeting and mingling at the same time. But the ego is not annihilated forever but rather merged into the subconscious where it remains as a latent possibility. The power of karma, which is itself a power of the subconscious mind, takes up the latter at the appropriate time and converts it into actuality, that is a new reincarnation, whilst dictating the character of the body and fortune according to the past lives. It is not an entity which transmigrates from one body to another, but a mental process.

The troubles of life largely originate in our individual fate, the latter being predetermined by our own thoughts and deeds of earlier lives. The way out of many of these troubles is to remove their root causes, in other words the power of this past karma. The latter lives on only because we as individuals live on. The removal of the sense of individuality therefore should be our chief goal, but such removal can be effected only after we have discovered what individuality really is.

Learning through experience means learning through a long

succession of trials and errors. Through the consequent suffering we are forced to arouse discrimination and by this to move upward from imperfect and incorrect attitudes of thought. Man is educated by events, and he cannot hope to master in one lifetime all the lessons which life offers.

Even in the midst of horrors that threaten the life of man today from sea and air and earth, it is well to remember that whatever happens this incarnation does not exhaust the possibilities of human life. We shall return again to take up the old quest, to carry it a step futher; and all that we have mastered in thought and achieved in deed will be gathered anew ere long. Nothing that is of the mind will be lost, aye, even the strong loves and hard hates will draw friendly and unfriendly faces across our orbit once again. The pupils will seek higher and higher for their true teacher and find no rest until the right words sound in their ears; the teacher will be compelled to wait calmly but compassionately for their slow recovery of ancient memory and spiritual ripeness.

Man quickly forgets but karma always remembers. The brain through which mind has to work, being new with every new body, cannot share this vast store of memories. The possibility of sometimes recovering any of them exists only for a person trained in a peculiar method of meditation which demands intense concentration upon memories of the present life; but occasionally fragments of such memories also present themselves spontaneously to untrained but sensitive persons.

In certain cases where one destined for great advancement on the spiritual path wilfully refuses to enter upon it or impatiently postpones such entrance for a later period, the Overself will often take a hand in the game and release karma of frustrated ambitions, disappointed hopes and even broken health. Then in despair, agony or pain, the wayfarer will drink the cup of voluntary renunciation or wear the shabby clothes of self-denial. His ego diminishes its strength out of suffering. His real enemy on the path is the 'I', for it is the cause of both material suffering and mental anguish, whilst it blocks the gate to truth. The more the course of worldly events depresses him, the more he will learn to withdraw from his depression into the forgetfulness of spiritual contemplation. It is enough for a votary of mysticism to find temporary peace in this way; but for a votary of philosophical mysticism, it is not. Such a one must insert reflection upon the meaning of those events into his contemplation. When he has attained to this impersonal insight, he may look back upon his past life and understand why so much of what happened had to happen.

The doctrine of karma clarifies the meaning of an unfortunate situation in which a man finds himself. Without its light he will often think, but think wrongly, that the fault lies wholly with others – and fail to see that he is at least partly responsible for it.

The gifts of fate and the reverses of fortune alike are to be regarded as ideas. Thus only may we lift ourselves into a region of real tranquillity.

The foolishness and failures of the past will vanish from memory but not from character. Although the forces of heredity and the influence of environment seem to be the chief forces behind man's actions, there are also deep-rooted tendencies carried over from an unknown forgotten past. It is impossible for man to escape his past altogether; the effects are there in him and in his environment. The problems it created have not all been solved, nor all the debts paid. All past thoughts and previous experiences have brought his intelligence and character to their present point. All karma from earlier incarnations has led him to the point where he now stands as a particular human being. He cannot now help being what he is. He is today the sum total of a myriad past impressions.

Man is the deposit of his own past and in turn as he lives gives rise to a fresh deposit. It is thus that the human race is subject to the process of physical rebirth. 'Let us open our eyes lest they be painfully opened for us,' pleaded the Turkish writer Albitis.

Buddha said,

'It happens, my disciples, that a Bhikshu, endowed with faith, endowed with righteousness, endowed with knowledge of the Doctrine, with resignation, with wisdom, communes thus with himself. "Now then could I, when my body is dissolved in death, obtain rebirth in a powerful princely family?" He thinks this thought, dwells on this thought, cherishes this thought. The Shankaras and Viharas (internal condition) which he has thus cherished within him and fostered, lead to his rebirth in such an existence. This, O Disciples is the avenue, this is the path, which leads to rebirth in such an existence.'

There is no simpler or more satisfactory explanation of the rags or riches which mark out one human birth from another, and no more logical solution of the divergences and differences which abound in human character. We keep on coming to earth because this is the most effective way to learn wisdom. We form friendships at first sight because we are merely picking up the threads of a hidden past.

Karma and Religious Teachings

Professor Hocking is reported to have said that Christianity cannot become a world faith unless Christians accept the idea of reincarnation from the Hindus, and that without this belief the Sermon on the Mount is not to be understood.

The first faiths inculcated ethical injunctions through the use of historical myths and legendary characters and through the appeal to fear or hope; the latest faith will tell the plain unvarnished truth that man must live rightly because he will have to eat the fruit of his own deeds. The mature mind needs a philosophical explanation of the world, whereas the childish mind, befogged by superstition, is satisfied with a fabled one. The ethics of former centuries were founded on uncertain fears of a probably existent God; the ethics of the present are founded on complete indifference to a non-existent God. The first led to some restraint on conduct, the second leads to none. The ethics of the future will be founded on rational understanding of the power of karma, the law of personal responsibility; and this will lead to right restraint on conduct. For when we contemplate the environmental limitations of life, the unsought pleasures and inescapable hardships, we come quietly into a perception of the power of karma.

Karma in the sphere of human conduct is neither more nor less than character. We really have as much free will as we need. If we do not avail ourselves of proffered opportunities because we are too blind to recognize them, the fault lies in ourselves. If we embark on an action which is initially and superficially profitable, but ultimately and profoundly inimical to our own interests, and it brings in its train a whole line of other undesirable actions as the sequence, we should not weep at karma's cruelty but at our own lack of intelligence. Those who practise self-pity as a habit may find a convenient scapegoat in karma, but the truth is that the ethical standards and mental qualities of man are the hidden factors which predetermine his fate. Karma is not an idea which need dull men's minds or paralyse their hands. It has a positive value and a regenerating influence by awakening both in nations and in

63

individuals a sense of ethical responsibility, thus inducing them to heal voluntarily the wounds caused by past errors.

Sooner or later man is bound to give expression in action or in speech to the thoughts and emotions which dominate him. There is no escape from this because the world surrounding him is largely a reflection of his own character. Once the trigger of a gun has been pulled, no subsequent action on the part of the shooter can deflect the bullet from its ordained path. In other words, if you fire a bullet you cannot recall it to the gun; it must go on until it strikes somewhere. And the thoughts and feelings of men, when sufficiently intense and prolonged, strike somewhere in this material world and appear before them again, as either physical events or physical environments. The operations of karma belong to the realm of the conscious – that is, the realm of the individual, of space and time.

Cults which teach that destiny either does not matter or is non-existent are cults which can never lead man to true happiness, for they illustrate that blind leading of the blind of which we have heard before. Destiny exists, and it is wise to face and acknowledge the fact. The mere refusal to acknowledge its existence does not thereby dismiss it. It is there and no amount of prayer or concentration will dismiss it because it exists for the benefit of man – for his ethical and intellectual education – and because whilst living in this world he cannot have one without the other. Christian doctrine has become a spent force, because it lacks the appeal of actuality and immediacy. Few people are frightened today by the prospect of a sojourn in a problematical purgatory, nor can they be cajoled by the prospect of an incredibly monotonous sojourn in the orthodox heaven. What they need is something applicable to life here and now on this earth and not in invisible heavens. Modern man cannot now find in orthodox dogma sufficient driving power to make him live a good life rather than a bad one. The world's troubles can be traced to the lack of a sound basis for ethics to replace the crumbling one of religion. John Locke said, 'If God did not exist we should have to invent one in order to keep men orderly.' I believe, however, that such invention is unnecessary; the introduction of belief in the doctrine of karma would equally suffice to restrain the evil conduct of men. The current and ancient idea that atheism must lead to immorality and wickedness does not apply to the philosophic brand of atheism, because here the notion of karma is added, making man his own punisher.

It is of the utmost importance that the masses should not lose their faith that a moral purpose governs the world even though they lose their religion. There is no supernatural and external being who arbitrarily administers or controls karmic rewards or punishments. We unconsciously produce their seeds ourselves; when a favourable hour comes, they germinate and yield their own fruit.

Large numbers of men today practise morality without actively believing in religion. Those who doubt this have not inquired deeply enough into the facts. Morality is not so dependent on theology as it was in primitive communities which lacked culture. Men are imbibing effective guidance from the press articles of sensible men, from the books of rational men and from the scientists of the world – all this without listening to a word from the pulpit.

What then is the hope for the West? To propagate a new creed with its baseless promises of a heaven to come is merely to offer more religion, more of a medicine which has already failed to relieve the suffering of mankind. There is only one hope – to administer truth. The justification of religion has been that it has kept the masses within certain moral limits, but this was done through threat and fear. If superstition, which in plain language means falsehoods, can keep the masses within moral bounds, surely truth can do as much if not more. The answer is that it can. We need not give the masses the whole of truth, for they are not ready to receive it, but we can give them an important doctrine which does not conflict with reason or with science, and which will yet provide them with a solid foundation for a genuine morality. This is the doctrine of karma. At the same time, an ethical code based upon such teaching will possess all the force of one based upon religion – while it ought to succeed where religion has failed. Let us make the attempt to build such a code on this firmer basis. But there is no such thing as proselytism, and he who imagines he has made a convert fools himself. Experience moulds views, instruction merely confirms them.

If unerring karma were the only power behind human fortunes and misfortunes, it would be a sorry outlook for most of us. We have neither the knowledge, the strength nor the virtue to accumulate much good merit. On the contrary, we have all the ignorance, the weakness and the sinfulness to accumulate plenty of demerit. But such is the beneficence behind the universe that we are not left to the treatment of karma alone. Alongside it there exists another power, the power of grace. The two operate together, although nobody can predict how much or how little of one or the other will manifest itself in any particular case. But of the reality and activity of grace we may be firmly assured. If there were no final way of deliverance from earthly bondage, our store of self-earned pain would accumulate to such an extent with every birth as to be inexhaustible. Our tremendous load of karmic sin could never be remitted, and man once lost in darkness would be lost forever. But redemption will be the ultimate lot of all, not the monopoly of a few; and none will be excluded from salvation, for all are enclosed within the circle of divine love.

Karma and Human Relationships

The situations peculiar to family life not infrequently bring together two souls whose karmic relation is not that of love but of enmity. They may be brought together as brother and sister, or even as husband and wife. What should be the philosophical attitude of one to the other? Taking a concrete example and assuming the case of marital discord, and without prejudice to the practical methods such as separation or divorce – which may be considered necessary – it may be said that the enlightened partner should regard the other first as a revealing agent to bring his or her own faults into sharp definition, and second as a laboratory wherein he or she can experiment with the eradication of such faults. Thus if the wife frequently flares into passionate anger, or constantly expresses nagging abuse, her provocations ought not to be allowed to call forth the husband's anger but rather his latent self-control; her lack of considerateness should arouse not a corresponding lack on his part but rather more considerateness. In this way the situation provided by her conduct can be converted into an opportunity to rise to higher things. Every domestic quarrel, however petty, should enable him to show forth something of the diviner aspects within himself. Again even assuming the two are radically unsuited to each other and sooner or later will have to part, the unhappiness thereby caused should be used by the enlightened partner to make him or her more determined to gain independence from external things for happiness, and to become more reliant upon those inner satisfactions which only the best in the mind can yield. Furthermore, they should make the person understand that he or she is expiating past karma which is self-earned through his or her own impulsiveness, stupidity or passion.

The worst physical karma is created by murder. There the penalty is inescapable, however delayed. The murderer will himself be murdered, although not necessarily in the same incarnation. The worst mental karma is created by hatred. If sufficiently intense and prolonged, it will give rise to destructive diseases which eat away the flesh.

It is hard to stop the flow of these thought-waves. We have built them up as habits through many incarnations. Those mental tendencies which have become our desires and passions are nothing else but ideas which are strongly implanted in us from our former births.

Gautama explained that one of the distinguishing marks of a Buddha is that he understands precisely how his thoughts, feelings and perceptions arise, continue and pass away, and consequently he is not swayed by them but is able to maintain complete control over them. Such an ideal perfection of self-observation and self-knowledge may not be possible for the average man, but he can at least achieve a little of it with a profit out of all proportion to the effort entailed.

Even if we have to undergo a sorrowful destiny connected with the body, our reaction should be different from that of the unawakened man. We may go through the same experiences as he does but we should remember always that we are not the ego and try to remain mentally uplifted by the unavoidable sufferings. At all times we should try to be the 'witness self' remaining calmly above it all.

The man who has lived for very many births on earth becomes rich with crowded experiences, and should be wiser than the man who has had but few births.

The extent of the karmic consequences of an act will be proportionate to the energy it holds. The World-Mind faithfully records the loftiest aspirations or the meanest desires. If, however, the thought, emotion or willed deed is only a passing idle one, then the impression remains dormant only and no karma is generated. Impressions which are very weak or unstrengthened by repetition are quite ineffective, but when they grow by repetition or collection they eventually become karmic and produce definite results. For this reason alone it is wisdom to nip a fault – when recognized – in the bud, and eliminate it before it becomes strong enough to do serious harm. It is also wise to remember that high ideals firmly held and lofty aspirations deeply rooted in the heart cannot fail to bear fruit of their kind in due course.

We should realize that each person thinks and acts according to the long life-experience which has brought him to the point of understanding where he now stands. Such a person therefore must inevitably be as he is and not otherwise. All the inner forces of his being, accumulated during many births, influence him to act as he does.

Observe too the karmic influences. What rich, envied family is there which is without a skeleton of suffering or misfortune or disease in its cupboard? Who does not know of some who have two or three skeletons? You may have found, as so many have done in these dark days, that life contains mysterious and potent karmic influences which reach out ominous hands to break the things you have set your heart upon; which permit you to achieve success and then destroy it before your eyes; which play havoc with the health and perhaps the lives of those near and dear to you. Your heart may often have bled in silence.

We create our own burdens of latent suffering when our deeds injure others, and we give birth to bitter ultimate consequences when we give birth to thoughts of hatred. The forces of lust, greed and anger are blind ones which uncontrolled, unleashed and unguided lead mankind to so much karmic trouble and misery.

A fire may be used to roast food or to roast a man at the stake. The fire itself is not an evil, but the use or abuse of it is good or evil; and this in its turn depends on what impulses are working in a man's heart, what tendencies he has brought over from past lives. Thus evil powers are after all our own evil thoughts. The world will be liberated from evil as soon as man liberates his mind. Mind is the agent whereby the working of karma is effected. There is no need to call in an extra-cosmic supernatural being to explain how man's deeds are requited.

National Karma

Karma is no dream. Those who want facts may have them. Russia built its large dam and hydroelectric station at Dnieperpetrovsk largely out of the forced labour of peasants and political prisoners. This construction job was the pride of the Communists. But they had to destroy it in a single day by their own hands when the German army approached. What they had built by such unethical means availed them nothing in the end. Karma is not a fossil doctrine. In their hearts men recognize that eternal justice rules the world and implacably pursues both good and evil doers; they have but to be reminded of the truth to accept it. Modern existence may repress it for the best part of a lifetime, but in the end most of us succumb to the belief that some part of the future is already foreordained and written invisibly across the brow of every person. Emerson said, 'If you put a chain round the neck of a slave the other end will fasten round your own neck.'

The use of brains or brutality or both may give a man success, but the matter does not end there. After the achievement of success, karma comes into operation and demands the price; and it may be paid by failure or suffering or both.

The stream of fate pursues its perennial course, halting now and then to find new historical channels which become necessary to its movement. The nation that first drops gas bombs on unarmed civilians drops them also on its own. Did it but know, the nation that breaks the rules of righteousness breaks also its own fortunes.

'He that loveth iniquity beckoneth to misfortune; it is, as it were, the echo answering to his own voice.' If the Japanese had heeded this wise counsel from one of their old books, the ninth-century *Teaching of the words of Truth*, they would not have encountered such a sorry plight as was theirs at the end of the Second World War.

If we wish to understand what has been happening in the world, we must first understand that continental and national karma are hidden causes of its distresses.

A nation arises by the adding together of every individual in it. You are one of those individuals whose thought and conduct will help to make your nation's karma. The subject of collective destiny is very complicated because it is composed of many more elements than individual destiny. The individual who is born into a particular nation has to share the general destiny of that nation as well as his own individual karma. If however he withdraws from that nation by his own choice and migrates to another country, he will then share a new collective destiny which is bound to modify his own and put its mark upon it, either improving it by giving him more opportunity or causing it to deteriorate.

There is a collective national karma which gradually grows and then materializes. When a group of people live together and work together, either in a country or a city, they gradually form for themselves a national or a municipal destiny which they have to bear. Sometimes this result is good, sometimes it is bad, but generally it is a mixture of both. Hence we find in history such things as a national destiny and a racial fate. Karma operates no less among the societies of mankind than among individuals themselves. The life of nations, as of individuals, is an alternating rhythm of darkness and light. Epochs of great retrogression are followed by epochs of great advance.

Would the history of India have taken an entirely different direction if Clive had not been there to lead British arms to victory? Was its history so fated beforehand that when the young Clive tried twice to shoot himself in Madras, the pistol refused to fire and Clive gave up further attempts at suicide?

When a whole people move along the road of wrong-doing, then they invite suffering for their purification and enlightenment. So long as selfishness rules society, so long will society have its sufferings. So long as nations are indifferent to the woes of other nations, so long will they themselves sooner or later share those woes. A wealthy people cannot escape a partial responsibility for its refusal to help the poorer peoples, nor a powerful nation for its tolerance of the persecution of others, nor an aggressive race for its forcible domination over weaker races. The world wars have abundantly illustrated these truths. Great sins have brought great retributions. This is a period of vast purification through suffering.

But even amid the swirl of hatred and the sight of horror we must never forget the inward oneness of mankind, and that even tyrants share this ultimate divine unity with us in their innermost nature.

Ultimately, we must say that the sad situation in the world was a self-earned one; and because it was self-earned it was necessary. The world needed to undergo the experience which it has undergone because it needed ethical and intellectual education, even though that particular form of education has been unpleasant and painful. What mankind can learn clearly and obviously from its continued present sufferings is that without goodwill towards each other brought into external manifestation there is not actual peace but only its pretence, that outward peace may even be a cloak for the preparation of war. They have learned that treaties are nothing but scraps of paper when written in ink alone and not also in the heart. The cleverest men in Europe tried to solve the problems which bristled all around, but they failed. They had the brains but they did not have the goodwill; if they had had that, then the problems could have been solved easily. Goodwill was lacking and it was lacking because of man's innate greed and selfishness. So long as he feels that at all costs he must cling to what he calls his possessions, and that moreover he must constantly increase these possessions, he is hardly likely to be motivated by goodwill. Selfishness urges man to cling to and increase possessions; good reminds him he is but the steward of them. Only through repeated suffering is he beginning to learn that justice and goodwill, the attitude of give and take and even the spirit of generosity are essential to the maintenance of peace. These are merely ethical qualities, and yet without them there is not peace – there will always be war. If mankind wishes to avoid repeating this age-old destiny there is only one way, old-fashioned and very simple: a change of heart. Without this change of heart there can be only postponement of war, a temporary patching of problems but no genuinely peaceful solution. And so we come back to a very familiar position, that if we seek the Kingdom of Heaven first, all these things will be added unto us – even peace.

The West needs the notions of karma and rebirth if it is not to be destroyed by its own ignorance. Only such an intellectual basis can give effective force to the idea of morality in these intellectual times.

Karma and Non-violence

Because we hold that karma is the hidden ruler of man's fortunes and that force cannot be their final arbiter, we do not necessarily hold that force may therefore be dispensed with in favour of an ethic of non-violence. Soft, woolly and sentimental mystics repose a pathetic faith in the power of nonviolence to crush aggressive totalitarianism and armed brutality. Their attitude represents a failure to recognize unpalatable facts, while their remedy represents a journey into the absurd – however high-minded it be. If we put this doctrine to the practical test, which is the only certain test, what do we find? What happened more than a century ago when a couple of hundred young American negroes landed in West Africa to found the Liberian Republic? They were specially selected because of their religio-mystical tendencies and noble characters, most of them being Quakers in fact. It is well known that Quakers make non-violence a cardinal doctrine. They were unarmed and declared openly that they trusted in the Lord to protect them. In fact, neither their pacifism nor the Lord did so: they were brutally massacred to a man.

For a further instance, let us come closer to our own times and to an Indian who was not only a devoted follower of Gandhi but himself

71

renowned for his saintly character. This was Ganesh Shankar Vidyarthi. The story concerns one of several communal riots at Kanpur between the Muslims and Hindus. G. S. Vidyarthi firmly believed that by approaching a fanatical and frenzied Muslim mob unarmed except by this doctrine of non-violence he could pacify them and restore peace. What really happened was that they murdered him straightaway.

The sage does not accept the mystical doctrine of non-violence for various philosophical reasons. His principle practical reason, however, is because he does not wish to confirm the wrong-doer in his wrong-doing, and does not wish either to smooth the latter's path and thus encourage evil, or to practise partiality towards him. A meek submission to an aggressor's will makes the aggressor believe that his methods pay, whereas a determined resistance checks his downward course, arouses doubts and even provides instruction should he suffer punishment.

The doctrine of non-violence is derived from the ancient Indian rule of Ahimsa. Himsa means the causing of pain, suffering, injury or brutality to sentient creatures – animals as well as men. 'A' is the negative prefix which, of course, reverses the word's meaning. But is there warrant for the belief that such forbearance from inflicting injury or pain on others was taught by the sages as a universal and unqualified ethic for all persons? On the contrary, they made it clear that it was applicable only within certain limits so far as citizens of a state were concerned, while granting that it was to be adopted in its entirety by those monks and hermits who had renounced the world and were no longer concerned with the welfare of organized society. For those of us who have not retired from the struggle of existence there is a bounden duty to protect human life, because of its superior value, when it is endangered by wild beasts – even if we have to kill those beasts. Non-violence is therefore not an invariable rule of conduct so far as animals are concerned. Nor is it even so when we consider the case of human relations. Circumstances arise when it is right and proper to arm oneself in defence of one's country and slay aggressive invaders, or when it is ethically correct to destroy a murderous assailant. What must always be avoided is the infliction of unnecessary pain.

He who invokes the doctrine of pacifism for universal practice misapplies an ethical rule meant only for monks and ascetics who have renounced the world, and misconceives a mystical doctrine of unity meant only for inward realization. Pacifism is admirable in a mystic, but out of place in a man of the world.

Karma and Man's Reaction

The Pythagorean practice of nightly self-interrogation with such questions as 'What have I done wrongly?' and 'What duty have I left undone?' was an excellent one to counteract bad karma in the making, as was their other practice of saying and doing nothing whilst under the influence of passion.

Karma is reciprocal. It brings back what we put forth. If a man lives like an animal, he has abused his human birth and must thank only himself if he is reborn in an animal's body.

We hear in every religion, whether Eastern or Western, of the sufferings undergone by the wicked in the after-death state. They are supposed to dwell for a while in a nether world, a purgatory. The truth is that this is a primitive symbol of the higher doctrine that the wicked do suffer after death, but only when they are reborn on earth again.

Is karma so iron-bound that there is no hope for man to escape its strong mechanism? The answer is that we may assuredly cherish such a hope, if not for such escape or for the abolition of karmic suffering, at least for rendering it less painful and more bearable – as an anaesthetic renders a surgical operation less painful and more bearable – provided we fulfil the requisite preconditions of repentance, reparation and resignation. Karmic pressures do not *oblige* us to act in a particular way, although they do push us to do so. If we choose, we can set up inner resistance to these pressures and thus modify or even alter their effects.

To offset the karmic effects of a bad deed, do the contrary one; and of bad thought or speech we should deliberately cultivate the opposite kind. If something has been taken from a man, something should be given voluntarily which is of equal or greater value to him.

If it be true that we cannot wish our bad karma away, it is equally true that we can balance it with good karma and thus offset its results. Buddha, who was one of the greatest exponents of the karma doctrine, pointed out that right thinking and good deeds could change karmic curses into blessings.

The fixed focusing of a persistent concentrated idea will exert pressure from within, as it were, and may slowly alter the karmic physical fortunes of a man. Karma is thought as much as action, desire as much as deed. The one is the seed which fructifies into the other and cannot be separated from it. It is this silent, secret registration in the World-Mind which makes the working of karma possible, just as the sound tracks in a gramophone disc make possible the hearing of its song.

Fate often seems to act in an arbitrary fashion, favouring the wicked and striking down the undeserving, but this is an illusion born of the dark night in which we habitually move. For in the end their actions take root from out of the very nature of man himself, who is the ultimate and chief arbiter of his own destiny. Man is like a race of Lilliputians which lives in a narrow pass between the giant walls of Justice and beats its head ceaselessly against these stony barriers. The four gods stand by, hard or lenient at times, but always just. From every man they require a requital and an accounting for his deeds. And so high are these walls that no man has ever broken through them.

Things act according to their nature. Nature records these actions in a secret way and reflects back their appropriate results. And as with things, so with persons. Each of us sings out a note into the universe, and the universe answers us in the same key. Karma is the bed which we unconsciously make for ourselves and upon which we shall one day have to lie.

When rendering our account of good or bad fortune, we usually forget to include the ethical values which we acquired from each experience. Nevertheless, when a man has first attained some understanding he will involuntarily bring the great truth of karma into this light – not merely as an intellectual dogma but as a heartfelt conviction. He will then shrink with horror from the memory of his past wrong-doing. Yet he knows it cannot be evaded and must be faced. And then, not out of external bidding but out of his own inner being, he will lay a duty upon himself – the duty of atonement. So far as he can, he will seek out those whom he has wronged and make fit reparation. If he refuses this task he will find his peace violated by those memories which will spring up unbidden again and again.

We may take defeat in a spirit of either bitter resentment or melancholy pessimism. Both these attitudes are wholly unprofitable. There is a third and better way – to make defeat serve as the starting point of a different advance. This can be done by, first, a frank ungrudging and searching self-examination to discover faults and confess wrongs, and second, by deeds of repentant amends and the pioneering of a new outlook.

'No man knows his own strength or value but by being put to the proof. Calamity is the spur to a great mind.' If Seneca could write these words when the tyrant Nero was his ruler, we too can find out their truth when modern tyrants turn the world upside down.

'Looking back from this my seventieth year, it seems to me that every card in my working life has been dealt to me in such a manner that I had but to play it as it came.' This confession by Rudyard Kipling reveals how destiny so largely made his life.

Karma does not say that a man born in a slum must remain there till he dies. It puts him there, true; but it is up to him to get out of it by his use of intelligence and by his personal efforts. It is true, however, that he cannot do everything he wishes, for he has to start with the existing material and develop from that. 'No general can be lucky unless he is bold,' said General Sir Archibald Wavell. It is the same on the battle-field of life. We must be prepared to take a risk or two if we would leave the field in triumph.

People talk dolefully about their hard fate and their unfavourable karma. What will happen to them when they put on the philosophic mantle? Does truth mercifully cancel their unpleasant future and pro-vide them with a bed of roses in return for their acceptance of her? Do they paralyse their karma by their profound insight? Alas, these com-forting expectations are denied them. The charted karma still stands, but their attitude towards it performs a volte face. The shadows cast upon them by the stars do not change, but they themselves do change. They are resolved henceforth to accept their sorrows in sublime spirit of forbearance. They are determined to submit to their destiny, not from weakness but from strength. Sometimes they may even welcome misfortune when they know it can free their character from obstruc-tions to true growth. If suffering came in the past to educate them or to teach them to discriminate between what is permanent and what is ephemeral, it now comes to test them. It provides them with fit oppor-tunities to try their strength and to realize whether the House of Life they are erecting is built of solid brick or of fragile reeds.

This teaching does not turn a man into a lethargic fatalist as it does not permit him to swell into a conceited individualist. It neither offers any excuse for a miserable weakness, nor bolsters up an illusory strength. It does inspire him with a balanced view of his possibilities, a sane view of his powers.

He has to pass through the school of multiform experiences. He is not to glean his wisdom from books alone, nor solely from meditation, but also from life itself. He may find himself plunged into conditions which seem useless to his spiritual development and unjust to noble aims. But the overself in its far-seeing wisdom knows better. From the philosophic standpoint it is not a matter for regret when he has to face adverse circumstances, but rather a challenge as to what he can make of them. They represent a triple possibility: deterioration, stagnation or growth. When his mind has been accustomed sufficiently long to these ideas, and when they have been recreated as the product of his own thinking and the conclusions of his own experience, they will enable him to meet the challenges of destiny and the mutations of fortune with a strength and wisdom unknown before.

He will begin to see that underlying the obvious human purpose of the relationships with all those other men and women who cross or stay on his path, there is another and deeper one. Whether they be friends or enemies, whether they bring pleasure or anguish, the experience of meeting them is finally to teach lessons.

When someone on whom he has relied for happiness proves unfaithful, he may treat the episode in two different ways. He may react in the common manner and become resentful, bitter, hurt and agonized. Or he may react in an uncommon manner and become wiser if sadder, better instructed in his own values and other people's frailties. He may learn from such an episode that, whilst accepting every happiness that may come from external things and persons, he should not rely on them as fundamental and primary, and that only the divine inward self can hold such a rank safely. He may learn also that the more the ego resents the cause of its misery, the more it resists the lessons involved – the more it suffers. In short, the event will provide a chance to correct his values, jump to a higher standpoint and effect spiritual progress.

The past is wholly unalterable and the present is largely conditioned by it. But the future is less so and therefore more malleable. To grieve over past self-made misfortunes is useful only insofar as it leads to a confession of error, to the detection of weaknesses in character which led to the error, and to active effort to eliminate those weaknesses. How far past deeds may be countered by present thinking is both a variable and indeterminate point. In the study of our own past experiences there is wisdom waiting for us. In the acceptance of its lessons there is strength to be got by us, and in the endeavour to comprehend why certain misfortunes have happened to us there is a practicality to be acquired.

If we go out of our way to do good to others and impose restraint upon ourselves, we thereby help to atone for past sins and to lessen the karma they would otherwise have brought us.

Karma and Right Timing

We learn from karma the grave importance of right timing. He who does the correct thing at the wrong time is not far from the position of the man who does the wrong thing altogether.

There are forces which predetermine our destiny and we must know when to win battles – like Napoleon – by retreating, by submitting to Fate's decree. In the last chapter of *The Hidden Teaching Beyond Yoga*, a technique used by expert boxers was recommended as supplying an excellent principle wherewith to meet the unavoidable blows of a bad karmic cycle. Another illustration of this point which will be helpful is ju-jutsu, whose principle is to conquer an adversary by giving way to him in so skilful a manner that he is forced to use his own strength either to defeat himself or to injure his own muscles. So we may conquer unalterable bad karma by yielding to it for a time but finally drawing from it such wisdom and reaction that we rise higher than before.

'When the superior man gets his time, he mounts aloft; but when the time is against him he moves as if his feet were entangled.' Thus spoke Lao Tzu to Confucius during a memorable interview.

As a man grows older – whether in years or in earthly embodiments – he will begin to pay attention to the invisible line of cause and effect which exists between his deeds and their later consequences upon himself and upon others, which means that he will become more prudent and more deliberate, less likely to act upon mere impulse and more likely to act upon calm consideration.

For the student all life must be a process of trial and error, repeated again and again although with diminishing frequency until at long last he matures into the ripe understanding of the sage. Meanwhile he should remember well those ethical errors which some call sins and reflect well over their lessons, as he should remember the sufferings which were their inevitable if belated fruit.

It is the part of wisdom to learn when to attack difficulties with a bold front and when to circumvent them by patience or cunning. There is a right time for all events. If they are brought about too early, then the consequences will be a mixture of good and bad, just as if they were brought about too late. If, however, one has the patience to wait for the right moment, and the wisdom to recognize it, then the results will be unmixed good. Karma comes into play as soon as a suitable combination of factors occurs. There is no real escape from the consequences of our deeds, therefore, but only an apparent escape.

Karma and Environment

Philosophy is not so foolish as to deny the power and importance of environment, but it adds that the mental attitude towards physical environment is still more important. If this be one of full dependence on it, then the man will be its slave and victim; but if his attitude is one of noble dependence on his inner self, then in part he will be its master. Some part of man is the product of his changing environment, but there is another part which most certainly is not. Sometimes the environment must needs be greater than the individual, but sometimes the individual can prove greater than the environment.

Even if no man should submit to domination by his environment, neither can he be divorced from it. Cruelly hindering or favourably helping him as it does, he cannot fail to be influenced by it. How much has it not meant to a tired, dispirited and depressed worker of the low-paid levels to find, on his return home in the evening, a bright cheerful room with soothing walls, shapely furniture and pleasantly patterned rugs? Environment does count.

A man's surroundings help to bring out his innate qualities or to prevent their manifestation, but they do not create such qualities. If they did, geniuses could be made to order in every school and studio.

Karma and Suffering

Suffering is the inescapable accompaniment to life. War merely throws this truth in vivid and spectacular fashion upon the screen of human consciousness whereas its ordinary operation is slow grinding and sporadic.

Once a man has been burnt by fire he cannot be tempted to put his fingers into a flame – no matter how beautiful its colour or how attractive its warm glow. The suffering and pain of his previous error live too strongly within his memory because they live in the form of knowledge. He does not merely believe but he knows that fire will burn and cause him pain. He does not even have to experiment a second time with the same error, because the knowledge has sunk into his very being. In the same way, the man who knows his essential unity through the Overself with all other men will not commit the error of injuring even a single person; on the contrary he will find powerful motivation for altruistic behaviour. He knows that in injuring others he will ultimately injure himself; for the infallible law of retribution will bring back to him either the pain or the blessings which he bestows on others. So perfect is his sympathy with all living creatures, whether human or non-human, that he seeks to avoid bringing hurt to any of them; on the contrary he takes pleasure in improving their welfare. This attitude comes through a knowledge of the reality of the underlying oneness of life, a knowledge which is neither blind faith nor pious hope and can be discovered through the ultimate path alone. The unfortunate ignorance of this all-important truth is responsible for the awful spectacle of a world arrayed in two camps ready to annihilate each other out of existence. No amount of prayers to an all-too-distant God can save mankind from such catastrophes, but it certainly can be saved by the intellectual acceptance of the truth of unity as a preliminary step towards its ultimate realization. It therefore becomes the bounden duty of every one of us who has intellectually perceived this truth to devote some fragment of his time at least towards giving others an opportunity of becoming acquainted with it. If a man's destiny – the fragment of fate apportioned to him – desires him to achieve a certain task, a particular mission, then – however much he may dally in secluded retreat – it will provide him with an inner compulsion that at the appointed hour will drag him from retirement into the public arena again. Even if the task has been distant from his desire and concealed from his conscious mind during all previous years, he will still have to obey this unexpected inner force, this overwhelming bidding which is but the voice of destiny making itself heard in this way. Yes, paradoxically one carries one's fate within one's self. Karma needs to send no attorney to plead its cause at the bar of man. All history reveals the truth in the long run. The world must learn and those of us who know must teach that every evil deed will infallibly bring an aftermath of suffering. 'What will be the next form of religion?' A. E. was asked a few days before he died. 'A religion of ethics,' he replied. This means a religion based on the doctrine of karma.

'The wicked deed which was done by the wicked hearted in glee; its consequences are reaped by them in the fulness of time with cries,' said Buddha.

Every deed carries its own consequences with it. If we have made a mistake or wronged someone by any course of action, then the sooner trouble comes to warn us off further errors along the same road, the better. We should welcome it as a guiding finger. When life is hard and trying we must peer beneath its surface. Is a bad attitude or bad outlook holding us in chains? The real self may be rejoicing while the surface self is weeping. For we are put here on earth to seek the perfect. As personalities we are certainly sufferers, but as the cosmic self we are sublime spectators.

Experience enlightens man, but it may do so with exasperating slowness if the man is ethically immature and mentally unevolved. He does not really need new experience so much as a right understanding of old experience. If he is unresponsive, stubborn or foolish, then nothing but further experience will teach him. Therefore it is our task to assist him by explaining to him the inner significance of his own experiences, by making available to him in simple form the philosophic fruits of our own wealthier and lengthier experience.

If a man learns the lessons of his past mistakes, then the suffering they brought him will not have been in vain. If he does not learn, then he will go on from disaster to disaster. When he becomes truly teachable, then he can retrieve disaster. If we do not bring reason to our experience it remains barren. Both joy and suffering fail to yield up their secret and the heart is devastated by periodic tumults in vain. Joy rarely comes alone. It is as often followed by sorrow as a man walking in sunlight is followed by his shadow. The foolish are always embittered and unenlightened by such suffering, whereas the wise are always mellowed and instructed by it. The misfortunes of life come from our past karma; the misery that we feel because of them comes from our own blindness. We beat our breasts because we do not understand.

The general conditions of the wars with their aftermath have brought the problem of suffering to the forefront of thinking. Why do we suffer? This becomes the question whose answer is being sought with an earnestness and sincerity which can find satisfaction only in the doctrines of karma.

How we react to the circumstances in which we find ourselves is a plain sign of our spiritual status. It is in times of stress that we are tested as to whether we have built into our character the qualities needful to deal wisely with life's difficulties, or are still depending on the many kinds of escapism. No human life is wholly free from trouble. God has ordained it to be part of our existence and no mystical path can alter this. What can be altered is our reaction to it.

Suffering is one of nature's processes for showing man where he has indulged in wrong-doing. If he will not give up his sins, nature brings their consequences home to him through painful experiences. The man who is incapable of self-rectification will be brought to it by external experience, and he who has failed to develop a sense of spiritual responsibility will be tested by suffering. Until a man adequately repents and tries to undo the harm he has caused, the troubles he has and will have to undergo are of his own making.

It would be unnatural and inhuman if those who seek a spiritual pathway out of their worldly woe did not feel so keenly about it. Nevertheless, it is for them to remember the eternal principles whilst the storms are raging, to remember that they are fundamentally divine and deathless, and to hold firmly to the faith that the ultimate triumph of good over evil is inescapable. The day will come when time shall have healed their deepest wound and when they shall view their world-experience serenely from the mountaintop, as in their Overself they already do. In the end such experience teaches them to depend on nothing and nobody for their happiness.

When a dark hour descends on us we should turn inward at once and there find the true help. When some dark trouble touches our life, when depression, suffering, anxiety, fear, or even temptation threaten to overwhelm us, we must follow this practice of instantly turning inward and seeking the true Self. We shall find at the end of our search peace, contentment, wisdom, strength, courage and love. In short, we have to train ourselves automatically to turn inward whenever we are confronted by seeming misfortune, apparent injustice or undue temptation. Then whatever action we are to take will be guided from within and will necessarily be right because dictated not by human intellect but by higher wisdom. It is not that the divine self will always put matters right for us of its own accord when we turn to it in thought, but that it will often inspire us to take the necessary physical measures which will produce successful results.

The day will come when we shall see this life in a new light and with that resign it to a higher power. In our innermost being there is the Real – unaffected, eternal, sublime. It seeks our love and gives to us its own. It wishes us to sacrifice to itself, but the sacrifice is to be deep in the heart, secret and unspoken. It is the Overself. Offer everything on the altar, prayerfully, and include all those problems of frustration and defeat. When the answer comes, as it must eventually, we shall experience a tremendous relief. It will be as a burden vanished.

The enforced cessation from external activity which illness or imprisonment may bring can be a help to spiritual awakening. A few months before he died, Oscar Wilde said, 'I have lived all there was to live. I found the sweet bitter and the bitter sweet. I was happy in prison because there I found my soul.' Illness is a bitter karma which must be worked out, but if this lesson is learnt the suffering is not in vain.

Man makes some of his troubles by negative thinking, by being too egoistic in his human relationships, by failing to sink the 'I' and to put himself in the other man's position. When he admits the source of many troubles to be within himself, then his chance of banishing them becomes brighter. Troubles are the outer sign of inward malady.

A man must have the courage to refuse to make something else the scapegoat for his own guilt. It is an equally grave error to ascribe to fate's compulsion or God's will what is merely man's way.

It is when outer torments of life shatter inner resistance that the need for spiritual things is acknowledged. And the more unsatisfactory outward life becomes, the more satisfactory will the blessed inward life seem both by contrast and in itself.

Those who have enough of the good things of life, or those who have made an easy passage through circumstances, are usually sufficiently satisfied with themselves and with the external world. Whilst they are running from one different satisfaction to another, beginning each experience under the pathetic delusion that it is the ultimate one and ending with the rueful knowledge that it is not, they are unable to listen to the voice of a wisdom immeasurably older than they are. It is those who have suffered frustration, deprivation and misfortune who want to escape from themselves and the world. Their hopes have died and their courage has departed. When their disappointment is deep and permanent, they will have the ears to hear.

The true seers always have the courage to look facts in the face and to admit that life on earth must touch suffering at some point. They teach man how to sustain himself when this happens, and how so to instruct himself by its lessons that the troubles of this earthly life are transmuted into wisdom and strength.

They who do not yet aspire to be delivered from animal enslavement and human ignorance cannot fail to be goaded into such aspiration by life itself. If they could understand aright their experiences of good and evil, of mind and body, as in the course of evolutionary flow they certainly shall one day, they would understand that they were trying to find themselves. The quest of the Overself may not be clearly conscious in their minds, but it is there nevertheless and actuating the whole life movement.

Man does not endure certain troubles or disappointing experiences during life without a particular reason for each one. If he takes the trouble to learn the reason he can conquer the experience and strengthen his character, or he can permit the experience to conquer him and to worsen his character. Through many and widely varied experiences man is given opportunity to build his capacities of thought and judgement, will and intuition. Experiences rightly handled can become effective means for his passing from a lower to a higher stand-point. Every experience should be exploited for its lessons, whether it be painful or pleasurable, as a novelist might exploit it for story material.

It should be realized that the situations which arise in life are often in some obvious or hidden way self-created, and should therefore be faced courageously and correctly analysed. They may then throw significant light upon character; and although it may not be possible to change them overnight, it is possible to experiment upon them with a different mental attitude and to perceive the helpfulness to inner development of outward adversity, personal antagonisms and peril.

Mental peace can come only by paying the price for it, and part of that price is the freeing of oneself from over-dependence on externals. The mind must be freed from worry and anxiety instead of yielding in hopeless submission to them. This will invoke and assist the protective forces. All bitter thoughts towards other individuals must be banished. Love must be given whether or not it is returned, and given equally to the weak and the strong. A rich inner compensation awaits those who can endure in this way.

Everything that happens to us teaches this lesson of non-attachment, which must be learnt through reflection and tested by experience. As the Buddha taught, we must learn and relearn to let things go and keep unattached, recognizing the evanescent quality of all earthly existence. It is the mercy of mother nature that all suffering, however hard, shares

83

this evanescence. At the end – as now for the few – there is unbroken calm, the eternal peace of a consciousness that is not personal self-consciousness.

Everyone has something to teach us. The lives, perceptions and experience of other men, and the lessons of past events when remembered and reflected upon, may contribute towards our guidance and help to point out to reason the proper course that should be followed in the future.

It must needs be that we acquire our virtues through struggle and pain when we fail to acquire them through reflection and perception. Thoughtlessness and carelessness have to be paid for. If we will not heed the voice of reason and goodwill, we must suffer the whip of affliction. But we are not compelled to wait for painful blunders to show us our folly. Reason is a pleasanter way and a shorter route than the long circle of satiety, repulsion and equilibrium.

Although one of the first qualities a man must foster is the capacity to learn from his past mistakes, he should not allow the past to imprison him. He should look backward only that he may look forward more clearly when considering what his duty is. The man who has the capacity to make new beginnings which cut across a faulty past is the man who can go far on this path.

There is no absolute certainty about anything in this life and no security in any situation. Such things are unattainable. Only relative certainty and security are possible, but if merely external they will prove inadequate. They must also be gained in an inward sense by keen thought and controlled emotion, by communion with the diviner self.

The philosophic prize of utter self-possession is far greater and more to be treasured than any which ambition can offer or desire suggest. It holds a happiness unknown in other ways, and against the misfortunes and difficulties of worldly existence it gives inner reserves of a kind unknown to materialistically minded men. He who has gained this prize is inwardly protected against the buffeting of fortune's waves or the arrows of human malice. 'He who hopes for nothing can never know despair' are words spoken by Caesar in Egypt. Where there are neither desires nor expectations there can be no disappointments.

Misery will be the result of continuing to ignore philosophy. Serenity will be the result of living by its teaching.

When a man turns in full surrender towards his Overself, he can learn of its power to overcome trouble by the poise which descends upon him and by the change in material things. He may not always come successfully out of any situation, in a material sense, but he will do so always in a spiritual sense.

The Overself speaking as the Christ in man says, 'Come unto me all ye that are heavy laden and I will give you rest.' And speaking as the Krishna in man it says, 'Take refuge in me alone. I will liberate thee from all sins, grieve not.'

Nothing but the soul's realization can bring man a total happiness. It releases him from hidden fears of the woes of terrestrial existence; it frees his mind about all concern for the future, and out of the vast depths of his own being he can draw all the wisdom he needs to meet it. In gaining this knowledge of the hidden truth of his own being he enters into real freedom.

Karma and Prediction

In recent years the world has witnessed such a large and rapid growth of belief in astrology as must stagger a sober historian. So many popular newspapers have devoted a column to it, so many astrological booklets emulating *Old Moore's Almanac* have appeared, that it is not too much to say the interest in the subject has assumed the proportions of a flood. One explanation is the general state of international insecurity and instability, and the private anxiety and worry which prevailed after the world economic depression. But there are other reasons for the great uprising of belief in astrology. There is the unconscious or half-conscious need of the masses for a means of interpreting both the stirring world-events and their own personal distresses on lines more satisfactory than the traditional religious or contemporary scientific ones. The religious viewpoint is inadequate intellectually and the scientific one is inadequate emotionally. Most other old standbys have also proved insufficient. Astrology helps them arrive at such an interpretation because of its chief implications, which are supposedly proved every time a prediction is fufilled. These are (a) that there is a higher power guiding the destinies of mankind, (b) that life survives after death, and (c) that there is a rough justice in life. Without endorsing the mass of superstitious rubbish which takes shelter under the name, nor the mass of charlatanic practice and exploitation accompanying it, it is true to say that astrology demands as a complementary doctrine the teaching of karma and rebirth. Therefore the present wave of interest in star lore is an oblique attempt to satisfy human need for this important teaching of which the Western world has been so cruelly robbed for many centuries.

Astrology cannot be considered a completely reliable guide in every-day life, despite the exaggerated claims made by astrologers. As a body of knowledge it is imperfect and incomplete. As a practical art of prediction it is inefficient and uncertain. Therefore nobody should stake all his faith in astrological readings and prophecies alone or he will be taking terrible risks. But this is not to say that astrology is mere superstition as its opponents claim, or utter humbug as the worldly-wise assert. It can provide, if the exact moment of birth be known, many useful indications about a person's character, capacities, tendencies and temperament. To a much lesser extent it can provide also indications of some – but not all – of the major karmic oppor-tunities, difficulties, etc. likely to occur.

The correct appraisal of a horoscope is to regard it as an *indicator* of circumstances earned and character formed in earlier births. It is delu-sion to regard its planetary positions as irresistible forces driving a man unfailingly into those experiences and that character.

We may watch our horoscope if we please, take note of the fate written in our palm if we wish, but we must remember that these things do not displace the need for wise living, moral discipline and right thinking. We should keep first things first and trust the soul's leadings more than the astrologers' warnings or the palmists' promises. The grace of God sought and found, good character and high ideals will be better safeguards through life's maze than any fortune-teller's predictive counsel.

'I forbid you, O Bhikshus, to employ any spells or supplication, for they are useless, since the law of karma governs all things. That mendi-cant does right to whom omens, meteors, dreams and signs are things abolished; he is free from all their evils.' So said the Buddha to a disciple when explaining 'Amitabha' to him.

'Star gazing and astrology, forecasting lucky or unfortunate events by signs, prognosticating good or evil, all these things are forbidden,' said the Buddha to Ananda.

When you become unconcerned about your horoscope; when you cease to run after fortune tellers; when you begin to let the future take care of itself, then you have found peace. But when you become anxious about the future, when you are filled with regrets about your past sufferings, then you are living in time; you become one of the creatures of time and you suffer the pains of time.

Gullible people gasp in awe when a prediction is fulfilled. They look upon it as a miracle. They do not know the immense number of predictions which were falsified by events and which passed in consequence into silent oblivion. It would be a miracle indeed if out of the mass of prophecies some proportion failed to obtain fulfilment.

Whoever expects anyone perfectly to predict all events expects him by implication to know everything that exists in the world, that is to be as omniscient as a God. No human being, not even a sage, could honestly claim such omniscience.

The old Hindu texts say astrology is no longer reliable when a person abandons his worldly life for a spiritual one. No astrological horoscope and no psychic clairvoyance dare utter any word about his future with certainty. From the moment when the Overself takes full possession of a man so that in the old sense his thoughts, feelings and acts are not really his own, it becomes responsible for the working out of his past karma. From that moment indeed the course of his external life and earthly fortunes is unpredictable.

4

Is the Soul in the Heart?

This question is really an ancient one. Centuries ago the Indian thinker Silanka sarcastically complained in his *Sutra Kritanga Tika*, that 'some posit a soul that has a form while others maintain that it is formless. Some point out that the heart is the seat of the immortal Self, while others oppose them by saying the forehead is the right place. How can there be an agreement of views among these philosophers? For us ignorance is far better than these follies.'

The master key to the comprehension of this difficult point is taken hold of when we grasp the notion of two standpoints and consequently discriminate between two levels of existence: the one apparently real and the other absolutely real, the one a transient appearance and the other an eternal substratum of this appearance.

Thus this apparent anomaly can be explained, thus and thus only can views so opposed be reconciled. The Overself of which the author wrote in earlier books represented the esoteric notion of it. Even so, he then pointed out the paradox of its being both inside the human heart simultaneously with its unbounded existence outside the human body. Such statements are perfectly correct from the standpoint of ordinary yogic existence because they describe the actual feelings of the mystic. If it be asked why the full ultimate truth about the Overself being entirely outside all considerations of spatial location was not then frankly given, the reply is that an ancient principle of tuition used by Asiatic teachers was followed, one which adapted truth to the capacities of different minds, unfolding knowledge only partially and progressively.

It is like the difference between gazing at an unopened nut for the first time in one's life and gazing at it when unhusked with the kernel lying revealed. At first we see the husk but believe we are seeing the nut; later we see the real nut and only then know that our discovery of the husk was but a stage – yet a necessary stage – towards our discovery of the kernel.

Spiritual *feeling* does centre itself in the mid-sternal region of the chest. As practical men we must experientially affirm that the Overself has its habitat in the heart, but as metaphysical men we must flatly deny the existence of any special point wherein it could be cramped. Only the sage who has mastered philosophy, who has harmoniously perfected himself in ego-less action yoga and metaphysics, can afford to dismiss all sectional viewpoints; others must attend to them or else unbalance their progress. When meditation succeeds in attaining its objective, the yogi does have a definite experience of bliss, a joy of liberation from matter and ego. Such an experience transcends any that he has ever had before and is so exalted that he believes he has entered into union with the Overself. Indeed he has really achieved his goal, but it is only as seen from an earlier standpoint, like a mountain seen from far off. He has approached immeasurably nearer to the realization of the Overself than the ordinary religionist with his remote anthropomorphic God, for he has found his Deity within himself. Nevertheless it is still not the ultimate realization. He has yet to pass through the metaphysical discipline and the ultramystic contemplations before this union is finally consummated in the discovery of the Overself as it is in itself, not as seen from any standpoint. With this discovery, he is delivered from the need of further meditation because the Overself is then found anywhere – not merely in the heart alone. And this is not a transient experience but a permanent insight.

The mystic view of the matter is not inconsistent and need not be negatived; it can be kept where it belongs and yet be included in and harmonized with the higher philosophic view. For no practical yoga system can be devised which does not in its earlier stages demand some focus for concentrating the thoughts. And in placing that focus within the heart region, the mystic follows the best means of withdrawing his attention from external surroundings. Hence the Svetasvatara Upanishad says: 'placing the body in a straight posture, with the chest, throat, and head held erect making the senses and the mind enter the heart, the knowing one should cross over all the fearful currents.' The Mundaka Upanishad also counsels: 'Just in the heart, where all the blood-vessels meet, very much like the spokes of a wheel meeting in the navel or the centre, resides the interiorly-governing Divine Spirit, manifesting His glory in ways multifarious. Contemplate Him, this interiorly-governing spirit, for, thus alone can you reach, with safety, the blissful haven, far beyond the ignorance-begotten miseries of this troubled ocean of life.' The Gita XVIII, 6, says the region around the heart is the divine centre. 'He has set eternity in their hearts,' says the Biblical Ecclesiastes. 'The Heart is the greatest, the most primal cavity Residence of the Self; the body of bones and flesh is Its temple. Those who study this Secret Path realize that the individual is that Self and nothing else. The five senses which are robbing an aspirant of his robust Self, are the candles to exhibit the Inner Light,' wrote Tirumoolar, a Tamil mystic of the seventeenth century.

It is an indisputable fact that although visions of divine figures or the Light of the Overself are clairvoyantly *seen* in the head, the presence of what is most divine *in* man is mystically *felt* in the heart; for Nature herself has made a mysterious and holy vacuum therein. The Overself as such is formless, but its *manifestation* within the heart possesses form. In the unimaginably minute airless space within the heart where this manifestation abides throughout the the whole length of an incarnation, there appears a picture formed of light, a picture which outlines the precise prototype of physical body of the man concerned. In our measure it is but a fraction of a fraction of a dot in size. Yet it is there. This is the 'little man within the heart' of whom Tibetan occultism speaks, the 'figure in the heart' space of Indian mystical Upanishads. In *The Quest of the Overself* it was explained that the divine habitat within the heart was not a thing but a space, symbolically called a 'cave' by the ancients and in reality a kind of vacuum.

The authoritative Pali commentators on Buddhist texts expounded that the mind or consciousness is in dependence on the heart-base, although the Buddha himself never stated the organ in which it existed. They must have had their reasons for doing so. One school of Vedanta teaches that Brahma's abode in man is in his vital centre, in the smallest ventricle of the heart. On the other hand, some yoga teachers place it variously in the top, centre, or base of the head. Shankara, the sage and commentator, reconciles these seemingly contradictory teachings about the seat of the spiritual self. He shows that in deep sleep the different places are entered in gradual succession. This does not mean that each has the same purpose or importance. Shankara points out that they fulfil different ends. Thus the spirit occupies the heart at one point of time and the head at another.

The actual place in the physical body where awareness of the Soul seems to come to birth differs according to the particular exercise in meditation deliberately practised, or according to the particular kind of mystical experience involuntarily and spontaneously received.

It is a fact however that in most cases the feeling of the Soul's presence is first felt in the heart or breast region. But if the mystic should pass into a deep meditation akin to half-trance, as the feeling deepens and strengthens itself it also spreads itself out into the Infinite. It is then no longer limited to the heart or the head, in whichever place it first made itself felt.

It is a tenet of the hidden teaching that Mind has two phases: conscious and the unconscious, or active and the inactive. The second is the root and determinant of the first phase. And it is a further tenet of this teaching that the conscious mind is correlated with the brain. Science can find corresponding changes in the brain for every change in sensation, that is, in consciousness; but science cannot find any such physical change in the brain for the principle of awareness itself, that is, for the unconscious. If it were to direct its researches in this regard towards the heart, its efforts might hope for better chance of success, because it is there only that the corresponding bodily changes could ever take place. But as the principle of awareness is an unchanging one, no physical changes ever correspond to it in actuality. It is everpresent during life. It is like a circle whose circumference is the entire body and whose centre is the heart. A shot through the heart is fatal not only in a physical but also in a mental sense.

What is achieved during odd illumined moments, however, is not enough, for these moments are at first but intermittent. The habit of descending into the heart must be rendered habitual; man's central consciousness must be transferred from the brain to the heart. This does not mean to say that he is to become incapable of thought; only that thought will assume a secondary and subordinate importance in his life, and that the supreme place will be given to a focused attention upon and enjoyment of the peace within the Divine Atom resident in the Heart. He may then use the brain at will and think no less clearly, no less efficiently, than he formerly did; only he will no longer become the hapless victim of thought's tyranny.

When we still the active intellect, we feel the pressure in the head relax and a feeling of peace begins to suffuse the heart. This is also a physical feeling, so that there is really a descent from the busy intellectual region of the head to the quiet spiritual region of the heart. The

Mystic rests his consciousness in the heart habitually, except when he has to enter intellectual activity for a time.

We descend from meditation in the brain to meditating in the breast. Such a statement may be incomprehensible to those whose thoughts and meditations have forever revolved within the sphere of cold ratiocination alone, but it will make some sense to the few who have begun to feel the first and almost impalpable radiations of the divinity which the heart harbours. For man's real home is in the heart, not the head. He has strayed afar.

5

The Interior Word

If thou would'st hear the Nameless and wilt dive
Into the Temple-cave of thine own self,
There brooding by the central altar, thou
May'st haply learn the Nameless hath a voice
————Tennyson 'The Ancient Sage'

When He, the Spirit of Truth is come, He shall guide
you into all truth; for He shall not speak from Himself: but whatsoever He shall hear, these shall he
speak.
————Jesus

Which things we also speak, not in the words which
man's wisdom teacheth but which the Holy Spirit
teacheth.
————St. Paul

If thou can'st do what He enjoins on thee, He will do
what thou dost ask assuredly;
————Awhadi (Medieval Persian mystic)

A striking mystical phenomenon is the 'living word' as some have
called it. This is the interior communication through clearly framed
messages from the Overself. It is a form of speech where every sentence
is endowed with magic, where every word is a vital force and where
definite effects flow from each communication. It works in and on the
heart and sheds wisdom's light on the mind.

All inspired bibles are the records of this inner utterance. They are
the echoes of this same speech, but drained of its life-giving power, its

93

supernal, over-worldly tone, and its vivid authority. All *true* gospels are spoken in this mystical inner language, are heard only in the heart and not with the ears, are creative transfiguring forces and not mere intellectual statements. What is heard within the heart is indeed the Logos, the Divine Word, which can be heard only in this way. That which is written or printed on paper can be no more than the word of Man, not God.

This mysterious power of the deep silence within himself to break into speech will at first astonish and then delight the aspirant. If he perseveres in his practice, the silence within will little by little take voice and guide his further efforts. Its words may reveal divine truths, afford spiritual guidance or explain the inner significance of situations and events. Negatively, it will reprove his sins, warn him of his errors, and humiliate his egoism. Positively, it will lead him to higher standpoints, show him the right path to follow and illuminate the true meaning of all scriptures. It will correct his attitudes, direct his behaviour, and instruct his mind. And he who has attained to the hearing of this inner voice will always be glad and willing to obey such commands. He must learn to listen to the inner voice and heed the inner light rather than the teachings and guidance of other men. It will come to possess for him an indisputable authority and a supreme truth. But it can do so only after he has learned to distinguish it clearly from its rivals and enemies – only with time, experience and constant self-examination.

After he has won through to the stabilization of this experience of the inner voice, he will find an inward teacher perpetually within his heart. Henceforth the higher self will impart knowledge steadily to him, either in the midst of activity through *intuitions* or in the depths of self-absorptions through *inspirations*.

By this method he will be taught continuously and instructed progressively. He will be led by a voice speaking in his heart, from stage to stage, truth to truth and perception to perception.

It is a mysterious voice that breaks the silence of ignorance which reigns in other men and whose every word is creative, dynamic and loving. The voice which now speaks perpetually to him is no metaphorical one. It is so real that even once heard it is more unforgettable than any human voice – however beautiful – could be. It is so sacred that he receives its utterances with the reverence accorded to scripture, for they are nothing less.

When inward converse with the higher self develops, the ego vividly feels the presence of its Beloved and expresses its longings and prayers, its joys and reverence. Through the Interior Word the soul responds. These interior conversations may become a feature of his life for a certain time, the ego addressing its higher self on some occasions, the higher self addressing the ego on others. He may often have the strange experience of participating in dialogues between the familiar ego and what seems to be a higher one. That he is receiving communications from the divine may well be a genuine fact. But the form they take is inevitably imposed on them and coloured by his own personality.

And I make it my business only to persevere in His Holy presence, wherein I keep myself by a simple attention, and a general fond regard to God, which I may call an *actual presence* of God; or to speak better, an habitual silent and secret conversation of the soul with God, which often causes in me joys and raptures inwardly.

——Brother Lawrence (17th century mystic), *Practice of the Presence of God* Translated from the French

That we need only to recognize God intimately present with us to address ourselves to Him every moment, that we may beg His assistance for knowing His will in things doubtful, and for rightly performing these, which we plainly see he requires of us, offering them to Him before we do them, and giving Him thanks when we have done.

——Ibid

The dialogues may develop spontaneously, and it will be a useful exercise to cultivate silent conversations with the sacred presence whenever the slightest tremor of its nearness is felt. Dialogue form often concerns revelations, guidance, counsel, encouragement and the answering of questions. There are fine specimens of this form in the third part of *The Imitation of Christ*.

A kindred phenomenon to the Interior Word is the dialogue between some higher being, often regarded as God or as an angel, and the mystic himself. He will receive the words but will not see their speaker. For the Interior Word is a different phenomenon from that where some spiritual personage of the past or present appears in vision. The first is more reliable than and always to be preferred to the second. This is because it is a communication to the mind alone, whereas the other is also a communication to the senses, which, being on a lower level than its source, are far less fit to judge it. The mystic is aware of

95

another presence, a holy entity, somewhere within him, and a beautiful fellowship with it gradually develops. It speaks to him within his mind, and not to his bodily ears, so distinctly and so spontaneously that he feels he cannot doubt its real existence. This mysterious entity within his heart has life but not shape, voice but not face.

Once he truly awakens to the god who sits concealed in his inmost heart, once he has learnt how to enter the silence and pass through it, then out of the interior silence there will sound forth the Interior Word. This amazing moment when the silence of the higher self is dramatically broken, when its voice speaks in his heart, will repeat itself at intervals, first in his periods of withdrawal for prayer and meditation, then at any time. This is the mystic voice heard by Samuel and by all inspired prophets. 'Speak Lord, for thy servant heareth,' was Muhammed's response to it. It will bring healing to his nerves and bear its own authority to his mind. Authoritative messages may thus be received from his higher self, formulated in distinct words but without any sound. During sessions of mental quiet the Overself may reach the ego in either a wordless or wordful way. A presence is felt, an inner voice is heard, an uplifting ideal is presented. Some have called this striking mystical phenomenon 'the living word'. Speech forms itself in the mystic's heart, he knows not how, and communicates revelations or gives counsel. What we have elsewhere called intuition, which more than anything else is a feeling inside him, is not the same as this, which is more like someone speaking to him. It is an aspect of the Overself's power.

The mysterious inner voice, which utters no sound that the ears could hear yet formulates messages and communicates guidance of spiritual importance, arises within him during trance. They will, however, refer only to the inner life. They will give no guidance for the outer life.

The aspirant should listen intently to the silence that he will find deep within his heart, deeper than all the passions, emotions, instincts, desires, attractions and repulsions which usually pulsate tumultuously there. No one else can do this for him. The voice which will presently make itself faintly felt will seem like a messenger from another world. Something or someone will begin to stir in his inner being and address itself to him. Wise and instructive, warning or inspiring, this mental voice will seem to be another's. Yet later he will become aware that it is not so, that it is, indeed, the voice of his own best mind.

Although the experience may not be in store for everyone, it is possible that some aspirant who is sufficiently advanced may find himself gradually entering into a heritage of great powers which have awaited him since his dim evolutionary past and which have slowly germinated deep down within his being during all these mystical efforts. The first of these mystical powers is to hear the Voice of the Silence.

It is needful to learn the art of distinguishing between the true and the pseudo Interior Word. If it manifests itself during the second stage and before he has ever been able to touch the third stage, it most probably is the pseudo-word. It may then be a result of mental activity on the ego's part mixed with a little reflected light from the Overself. The true word comes after the third stage. It speaks out of the mental stillness of contemplation, and is indeed one of its striking effects. It is 'The Voice of the Silence.'

'I will hearken what the Lord God will speak in me.' Psalm 85 testifies to the truth of this same experience. Similar testimony is found in Oriental scripture.

Dr Singh has translated the *Gorakha-Bodh*, a dialogue between Gorakhnath and his teacher, Machendra which bears comparison in style and importance to the yoga Upanishads. An extract follows:

QUESTION. Who can tread a path without feet? Who can see without eyes? Who can hear without ears? Who can speak without words?
ANSWER. Contemplation can tread without feet; discrimination can see without eyes; attention can hear without ears; the self-born can speak without words.

Eternal wordless truth is brought into time and expressed in space.

6

Is the World an Illusion?

It is not surprising that when mystics in East and West come to regard as their loftiest wisdom a metaphysic which is statically perched on an altitude of the most abstractly conceived ideas, which is void of human relations and human interest and which disdains the entire world as being non-existent, they also come to be regarded by the critics of mysticism as impractical dreamers. The consequences of such a degeneration are serious. Men with brains put them to no better use than wasting whole lifetimes in interminable discussions of a purely logical character, discussions which are devoid on the one hand of human colouring and divorced on the other from human needs.

But we ought first to inquire whether this really is their loftiest ancient wisdom or whether it is merely the degeneration of it.

The doctrine of world illusion is a stumbling block to most Western students, and this is understandable. Many Indians themselves expound this remarkable doctrine in a manner so airy and a speech so glib that one feels intuitively that to them it is only a bit of verbiage. A courageous and penetrating few have grasped the true thought of their masters; the rest repeat words and sentences like so many parrots. When we inquire as to what is the highest wisdom attained by Oriental sages, we are informed by many metaphysicians and several mystics that it consists in regarding a mysterious entity, Spirit, as the only reality and the universe itself as a mere illusion. When we ask them how this illusion originated, they reply that because this entity alone exists there are no individuals in existence and consequently nobody to be caught in illusion! When, further, we ask them what is the purpose of human existence, they answer that it is to discover reality; yet in the same breath they say that reality is totally unrelated to the universe and consequently to such existence! Nor is the current Western religious belief that this world is principally a material one with a kind of incidental spiritual 'ghost' somewhere inside it any better. It is only one step less materialistic than the atheistic belief that there is no other world at all.

A doctrine which says that the Perfect alone exists, that the Absolute alone is real, that the universe is illusory and that our knowledge of it is false – such a doctrine unconsciously and unsatisfactorily commits itself to the conclusion that the Godhead is eternally engaged in the act of self-deception! This doctrine which makes the world non-existent, although drawn from the undeniable fact that the testimony of the senses is sometimes refuted by the testimony of reason, is a false conclusion reached by confused rational thinking or obscure mystical feeling. Nevertheless, the idea-intoxicated metaphysician or self-deceived mystic who dismisses the universe as an ungrounded illusion does not dismiss himself thereby. He too is a part of this illusion. Yet he continues to treat himself as a reality. Such inconsistency alone would show the futility of his efforts and the illogicality of his thinking.

The orthodox doctrine of an immobilized, inactive Reality can never explain why the universe is present in experience nor why we feel we are here at all. But we need not accept this doctrine as being the best that mysticism has to offer. Quite correctly this metaphysic proclaimed that man attained his higher goal when he came to recognize his true being as rooted in or identical with the Absolute being. Quite incorrectly, however, through losing itself in queer and questionable logical abstractions, it converted the individual Self into a pale fiction and the physical world into a grotesque hallucination. The truth is that neither is the one a fiction nor the other a hallucination, but both are a *manifestation*. However insufficiently, the Real reveals itself in them. It cannot be sundered from them.

Those among the Greek, the Alexandrian and the Indian mystical metaphysicians who opposed the reality of Spirit to the illusion of Matter, were unable to explain how the two could be unified. Consequently, they placed the former on a pinnacle separated by an unbridgable chasm from the creative Universal Soul, from the material world and from the individual soul. All their ingenious explanations of existence either stopped at the edge of this chasm and there left the Absolute as an inexplicable mystery with whom the Relative had nothing to do, or left the manifested world as a purposeless creation drifting like a mist in mid-air. Only one bridge can be built across this chasm and only mentalism can build it.

We have seen that 'matter' is non-existent and we know that thoughts are transient. What is it then that we are dealing with as the stuff of our personal world experience? Mentalism answers that it is the permanent essence of all thoughts, that it is Mind. This discovery is as far as we can get when searching inwards. Mind-essence is the irreducible ultimate reality. It is itself empty of all forms, void of all individualization. But we have also to search outwards. And then, when we are able to see that it does not make any *intrinsic* difference to itself whether it be known as transient thoughts or as enduring Thought so long as it is *always* perceived as present, we see aright. The world is an appearance if it be viewed as a process, but it is the uniquely Real if viewed as a single substance.

When first the truth dawns on us that this mysterious all-enclosing yet paradoxically all-excluding Void is the Real; when second its blessed presence is felt as something living within us in all states and times and places and not merely in meditation alone; when third we see the universe in its Cause and its Cause in the universe – Matter in Spirit and Spirit in Matter, the two at once – we are said to possess insight. We then perceive that the broad brown earth, covered with green stuff and rolling through hills and valleys, is not less real in substance than the Void, not less divine in essence even though its form be but a mental image which must pass away. We feel that it is a part of the mysterious Whole, a part which can in no wise be separated from that which sustains and cherishes it. Thus we learn not only that there is no reality independent of Mind and no ultimate being apart from our own innermost egoless self, but also that there exists no formed thing in our external experience which does not get its essential being from the same source whence we derive our own.

The impenetrable and enigmatic problem of how the Absolute became the Relative is a manufactured one. It exists only in a wordy realm of a logic divorced from fact, of a metaphysic which has set up an artificial opposition between Spirit and Matter because it did not know that these were merely Mind and its Idea. For if we intellectually throw everything into Mind, we discover at once the unifying principle which can neatly contain them without doing violence to its own integrity. Mind thus becomes the first principle of all existence and, paradoxically, also the last. The ego and the ego's world are ideas of the Overself and the Overself in its turn is a ray of the Mind. Just as the sun appears to have split itself up into millions of rays but nevertheless.

remains the same single sun that it was before, so the ineffable Mind cannot be separated into parts except in appearance, and cannot be divided into individual entities except in human thinking of it. He who believes that Mind has ever lost anything by this self-giving, has ever become less than it ever was, does not comprehend it. It always keeps its pristine, undivided and integral character. We humans are in essence divine souls radiated from that central sun – a simile which is useful to help our thinking minds grasp, in the only way they can, both the intimacy and immediacy of our inner reality. We are sharers in the reflection of its glorious light.

The One does not *become* the Many, for the orders of being and consciousness are different. It remains what is is and from it *emanates* the Many. The universe is much more an emanation than a manifestation. Because it is an emanation rather than an illusion, the World-Idea is not to be treated as a non-entity. It is not to be sharply divided from reality. For it *is* the Real manifesting something of itself in a particular way. All events are only its activity as all things are only its attributes. Relativity exists between the ideas themselves but the substratum out of which they spring is the eternal and infinite, the self-existent and Absolute Mind. Matter thus becomes but a mental entity. The Absolute is not cleft inseparably from the Relative for the Relative is its own Idea. Mind itself is that which has always existed, which is the unique essence of all things and all beings, the first and last Principle of the world process. We may say of it what we may say of nothing else except Infinite Space: It *is*. And this will still be true even if the whole universe, including the conscious beings in it, disappears. Mind could not have come into existence at any specific time as it could not have come into existence from nothing; therefore, it must always have existed and there was never a moment when it was not.

By contrast, both our thoughts and the world which is inseparably associated with them are transient and changeful. But the mind which makes their appearance possible is not. It alone can stand the supreme test of ultimate reality, the test of whether it is changeless and ever-enduring. Whatever is real can never perish. Whatever is only an emanation from the Real will lose its form but nevertheless will not lose its essence. If it be true that the Godhead transcends all finite things, nevertheless it is inseparably immanent in them and is indeed the very foundation of their existence. As if this cosmos could lie outside the force whence it arose, or the force outside the cosmos! They are not really two things but two aspects of one thing. It is not that the world is non-existent; it is a thought and has mental existence. Our natural desire to be assured of our own and the world's existence, no less than of life's utility, is satisfied by the truth. Thus the world-problem that eluded these metaphysicians and mystics is smoothly elucidated by mentalism. But to achieve this success we must first clearly understand that mentalism is not merely the same as idealism but is a fuller doctrine. Whereas the latter would convert everything into separate ideas and leave the world as such, the former would convert them into ideas only to unify them again into this single stuff – Mind.

The Real and its appearance are the same thing seen from different sides. After all, the innumerable subjects in the latter are formed by a process of thought, which is a power belonging to the former. We cannot do violence to the world's existence by dismissing it as unreal. It is only an incomplete mysticism or an unillumined and merely intellectual metaphysics and not insight-based philosophy that attempts to do so. Philosophy, by dissolving the world's plurality into unity, reveals that it is ultimately made of the same stuff as its eternal ground. All the different space-time levels of the universe are inter-penetrated by Mind. Therefore, all worlds are one. Those who live in one particular space-time level will naturally have a different form of consciousness from those who live in another one. Consequently there can be – and are – numerous forms of consciousness, each one repre-senting a world to its inhabitants. But the ultimate 'stuff' of these worlds is one and the same – Mind – only the modes of apprehending it change from one space-time level to another. Each world is real in the experience of those in it, although vastly different from the others.

No world is an illusion, for every world is spun out of God's own being; but our particular space-time mode of experiencing and know-ing that world is illusory. The world appearance is real enough to those who have to live in it. Therefore the true position is not between it as illusion and something transcendental as reality, but between appear-ance and its hidden ground. Thus when we expand our understanding of the physical world we discover that it too is divine. So long as the myth of multiplicity holds sway over our mind, so long will we be confounded and bewildered. We must turn to the truth: unity. There is nothing but Mind.

When we can grasp this concept, that Mind is the only reality and that all else is but its appearance or manifestation, and when we grasp the corollary of this concept, that man himself is fundamentally rooted in Mind——we may then proceed to the further step that if human existence has any ultimate aim at all, it can only be to demonstrate the oneness of being and to enter consciously into its own hidden truth. Thus our final conclusion must be not that the world is an illusion, nor that it is unreal, but that its externality to mind is illusory and its independence of our own self is unreal. It does not exist in its own right. That stable reality which we believe to be in things but believe wrongly to be in their sense-experienced existence, actually resides therefore in the universal mind which manifests itself in them. Consequently our total impression of the world's reality is not illusory but it is misplaced. If we would lay hold of this reality in the right way we must rise above the level of sensed perceptions and attain the level of the one all-unifying universal Mind behind them.

This mentalist appraisal of the nature of the wakeful world of so-called illusion, and this realist appraisal of its worth, are not Western alone. Thousands of years ago some wise initiated commentators on the Mandukya Upanishad, including the most ancient of all, Guadapada, followed the same line. The teaching of the old Eastern masters was that the world does not exist except through the Self. Therefore they called the whole created universe 'Maya' – a word which we translate badly as 'illusion' but whose true meaning can be reached only by pondering over mentalism. They pointed out that our first and natural instinct is to accept the external world as the final reality, but since that world requires a conscious self to witness it and to receive the reports of the sense organs concerning its existence, the ultimate reality was then this conscious witnessing self. This declaration did not destroy the first acceptance of external reality; it simply supplemented and deepened it. The mentalist doctrine of Maya explains that if we are not aware of the world, then the world has no real existence *for us*. Those last two words need treble underlining, for most people conveniently forget them or stupidly ignore them. Consciousness is thus shown to be the basic reality. Hence the Upanishad verse:

> In me arose the whole world:
> In me exists the All
> In me it passes.

The false opposition of Spirit and Matter, the disheartening tenet that the material universe is without significance, and the pitiful belief that all existence is mere illusion represent the lamentable result of the impact of the full truth upon half-prepared minds.

If these views were ever to be carried into practical life, they would smite their holders with complete paralysis. The intellect would cease to move, the heart to feel and the body to act. But whatever may have been the case in ancient or medieval times, if we look into the practical life of their present-day advocates we find that all this talk of a futile Absolute, eternally divorced from a meaningless universe, is mere syllogistic jugglery and logical gymnastics; for they usually take as much interest in securing 'illusory' earthly benefits for themselves as do the much despised realists. Whilst they insist for the benefit of other persons on the nothingness of the common world, actually they show no less insistence than others on treating it in terms of the utmost reality. This is an evidence of the uselessness of a metaphysic divorced from mystical science and of the danger of exaggerating a single aspect of existence at the cost of all the others. In any case, it is clear enough that the only reasonable goal of one who sincerely follows out the consequences of all such teaching is to renounce the active world and become a carefree lotus-eater, a body-hating monk or a self-centred dreamer.

Such a complete splitting of life from wisdom, of truth from experience, as is represented by the basic doctrine of this so-called highest wisdom is not likely to be acceptable to the West as a contribution from the East. Fortunately, this teaching is not worthy of the title. In the East's own hidden teaching lies a superior doctrine which satisfies alike the demands of reason, the dictates of the heart, the promptings of intuition and the needs of practical activity. Whilst it rigorously refuses to accept the finality and errors of sense-experience, it does not pessimistically alienate man from the ultimate values of such experience. There is no rest, no peace, no truth, no life even, certainly no happiness, while we cling to the phenomenal passing show *for its own sake*; but there is final peace and complete fulfilment when we can accept it as a fleeting manifestation of the deathless Real. Then we can convert all things and all creatures into thoughts; the myriad of thoughts into their single element, mind; and mind into its unmanifest, un-individuated infinite essence or reality, Mind. We arise to a region where all exists within ourself and nothing can therefore be lost, where death is a fiction and suffering a phase that will pass. This is God, Nirvana, Overself – any name we wish to give it, although no name can ever reach it. It is not to be thought of as a second thing apart from ourself, but as our very being. We are here on earth to find that.

This quest cannot be finished merely by an intellectualist abstraction of what are thought to be the illusions of the terrestrial sphere, and certainly not by ascetic flight from them. It can come to a final terminus only when insight into the Real is gained from and amid the fullest activity in the terrestrial sphere itself.

If we want to think truly of the supreme reality, we must think of it under two aspects: the ever-resting and the ever-working, and under two forms: stillness and motion. Nor can we stop our understanding of this great truth at this point. For if we want to live more truly in accordance with the way in which the life of God itself is lived, if we aspire to imitate the divine existence so far and so humbly as we dare, then we too must bring our little lives into this same twofold rhythm of quiescent stillness and busy activity, of inward contemplation and outward struggle, of self-regarding satisfaction and altruistic service.

This remembrance of and concentration on the silent void whilst engaged in the midst of bustling activity is admittedly not easy and requires nothing less than genius for its successful consummation. It is called in the Chinese hidden teaching 'Wu Wei'. An adulterated fragment of this teaching exists in Lao Tzu's little text entitled Tao Teh King and the phrase is usefully translated as meaning 'non-doing' or 'inaction'. Both Western and Eastern mystics have erroneously thought this means to refrain from action by living in monastic retreat. The correct meaning is the inner realization of the basic voidness, the immateriality of existence, while outwardly taking that materiality as real for practical purposes. To practise inaction, in the sense in which it has been used in Oriental mystical works like the Bhagavad Gita and the Tao Teh King, does not mean physical inertia. This is a materialistic misapprehension. It means to effect an entrance into the Void *and then* to carry the sense of its emptiness into the very midst of activity, into the heart of physical existence. We have to comprehend that despite appearances the hidden teaching does not lead to utter nihilism or to blank negativism, but rather to what is most real in life. Hence if most mystics envisage their ultimate physical goal as a state of inspired inactivity, all philosophers envisage their ultimate physical goal as a state of inspired action.

If it be true that we all live and move and have our being in the Infinite Mind, it must be equally true that the presence of that Mind is not confined to any ashram, mountain cave or cloistered retreat. It is here in

London, here in Chicago and here in Chungking, too. It is just as much here in the midst of Broadway's bustle and London's teeming life as it is in any far-off Tibetan monastery. If we could not find it whilst attending to our everyday practical interests, if it were utterly outside and forever beyond them, then it would not be the Real. If the start of outward activity annuls the inward peace, then the true transcendence has not been found. When we understand that this world is a manifestation of divine reality itself, then this earthly life is emphatically not a trap set by Satan as some believe, nor a mirage made of cloud as others say. It is not only something which does matter but, on the contrary, something which must matter even more to the truth-finder than it does to the materialist.

7

Ascetic Mysticism Reconsidered

We often hear that all religious and mystical paths lead to the same goal – God. This is doubtless true if we take a long-range evolutionary view of existence, if we think in terms of hundreds of lifetimes rather than a single one. But if we descend from ultimate to immediate considerations, we shall find that there are important differences among the attainments of the different paths. Mysticism is a strange country. It is no less important to find out the hidden goal or intrinsic purpose of a mystical technique than it is to understand the man who has originated it. For in this elusive terrain, it is easy to jump to a superficial estimate but hard to descend to a scientific one. It is not enough to accept the asserted objective of any such path. Its examination is equally necessary. 'Does it really lead to such an objective?' is the question which must start this examination, and not only by the declared theories behind it but much more by its ascertained results are we to find a correct answer. It is thus that our own new pilgrimage was born.

It all began with the framing of a single and simple question which experience, reflection and other men had suggested to us. We wanted to know why mystics play such an insignificant part in the collective life of mankind when, if their theories are true and their powers exist, they ought to be playing a leading part. For we believed then, and even more so now, that the ultimate worth of an outlook on life which inculcates the hidden unity of the human family is its power to find expression in the earthly life of mankind. We believe that those who possess such an outlook should endeavour to render it effectual, first in their own everyday existence, and second in that of society, and not be content only with dreaming or talking about it. We believe that there is laid upon them the duty to *try* to mould, however slightly, the public mind; to *try* to guide the contemporary public welfare movements and

107

to inspire; to *try* to influence or counsel the leaders and intelligentsia. They should not find an excuse for their failure to do so in the public distaste for mysticism, for they are not asked to obtrude the subject itself, but only its fruits in useful service and wise guidance. Nor ought they to refuse the task as foredoomed to failure in the face of evil public Karma. It is their duty to try, unconcernedly, leaving all results to the Overself. In short, if their claims to esoteric knowledge and extraordinary powers are worth anything at all and can be demonstrated by results, they ought to try to leave their mark on history in a most unmistakeable manner.

But when we gaze around at the contemporary world, we actually behold no such effective contribution, even though we are living in an epoch which has witnessed the most dramatic convulsions of human history. Whatever social benefit has been brought by the mystics to mankind has mostly been brought not because of their mystical outlook but in spite of it.

The mystical hermit who withdraws from his fellows physically may in time withdraw his fellow-feeling from them, too. When he settles down to enjoy the inward peace which world-shunning will admittedly yield him, there arises the danger of a complete introversion of the sympathies, a callous self-centredness in social relations and a cold indifference to the fate of mankind. We see it in the persons of ascetics and yogis especially, who – because they are so sublimely wrapped up in their own inner peace – are regarded as perfect sages by an ignorant populace and are honoured accordingly. We must not fail to note the implication that the millions of suffering human creatures would then share in this supposed non-existence. Such a crankily ascetic and confusedly metaphysical indifference to the world leads inevitably to an indifference towards all mankind. Its welfare is not his concern. Thus, from a social standpoint he becomes impotent. To show, in the face of world agony, an emotional callousness and an intellectual apathy is a spiritual greatness which we have no desire to attain. On the contrary, we would regard it as spiritual littleness.

Such reflections alone might have sufficed to persuade us to take up the pilgrim's staff again, but is a further defect of the mystical temperament (a defect which, of course, we ourself shared although fortunately our mental make-up was too rational and too complex not to be somewhat aware of it) that it is prone to fnd plausible esoteric excuses for the inexcusable. The destiny which has led us thus far had to step in, therefore, and bring us to the critical crossroads of a compulsory and decisive recognition of the need for further search for a higher source of truth. And she began to do this, firstly through a painful personal experience of monastic institutions which had quickly descended the way of most 'spiritual' institutions and secondly, by stripping away the façade of glamour which surrounded those whom we had taken at their reputed status of perfect sages when they were only perfect yogis at best. The consequence of this was a reorientation, or rather return, towards our early love of philosophy in an effort to correct and balance our mystical experience.

Before we can explain this observation, we must first pen a brief preamble. There is a common belief that writers on a higher thought should avoid politics, but it is a belief common only among the mystically inclined or monastically minded, not among the philosophically trained. We shall shortly explain that the only kind of mysticism we follow is the philosophical kind. Now it is, among several other things, part of the business of philosophy to examine political principles and ethical problems. It might, however, be advisable for mystics, religionists and ascetics to avoid political discussions, at least from the standpoint of practical policy, or they will run the risk of starting schisms and opening splits in their ranks and institutions because they distribute their political allegiance in various quarters. But such a risk does not detain the philosophically inclined for a moment. The latter are necessarily independent and subserve the interests of no racial group, no particular organization and no special political affiliation. They believe truth to be as necessary in this practical world as in the less-visited worlds of metaphysical doctrine. Truth is their primary business, but it is ample enough to include matters erroneously supposed to be remote from it.

Nevertheless, those accustomed to move in the fixed orbit of ascetic mysticism, with its aloofness from politics as an expression of its aloofness from all earthly things, may be surprised or even shocked at the thought that a professed mystic should put forth such ideas as will be found in the next few pages. Many may consequently misjudge them and think that we are stooping into the dust of politics or airing nationalistic prejudices. Those friends, however who really know us will not make this error. For we have come too often on this planetary scene and thus lived too long to care for the politics of a moment when eternity is our native atmosphere. We have travelled too widely and reflected too deeply to take root overmuch in any one land rather than another and can honestly say with Thomas Paine, 'The world is my country!' We have found loyal, loving friends and bitter malicious enemies in every continent, among the Orientals as among the Occidentals, among capitalists no less than communists, and have come to regard all peoples with a more or less equal and cosmopolitan eye, knowing that it is always and ever the individual *character* that counts. If a man has genuinely awakened into the Overself-consciousness, the experience will of itself annihilate his prejudices and unite him fundamentally with other men. If anyone speaks of God but dislikes another man merely because of racial or colour difference, be sure he is still living in darkness. The materialist who thinks he is the body and nothing else, naturally betrays racial prejudice. The mentalist who knows that he is mind more than flesh, naturally discards such prejudice as puerile. Our views are therefore quite detached and impartial. If we venture now into what seems like politics for a few minutes, it is only because we do not and cannot divorce anything – not even politics – from life and hence from truth and reality. We have no use for a goodness which wastes itself like a lonely flower in the desert air or for self-admiring monastic retreats, as we have no use for a faith or doctrine which is to be confined to the inactive shelves of libraries or the fitful gossip of teatables.

We cannot fail to admit some justice in a further question, another which is often asked us by Western critics: why has Shangri-la, which is the traditional home of yoga and the reputed paradise of mystics, shown proportionately such little external benefit from their presence and powers? Such a question may irritate many Shangrians emotionally, but it always impresses itself intellectually on most Westerners.

Tibet, even more than any other part of Asia, has fallen victim to the seductions of ascetic and monastic mysticism. The grand spiritual goal is there thought to demand complete isolation for its attainment. The most advanced spiritual type is believed to be the complete recluse. What has been the practical social result of all this lofty aspiration? Dirt, semi-starvation, disease and superstition are the common heritage of the masses, for those who had the superior intelligence to instruct and help them did not care to do so, did not care to take an interest in such mundane matters. To varnish the picture of the 'Forbidden Land' with the romantic glamour of mystery is to deceive oneself.[1]

We came for the first time as a world-indifferent mystic, seeking to penetrate into the mystery of Shangri-la. We left for the last time as a world-observant philosopher, having penetrated into the misery of Shangri-la. Why have the yogis and lamas been so ineffectual in modern Asia, as the mystics have been so powerless in modern Europe? The idealism which places defective observation on the pedestal of virtue, which is unable to see what is happening all around it and which ignores all the realities of a situation when they do not fit in with its wishful thinking, is not the kind in which our search for truth could continually afford to indulge.

We foresee that quite a number of people, bewildered by what the West has spiritually *been* in the past and dazzled by what the East has spiritually *taught* in the past, will fall prey to an increasing flow of swamis and monks, gurus and yogis, who will either invade the West or else invite would-be followers to leave it altogether and enter their ashrams. And even those who fail to fall for the Oriental varieties may fall for their corresponding Occidental analogues; freak forms of mysticism and occultism are emerging for their benefit out of fertile Eur-American imaginations. Already some Shangrian gurus have appointed advance agents (who are Westerners themselves) in Western Lands, to collect followers, gather disciples, give 'initiations', or persuade aspirants to join their organizations. They are working without the benefit of publicity's limelight, partly in order to foster the give-inspiring illusion of representing a secret fraternity. And they are working with great success. It is enough for them to gain a single follower and then ask him to start the missionary snowball rolling. He at once informs his friends, who inform others and so on, *ad infinitum*. It is such a rare and thrilling opportunity, they tell themselves: 'Just fancy! to become the disciple of a real master while staying at home in America or England, without having to travel on a long journey to Shangri-la and live there for years. It is all so easy, too.' Hence they tumble over each other in their haste to join – and needless to say, everyone is accepted.

Those contemporaries – and they are few indeed – who fled from

---

[1] Editor's note: in a conversation in 1981, Dr Brunton expressed pleasure that the present Dalai Lama had not only recognized these problems but also had been successful in his efforts to reintroduce a more philosophical perspective to Tibetan Buddhist thought and practice.

the turmoil of life and have found satisfaction and peace in secluded Indian ashrams or their Western equivalents, do not represent modern mankind but are rather atavistic throwbacks to more primitive times and more obsolete outlooks, persons quite understandably repelled by the complexity and strain of present-day life. Unfortunately, they overlook the fact that it is precisely to understand such complexity and to master such struggle that the God they profess to obey has thrown them into modern Western bodies. Do they seriously believe that they are reborn on earth only to pass through the same experience and the same environment each time? No! Life is perennially fresh and they return to learn new lessons from new experiences in new surroundings. To shrink from the difficult present and call a retreat to the easier past, to evade the problems of modernity by taking refuge in antiquity, to gain no inspiration from our own resources and to lapse back into those of medieval men, is to become defeatists. But it would be utterly wrong for us to hinder such persons from making good their escape. Let them do so by all means, if they wish. Nothing here written is intended for them.

The war was their chance to wake up, to quicken their process of thought. If it did not open the eyes of these mystical Rip Van Winkles, then its bestial horror and fiery terror was for them in vain. If the war did not break their unhealthy bewitchment, then the postwar period certainly cannot do so. The mystic who remained a mere spectator of the world-conflict may have kept his inner peace undisturbed. But there is no need to practise yoga to obtain this kind of negative peace. Every inhabitant of a graveyard has it. We write only for the others – and they are the majority – who are sufficiently aroused not to fall into an escapism that merely evades the problems of living and does not solve them, who do not wish to revert to spiritual atavism in a progressive world, who have been stirred by mankind's wartime agonies to seek the rugged road to truth no less than the smoother path to peace, and who have come to understand that the only satisfactory question is the one which combines the pursuit of both truth and peace with the unselfish service of humanity.

Mysticism has been associated in the popular mind mostly with monasteries, retreats, ashrams, caves and similar places where novices and would-be yogis foregathered. Thus it came to be looked upon as a way of escape from the domestic difficulties, business troubles and emotional disappointments which seem so inseparable from human existence. Those who could not cope with the ups and downs of daily life, with the shocks of unexpected misfortune or the death of beloved relatives abruptly detached themselves from society and fled to the relative peace of monastic life. Those who could not qualify themselves to earn their livelihood by burdensome physical or mental labour, renounced further effort and raised both their failure and their incompetence to the pedestal of virtue by proclaiming that they had renounced the world with all its wickedness! Nevertheless, deviously or directly, all these types came to the world for alms and food and clothing, for which the world continued to struggle, thus rendering itself able to provide them with their needs. Nor did they hesitate to proclaim a lordly spiritual superiority – quite disproportionate at times to their own personal defects – over the worldlings who financed or fed them.

If a man has undergone great emotional disappointment or much worldly suffering, he has every excuse for fleeing away to the peaceful refuge of monasticism, usually symbolized in the East by the donning of a yellow robe. What cannot be excused is, first, if he rests for the remainder of his earthly existence in such 'escapism'; and second, the large number of unholy 'holy' men who hypocritically imitate such a man and put on yellow robes, cover their heads with ashes, or appoint themselves to manage ashrams in order to beg, covertly or openly, their way through life – or worse, so as to exploit the pious or the aspirational. They contribute nothing to society and follow no inner quest for themselves, but batten on the superstitious hopes and panicky fears of the ignorant multitude by bestowing utterly worthless pseudo-blessings. Thus they unconsciously exhibit the very materialism which they are supposed to avoid! And they have their parallel types in the mystic cults and occult circles of the West, too. When mysticism becomes merely a way of escape from difficulties that sharply demand to be faced, or when it breeds an atmosphere wherein pious charlatans can pretend to be hallowed mouthpieces for God, it is time to call a critical halt.

Mental quiet alone, however perfect, is of itself not enough. The man who is content with it is not a complete man. For life is here and now, and to live only in mystical delights in the belief that they are the ultimate goal is to live only at the dream level. The consequence is that the external everyday life of action is kept outside them and is left untouched or even regarded with positive hostility. If we understand with the philosophers that meditation is for life, it is well; but if we can understand only with the mystics that life is for meditation, then it is not well.

There are those who believe philosophy to be a synonym for idleness. Yet its quest is a virile affair – not a resignation to lethargy, a dissolution into inertia nor an excuse for inaction. This is a quest which does not lead into ascetic negation of the world but into philosophic mastery of such negation, not into self-centred apathy but into altruistic, wise and useful activity. Whereas ascetic mysticism rejects the world, integral philosophy annexes it. Mysticism must become a part of life, not an evasion of it.

Every man has to act in some way; it is impossible for anyone to live without action. The ascetic, who thinks he has renounced it, has merely substituted one kind of action for another. This being the case, philosophy says it is better to align the *motives* for action with the highest philosophic ideal. All lesser motives are merely means to some end, whereas this alone is an end in itself. The ascetic who as an end in itself cuts off contact with the world and shrinks from its affairs, will surely drift into sterile negation; whereas the one who regards it only as an instrumental aid to personal peace and mental self-discipline, will intermittently return to the world he has deserted and embrace its affairs. Thus, he may test the true worth of his attainment by adjusting it to active life, assure himself whether the calmness which he has gained in a quiet corner can be kept in a noisy one, and help those who are unable to escape even temporarily from the world.

Now the sheltered life of an ashram may weaken a man for the struggle of existence, or it may strengthen him. Everything depends on the instruction, or lack of it, given in the ashram, the breadth of the external experience and the internal status achieved by its director. In any case, such methods of mass retreat are unsuited to us of the modern world and especially the Western world. It is better at least to remain human beings, since our feet are still encased in shoe leather and we have to walk this earth. Was it not a wise German who said: 'He who has experienced nothing is made no wiser by solitude?'

Dwight Goddard, translator of *A Buddhist Bible*, after having qualified himself by study in China and Japan among the monks, ascetics, hermits and scholars, made several attempts to found an ashram, a Buddhist retreat, both in the mountains of Vermont at Thetford and on the shores of California at Santa Barbara. Later he wrote me that he had most unfortunate experiences in each case, so he decided in the end that America was not ready for such an experiment. This confirms my own view that it is not because the West is not ready for such things, but because it has outgrown them, that it refused to flee into asceticism and escapism. Each incarnation carries its special and necessary lessons for us, however disagreeable they may be. Therefore, the attempt to shirk those lessons by falling into an escapist attitude and environment is in no way praiseworthy.

We are not undervaluing the past however. It has a definite value. But if men are to progress, they have only to learn from it and then put it aside – not to live in it stubbornly, blindly. They must look to present needs. Modern men can find no foothold in systems which are based on antique needs and which seem so utterly remote from contemporary life; in fact, if they are wide-awake, they not only dislike them but frequently even distrust them. We must ourselves, however, beware of such atavism, such seeking to escape by a regression from the struggle of modern conditions to the shelter of primitive ones. The goal of our fitful human existence cannot be so narrow and so negative as to idolize the life of a lotuseater, to lull a man into continual trances or half-trances, or to let him meditate himself into a permanent condition of dreamy futility. Nor can it be to indulge all his years in the joyous hiatus of emotional titillations. Rare however are those determined mystics who succeed in emancipating themselves from the fanatical extreme of excessive meditation without, however, falling into the other error of abandoning it altogether. Great indeed is he who can escape from the pitfall of being carried away by his ecstatic feelings into an anaesthesis of social action. The ascetic who sits in negative virtue and safe isolation from the world's fray may feel happy, but the sage who spurns such egoistic satisfaction and serves others in its tumultuous midst provides a better ideal. Such a life is a creative one and is not stippled with the pale hues of futility.

The question therefore arises: are mystics to continue playing the old part of being passive spectators of the world-show or are they going to measure up to this unique opportunity to render timely service? Those who have been gifted with a glimpse of the far-off divine goal towards which all things are moving, should realize that they have a worthwhile place in the present scheme, a place which they alone can fill. They can contribute what no one else can. They can not only help, as every decent person is helping, the forces of righteousness to secure outward victory over the forces of wickedness, but they can also assist in the equally important inward struggle of the forces of knowledge against those of ignorance.

The anchorite who sits in a vacuum cut off from a world which he cannot cope with and which he lacks the imaginative sympathy to understand, has, if he is sufficiently intelligent and sufficiently developed, to face an inner crisis today. The world war and its aftermath involves us all, including him. Either he must be stirred by the tremendous happenings into a realization of his social responsibility and moral duty, or he must be written off humanity's account as a contemporary failure. He must wake up to the new world-situation. How can the man of head and heart remain a foreigner to the tragic external forces around him today?

How can those who feel with and for their suffering fellows, who recognize this unique war for the spiritual conflict which it really is and understand the tremendous moral consequences for mankind's future involved in its outcome; how can such persons shut themselves up in the ivory towers of yogic ashrams and monastic retreats? This callous disregard of other people's miseries, this encampment in a splendid oasis kept all to oneself, this ostrich-like immurement in a cold ivory tower, is not a sign of sagehood whatever the populace believe. It was Vasishta, an ancient sage not an ascetic, who said: 'Unless the good of all becomes your good, you will add only fetters to your feet,' when urging a young prince who Buddha-like sought to renounce the world and escape its duties to gain an egocentric peace. Whoever truly understands and deeply feels his inner relationship with and his shared responsibility for his fellow creatures can never subscribe to the cult of indifferentism. In a world crisis like the present one, for example, he could never bring himself to sit idly by, babbling with shrugged shoulders of people having to bear their karma and of everything being just as God wishes it to be, while aggressive human instruments of unseen evil forces strive to fix spiked manacles upon the human race and mind. On the contrary, he will rise to the imperative call of the hour.

It is on this point of the necessity for altruistic service that the philosophic path diverges strikingly from the mystic path. Such a divergence, needful though it was at all times, became more needful than ever in our own times. The day of spiritual isolationism has passed. Such a self-centred doctrine can make little appeal to those who have been touched by the desperate and urgent needs of modern mankind. Mysticism seeks a static condition, whereas philosophy seeks a dynamic one. Mysticism is content with withdrawal from life, but philosophy would embrace all life. The mystic is happy when he obtains his *own* inner peace, but the philosopher will be happy only when all men get such peace. The serene state which mantles the philosopher is not bought at the price of self-centred indifference to his fellows and does not isolate him from their struggles. He is subject to an inner necessity to serve mankind.

The great sages saw the desperate need of mankind and compassionately gave what help they could. They never stood aloof; they did not despise those who had to participate in worldly life and flee from them accordingly, but understood their situation and helped them. They did not spend their lives sitting apart in mountain caves and forest retreats, in ashrams and monastic hideouts, but went where the crowds were – where they were needed, in fact. This is what Jesus did. This is what Buddha did. Jesus indeed worked so untiringly for the enlightenment of others that he often took no time to eat. These verses represent accurately the feeling which suffuses the heart of such a man. This, indeed, is the outstanding characteristic which distinguishes them from mere yogis. They had pity; they had fellow feeling. In the Bhagavad Gita, Krishna makes it perfectly plain that the yogi who lives in and serves the world is far superior to the yogi who flees from and renounces it. Yet despite this explicit teaching by the one most-revered Indian sage, many Hindu ascetics will tell you that self-centred monasticism is superior!

Whoever has attained true and permanent insight does not need to spend his time always in meditation. For meditation is a form of mental exercise to help its practiser get into the transcendent consciousness of pure Mind. He who sees pure Mind all the time does not need to practise any exercise for its possible perception. When, therefore, we are told that a sage lives in remote places and mountain caves in order to practise his meditations undisturbed, we may be sure that he is only an aspirant, only a would-be sage. The populace, impressed by his asceticism and awed by his trace, often regard such a yogi as a sage. He may himself accept such a valuation. But he will really possess the status only of a mystic, perhaps even a perfect one. If he reaches such perfection and is bewitched by his transient trances, he will feel that he is all-sufficient in himself and that he does not need anything from the world. The corollary of this, unfortunately, is that the woes of his fellow creatures have nothing to do with him also. If he begins fascinated by the emotional satisfaction which envelops his achievement, he develops an indifference toward suffering mankind and ends by becoming a complacent recluse and nothing more. This does not mean that a sage will never practise meditation. He will. But he will do so more for the benefit of others than for his own. He will carry out all his other personal and social responsibilities, as his wisdom and karmic circumstances dictate; he will certainly not seek to run away from them nor believe that his enlightenment has relieved him of them.

An appreciation of all the admirable benefits of mystic practice should not blind us to its limitations and make us commit the error of setting it up as the only goal for all mankind. The reflective man will sooner or later come up against these limitations and the discontent thus generated will cause him to bestir himself once more upon this quest of the Overself. Thus he may eventually enlarge his horizon and perceive that the ideal type is not the mystic but the sage.

What is a sage? He is the man who has finished all three stages of religion, yoga and philosophy, has realized the Overself and has come in consequence to a wide compassion for his fellow creatures. Because he comprehends that the root of most human troubles and sufferings is ignorance, he likewise comprehends that the best form of service he can render is to enlighten others. Hence so far as his own circumstances and capacities permit, and so far as the aspiration of others indicates, he devotes himself to their inner welfare. In such a beneficent occupation he will therefore incessantly engage himself. Through all history the mystic has been confused with the sage simply because the latter has rarely existed, being usually an aspirational ideal rather than a realized possibility. The highest type of the former achieves what may be called 'yogic immobilization', which is brought about by following a path of *abstraction* from entanglements, a path which is a necessary mental and physical discipline but still a negative one. It is not enough. Beyond it lies the ultimate path, which leads the man back into the world again but allows him to keep a secret interior detachment. The aura of intense mental peace which is felt in the presence of a perfect mystic is not necessarily a sign of perfection, as the ignorant think, but a sign of successful inward-turned concentration. He consciously exerts a mesmeric force on the disciples who sit passively around him. The sage, on the other hand, spends all this concentrative force in action intended to

118

render real service to others whilst at the same time spontaneously and effortlessly also giving that which is given by the mystic to those who search.

The mental differences between them are too subtle and complex for the uninitiated multitude to grasp, but it is easy to understand the *practical* difference between them. A simple analogy will help us here. There are two kinds of electricity: static and dynamic. The first yields at best a single useless spark, whereas the second yields a flow of continuous useful power. The electric current which we tap for light, heat and power belongs to the second category. The mystic, seeking to contract his activities to a minimum, is like the static electricity. The sage, seeking to render the utmost possible service during his lifetimes, is like dynamic electricity.

The mystic, in his genuine need for solitude and silence, deliberately turns his head away from the world. The sage, in his compassionate consciousness of the darkness that overspreads it, deliberately turns his head toward the world. Psychologically, the mystic is at the stage where he needs to silence thinking and refrain from action in order to eliminate their disturbances, whereas the sage has long passed that point and can afford to let both thinking and action have full free play without harm. The squatting mystic has to neglect the earth because he seeks to soar in the heavenly sky; the working sage has to stand upon the earth because he finds it mirrors that sky! And whereas the first finds God within himself and Satan outside in the world, the second finds God everywhere. The mystic takes pride in his negligence of material affairs and in the half-heartedness with which he attends to material duties. The sage takes pride in the efficiency and concentration with which he attends to material responsibilities. The mystic may self-righteously believe that paying proper attention to material life is the same as practising materialism. The sage will sensibly believe that failing to do so is practising foolishness. Thus the aim of philosophy is not, like that of mysticism, to turn men away from the world – quite the contrary. It wishes them to embrace life fully, but to do so with self-mastery, complete understanding and disinterested helpfulness.

According to this teaching, it is the harmonious development and maintenance of a wise balance among three factors which, in their ultimate synthesis, yield realization of the philosophic ideal and thus make the sage. These are: mystical feeling, metaphysical thinking and disinterested action. It is only in mediocre mentalities that these

119

tendencies disagree with each other. In superior souls they complement and help each other. Why is such stress laid on the last factor? This is done not only because the integral – that is, physical, ethical, and mental welfare of mankind becomes inseparable from one's own; not only because the waking state – that is, the world wherein activity attains its climax and possesses a peculiar importance of its own as will be ascertained in our study of sleep; but also because action is intimately connected with karma. Action is the force which bestows the final propulsion to karma. We take the last step to make or mar our ordinary life by our deeds, too. An old Sanskrit text pithily explains the point thus: 'According to his desire is his habit of thinking, according to his habit of thinking he enacts a deed, according to the deed enacted is his karmic lot in life.'

Thought however exalted, and feeling however purified, are not of themselves enough to perfect a man in the realization of the Overself. They are the seeds which must grow until they blossom into the flower of disinterested action. Therefore, the philosophy of truth knows no difference between theory and practice, for to it both are really one. The student has every right to ask what practical purpose, what human benefit, what tangible result is to be looked for from these studies. No better test of a teaching can be devised than that simple one which Jesus bade his hearers apply: 'By their fruits shall ye know them.' It is as sound and effective today as it was in his own time.

These same points are thrown into high relief by the two world wars and their aftermath. How can a man remain indifferent or even indolent, isolated in his own peace, in the face of a world suffering as it never suffered before, if he really feels his mystical oneness with mankind? The answer, glibly given and gullibly accepted, is that the mystics know best what they ought to do, that it suffices for them to work on mysterious 'spiritual' planes of being, and that it is sacrilege for us to criticize them. But our answer is that the dreams become actual when they leave the head and reach the hand and that in Buddha's words: 'A beautiful thought or word which is not followed by a corresponding action, is like a bright-hued flower that will bear no fruit.' It is generally not within the average aspirant's competence to judge correctly who is or who is not a realized sage, but it is within his right to form a working and tentative judgement for the sake of his own personal and practical life. The mystical ascetic may stand indifferently aside, but the philosophic student cannot do so nor use the quest as an apology for inertia when faced with social responsibilities. The ascetic striving to detach himself from sense activity, the mystic seeking to turn his interests wholly inward, the atavist sheltering in an Indian ashram from the complex strain of Western life – all these are entitled by their standpoint, by their cloistral outlook which is so unsympathetic toward a practical and human teaching such as ours, to turn aside; but not he who would use his higher intelligence and master true philosophy. The value of such teaching proves itself best under the stern pressure of terrific events; it reveals its practical worth most when he who has mastered it has to withstand the impact of a war like the last one.

Philosophy cannot fulfil itself in the individual alone. It must work through society also. The interaction of both, in obedience to the higher laws of life, provides the field for its complete expression. This is a fundamental difference between the ancient and the modern teaching. The first usually separated the contemplative from the active life, whereas the second always unites them. The Christian, the Hindu, the Buddhist mystic usually had to withdraw himself from society's fold if he wished to pursue his inner life to its logical end, whereas the philosophic mystic of today throws himself ardently into the world arena to serve mankind. Everybody sees the historic struggle between the malefic and benefic forces in life, between what would arouse antipathy and stimulate selfishness amongst men and what would arouse sympathy and stimulate selflessness; but only the sage sees both this struggle and the concealed oneness beneath it. Whereas the mystic, when he gets a glimpse of this hidden unity of life, becomes emotionally mesmerized and physically immobilized by it and ascetically deserts the fight in consequence, the sage continues to take his part and contribute his help to the strengthening of the good forces. The disciples of philosophy should not hesitate to become a power in the world, utilizing that power not only for their personal benefit but equally and even more for humanity's benefit. Their social task is to adjust personal welfare to the common welfare and not to ignore either at the expense of the other. To do something worthwhile in life for themselves is the fruit of ambition, but to do something worthwhile for humanity also is the fruit of aspiration. It is the nature of manifestation to be ever-active. Hence man cannot escape being involved in action of some kind. But what he can and should escape is being attached to his actions.

We are merely warning, as it were, the less experienced man from the country, who is travelling for the first time to a metropolitan city, of the dangers which will confront him there and of the errors he is likely to make on the way. *We are not telling him not to visit the metropolis*! Would-be mystics, therefore, ought not to become disheartened at the critical note which has deliberately been introduced into this essay as a protest against those monastically minded teachers who would arrogate the kingdom of heaven to chronic recluses like themselves and their followers, leaving us – the unfortunate captives of social circumstances and human duty – outside! Let them enter this path and pursue it assiduously, for it will well repay their effort; but let them take our criticisms as useful advice on what to avoid, ever remembering that mind is more than habiliment. If we have administered a shock to them, it is also true that those who faithfully endure must one day come to bless the hand that gave it. For they are being asked not to mistake a half-truth for a whole one. And we have sought to shame them into higher ideals of usefulness to suffering humanity.

8
Insight

If reality exists anywhere it must exist in an irreducible infinitude. But such a character places it beyond ordinary finite perceptions. A transcendental insight is therefore needful to bring man into relation with it. When the Supreme Reality is declared to be unknowable and unthinkable, we mean that it is unknowable only to physical sense-perception and unthinkable only by intellectual consciousness. Although the Absolute is beyond man's ordinary means of comprehension it is not beyond his extraordinary means. For there is in man a faculty which he may unfold that is higher than his ordinary means of comprehension: it is the faculty of transcendental insight, which can enable him to know and to experience this Reality. The quest consummates itself in the philosophic experience, which is this unbroken enduring insight into the inner reality.

Man discovers himself as a body through the eyes but discovers himself as the Overself through insight. Thus, when experience has developed and perfected its own fullest self-comprehension, it has developed the instrument of insight. When man is so mesmerized by his personality that he regards the Overself as non-existent and so mesmerized by the world-appearance that he regards Mind as a mere illusion, he is said to be dwelling in ignorance. When however he is aware of reality as intimately as he is aware of his own body, then only has he authentic insight. His struggle to attain an understanding of life will not be brought to a decisive issue before insight has fully flowered.

This faculty must not be confused with a merely intellectual, one-sided, so-called insight. For the whole of a man's being shares in its operations, as the whole of his feeling-nature is penetrated by it. Whoever possesses this understanding possesses inextinguishable light. When reason can conquer its one-sidedness and admit the play of other elements, it will itself be absorbed in the higher and richer all-embracing faculty of immediate insight. In one sense insight is a synthetic faculty, for it blends the abstract reason of the metaphysician, the feeling of the artist, the intuition of the mystic, the concrete reason of the scientist and the practical will of the active man. It fuses all these and yet it is also something higher which transcends them all. What the metaphysician only recognizes intellectually and what the mystic only feels emotionally are contained, combined and yet transcended in the philosophical insight.

Nor should it be confounded with intuition, of which it is the higher octave. Nor is it to be confused with mere clairvoyant vision.

Insight is a three-in-one faculty: it sees, it knows, and it is, all at the same time. Because knowing involves a duality of knower and known, it disappears at this point and merges into being. Realization is not a personal experience, for there is nothing personal in the real. Nor does it consist of an intellectual activity, although the pressure of right intellectual activity is one of the factors which helps us to arrive at it. Its decree is alone authentic. He who has this sure insight is liberated from the dogmas of ecclesiastics and the speculations of theologians, as well as from the aberrations of mystics and the imaginations of visionaries. Once he has attained to this higher consciousness, man's world-view will possess a certitude superior even to that of mathematicians.

How can we be assured of the truth of insight? By the disappearance of ignorance, its opposite number. The two cannot co-exist. Its truth is not an argument but an achievement. The coming of insight means that blindness has gone. The man can see where before his eyes were firmly shut by illusion. Henceforth there is that in him which fixes its gaze steadfastly upon the Timeless, the Real and the Impersonal. Insight alone has the power to pronounce on the universal truth and eternal reality of existence, because it alone has the power to penetrate the world appearance and to contemplate that bliss behind it. To this unveiled faculty, Reality will then be self-evident in the sense that man needs no outside testimony or rational proof of the sun's existence: it is perfectly self-evident in his own experience.

Illumination starts as an advancing process but ends as a sudden event. He grows slowly into Overself-discovery but the glorious bloom is abrupt. Insight arises of itself and without further striving when the needful preliminaries are finished. What then happens is that there is something like a veritable turning-around at the base of the whole consciousness. He realizes his own immediate oneness with the ultimate by a final flash of enlightenment which effectively removes all doubts and all ignorance for ever. This very first glimpse will be such a tremendous and scintillating revelation to the man that it will leave an ineradicable impression on his mind and he can never forget what he thus learns even if he were to try. His faith in the existence of the inner reality is thereafter absolutely unshakeable and his resolve to carry on with the quest is thereafter completely ineradicable.

Anyone who has had such a flash of insight, experience of reality or gleam of enlightenment will naturally desire its constant presence, or at least its continued return at will. But he will find that although insight deals with what is single, ultimate and final, there are separate graduated stages in its full unfoldment within man. The time it takes a rose to produce its buds is disproportionately longer than the time it takes these green cases themselves to open and burst into blossom. The unfoldment of insight is like that. The aspirant toils for long wearisome months or years amid emotional moods of darkness and failure, disheartenment and monotony. Suddenly the light breaks, his blindness vanishes and he begins to see again. The flashes of enlightenment swiftly pass, but the adjustment to it of his character and mentality, his life and personality spreads out over a disproportionately long period indeed. Years may often pass whilst he waits for the divine visitation to repeat itself. The full dawning of insight is a progressive graded event with time-lapses between each grade. This is better understood by pursuing an analogy by which insight is usually pictured in this teaching. No more time is needed for the first glimpse of reality than is needed by a flash of lightning to streak across the sky. Hence the first dawning of insight is called in this teaching 'the lightning flash'. Plato has similarly described this particular characteristic of the arisal of insight in his Seventh Epistle. He writes, 'It is brought to birth in the soul on a sudden, as light that is kindled by a leaping spark.' Indeed, the glimpse is so swift and hence so elusive that its recipient must be smart and alert to seize its dazzling significance before it is gone. It will not stay but vanishes in less than a second. Hence Augustine gives this advice: 'In this first flash when thou art as if struck by lightning, when thou hearest inwardly the affirmation "Truth", there remain if thou canst.' The intellect must handle this mystical 'flash' as delicately as though it were a fragile orchid. Over-analysis may lead to its destruction, under-analysis to its incomprehension.

The student first sees reality as a man sitting in a dark room sees some of the objects therein when they are suddenly lit up by lightning, which is too swift to do more than outline the interior somewhat dimly. This degree of insight may be likened to seeing the figure of a human being from a distance but not being able to recognize whether it is a man or a woman. Hence if he misses, as he probably will, much of this significance on the first occasion, this should warn him to be better prepared when it comes again. Every further flash makes the different things more and more distinguishable from one another. Just as during the first flash of lightning an observer may see only the inside walls of a room, during the second flash he may also see a table and some chairs, during the third flash he may also see some persons who are present too, until he finally gets to understand what the room is really like, so the student discovers that each momentary flash of the philosophic insight as and when it occurs tends to round out and complete the visible picture.

Nevertheless the fact remains that these glimpses of reality are but momentary ones however many times they be repeated; that when each lightning-flash has passed the student has to live on and by its unforgettable remembrance in the form of a powerful intuition but not a steady perception. Thus the need arises of progression into the second stage when it is as though the same man who formerly saw a room lit up by single and fitful lightning-flashes now sees the same room lit up by a small oil lantern. The light is now steady and continuous for a few hours until the oil gives out. The first brilliant lightning-flash turns out to be but a foretaste of a stable state which will one day be kept as a permanent possession. Insight is brief at first, but it becomes more and more stretched out with further experience.

The third stage is when he sees reality as the man in the dark room sees the objects by the light of the full moon. The fourth and the last stage is when he sees reality as the same man sees the objects by the full light of the sun at midday.

This insight must be got whilst we are still in this world in whose depths the imageless intangible Real forever abides, and not only while we are out of it in a trance. For what we see as the world is not its real nature but only a thought-construction. The waking world is partly constructed by the individual, and the individual himself is partly a constructed entity. The same mind which co-constructs the one lays it before the other as an external but imagined thing. The world which is actually given in our experience is made up of millions of individual and independent items. The world which is rationally found by metaphysical examination is made of one stuff – Mind. The One appears as the Many! Thus the seeming variety of things melts down in the end to unity. All the myriad ideas not only exist for and to the mind but are in essence nothing else than mind. Every land, mountain and river, every wrought object, every living creature, even every human being is but a thought-structure whose form appears and vanishes like the waves on an infinite ocean. The waves may go out but the ocean remains. And the ideas may go but Mind remains. It is nothing more and nothing less than the first origin and final source of all thoughts, beings and things.

The world's objectivity and materiality exist for the individual, but for the mind underlying both they are known as mere appearances. When however the individual comes to comprehend this and turns his attention to this hidden mind and finally knows it for what it is – both when tranquilly abiding in itself or manifested in external activity – he is said to have attained supreme insight. All other kinds of experience deal with something as if it were apart from Mind. This alone deals with something purely pertaining to Mind itself. All other experiences deal with forms but this deals with the unique formless. The moment the mind realizes that it is itself the permanent reality behind transient appearance, the constant perceiver of its own changing thought-forms, in that moment the truth flashes across it and illusion is dispelled. For man's insight is Mind contemplating itself.

Does the teaching of mentalism make the manifold world only a mirage? No! Like the superficial study of this teaching, a superficial practice of yoga seems to rob the world of reality; but an advanced practice restores it. The world finds its reality in World-Mind, therefore the world is a dependent reality. Mentalism brings recognition of the physical world as being real in its own way, although only dependently real. Insight is realization of unity or spirit-matter. 'There is but one Nirvana, as there is but one Truth, not two or three,' Gautama Buddha told one whose mind was uncertain. The mystic has yet to see that Mind upholds all its thoughts, to feel that it is present in and as all his external experience. People look upon this world as being either a reality or an illusion, according to whether their standpoint is materialistic or spiritualistic. The philosophic insight, however, knows that matter is spirit and spirit is matter, because it knows that both are but Mind. Therefore this opposition becomes unintelligible and does not arise for it.

The Overself, when not under the limitations of being aware of dreaming or unconscious, is in the fourth state; it is then its own pure self, conscious in its own secondless way for itself, of itself, and of nothing else! The discovery of Mind in its naked pure aloneness is made in a self-absorbed psychological free state, in the thought-free, sense-free Void. But it is not enough to touch the Void although most mystics consider it to be sufficient. The Void must next be brought into the Full; the Light must descend into the Dark; the personality must not revel in the Void for its own ecstatic enjoyment, but must convert bliss into service. This consciousness of the Void must be carried not only into every wakeful instant but also into every dreaming one. The separation into Reality and Appearance, into Being and Becoming, must now be recognized for what it is – a tentative and not a final step. The student who can rise so high must now transcend even this distinction. He must see all things as not-different from the original Mind Essence, must embrace them in a single realization with the essence itself. Man attains the final stage of insight only *after* he has passed through this earlier experience of the Void. Only then may he return to the world of appearance and penetrate its profoundest secret. And this is to perceive its oneness with the Void, its not being different from the unseen and unseeable Infinite Space. After insight into the meaning of the Void, the Nought, flashes upon him, he travels onward to gain an understanding of the All, of the universal manifestation itself. When these two stages have been mastered, when insight attains its fullest bloom, the influx of separate thoughts will no longer break his transcendental consciousness and may therefore be accepted as a part of the Real. This, the highest grade of insight, is not something which happens now and then but something which indescribably is forever present, whether during sleep or wakefulness.

Enlightenment is not a process which occurs as the result of a single factor. If insight has been gained by purely mystical means – which is the shorter way – it is always partial and fitful. If it has been gained by philosophic means – which includes the mystical and is therefore the longer way – it is full and permanent. The science of biology has shown that Nature takes more time to bring the superior organisms to their full growth than to bring the inferior ones to the same point. In the same way she requires a longer period to bring to maturity the higher power of the human mind than the lower ones. And insight, being the highest, subtlest and most recondite of all such powers, can therefore come into being only long after they themselves have come into being. That is to say, scientific thought and metaphysical reflection, mundane emotion and mystical feeling, intellect and intuition must first proffer their contributions before insight can establish itself. Hence insight cannot be reached by intellect or emotion, intuition or will acting apart. None of these can of itself attain this goal. The whole man must advance towards it. When the faculty of reason is constantly exercised at its highest pitch, which means its most abstract and metaphysical pitch; if and when such exercise is conjoined in a certain way with the practice of mystical meditation; and when profound veneration and altruistic compassion is the atmosphere within which they move, they are one day suddenly and quite spontaneously replaced by the higher faculty of insight. The mystic finds his inner self. He discovers that personality is rooted in a deeper, wider being – the Overself. But he does not discover the significance of the not-self. He does not enter into comprehension of the All. Once a philosophic illumination has been gained, it shines steadily and enduringly. It is never clouded even for a moment. In other words, the philosopher walks in perpetual light and not in intermittent flashes of light as does the mystic. The philosophic knowledge is a well-established one, whereas the mystic knowledge is an occasional one. Philosophic truth is a constant and unclouded power of the one, whereas fleeting intuition or temporary ecstasy at best is the attainment of the other. When a steady enlightenment beats down upon your path of life, you have gained something which is unquestionably superior to the fitful feelings of ecstasy which visit the devotee or the mystic now and then. For these feelings will not of themselves be sufficient to keep you from going astray during the intervals when you do not have them, whereas the philosophic illumination shows you clearly every inch of the ground where you are walking. The mystic gets his fitful and partial glimpses of the Over-consciousness, whereas with the philosopher, like a lamp in a windless place, it burns steadily. The inner perception will finally become continuous and the insight into what both he and the world really is will be inseparable from him. His inward eye forever gazes into infinity whilst his physical eyes do not fail to see the world at the same time.

What are the inner characteristics whereby a man will know that he has attained insight? The development of the different stages of insight – if achieved by the philosophic way – necessarily brings about certain changes of moral character as well as mental understanding. In the first stage there are: morally, the permanent enfeeblement of self-ishness in the same way that a tree which has been struck by lightning is so enfeebled that it will not only stop growing but will also die sooner than it otherwise would have done; mentally, the permanent disappearance of wrong views about self and God and of old illusions about matter, time and space. In the second stage the moral result is a permanent enfeeblement of lust, anger and hate. That is to say, although he may sometimes be disturbed by rebellious thoughts of ill-will and sensual desire, the thoughts themselves will not attain any strength or intensity and will not be able to endure for more than a very short time. He will soon be ready to forgive critics, for example, or to be friendly with enemies. His partial apprehensions will be enlarged, his illusory beliefs will be eliminated and his long habits of wrong thinking will be corrected.

In the third stage all passions are utterly subdued; lust, anger and hate are completely effaced and can never again affect his feelings for even a moment. In the fourth stage there is a perfect balance between the just needs of egoism and the wise demands of altruism. Disinterested-ness marks all dealings with other persons; vanity is utterly extin-guished. There is a continuous unbroken feeling of exalted serenity which exists quite independently of the senses. All the finest tendencies of character which circumstances may have hitherto kept latent or only half-unfolded are now able to manifest themselves in their fullness without hindrance. Although the earlier stages of insight's develop-ment enable a student to intuit reality in ascending degrees of clearness, the experience is a fitful one and is necessarily followed by a recoil back into ordinary consciousness. The attainment of the fourth stage alone yields a permanent and unbroken realization throughout his lifetime. The mind is now always poised and calm and ever-concentrated on the Real. It possesses the power to enter at any moment into itself and remain rapt and thought-free. His consciousness of the Real will be an unwavering one. His perception of the transiency and insufficiency of form will be equally unwavering. His satisfaction with experience of the Divine will make him feel complete in himself.

Nevertheless the Absolute still remains a grand Mystery – even when we have won our way through to its presence and stand in its light. No human being ever becomes the Godhead. His highest pos-sible achievement is to stand in *the light* of the Godhead. Thereby the whole universe becomes revealed to him as itself a *divine* thought. This is insight.

Insight is something which cannot be communicated but must be personally realized. It is entirely experiential. The guru who claims that his mere wish for another's attainment can *enduringly* realize itself in him, is deceiving the other. It is a sure sign of such misleading doctrine when a guru declares that the path to realization leads to and through him alone. Just as no amount of instruction will show a man how to dream – for it must come naturally or not at all – so no amount of instruction will show a man the ultimate state. The experience must come spontaneously of itself. To expect spiritual attainment without having deserved it by his own exertions is as unreasonable as to expect engineering attainment without having worked with an engine. The personal favour of no master and no priest can grant it, whatever popular superstition of self-interested 'guides' may say to the contrary. The man who thinks that by wholly handing his life over to such a guru realization will come of itself one day without any or even a little effort on his own part, is going to receive a severe awakening. One great human delusion is that which fosters the desire to get something for nothing. The rich social parasite who is satisfied to contribute nothing but takes much from the common store merely because some family ancestor had once given something is one example; the religious devotee who expects, without any effort on his own part, some other man to give him God, is another. There are too many seekers in mystical circles who are waiting for a Master to appear on the horizon who will conveniently present them with what can only come as a result of their own endeavours.

A genuine teacher seeks to help the pupil unfold what is already within him; he does not pretend to perform a miracle. If any man could permanently lift another man into the Overself, if he could transfer his own consciousness of it to a second person, the feat would have been accomplished by all the great sages of the past; the history of mankind then would have been quite different and the present state of mankind far superior. It has never been done because it can never be a gift. Only through the processes of biological evolution does a sperm grow into an adult human being, and only through the processes of spiritual evolution does a man grow into a sage. There are no swift and sudden transformations. The transforming touch of grace will come at the right psychological moment of his history when it should come. But that moment is determined by a man's Overself, not by any other man – however be-lauded a teacher or saint he may be.

However useful and helpful they admittedly are in their own place, teachers cannot bring anyone to the one thing that matters most – to the established realization of the Overself. That can be done only by God's grace and in God's time – not ours or theirs. No embodied intermediary can do it for anyone else, can bestow the one initiation which, because it yields a permanent conscious and unbroken communion henceforth, counts above all other. In the end, instruction must come pure and undefiled by human limitations. No finite being can initiate man enduringly into the Infinite, only the Infinite itself can do that. Truth is best studied at its source. The aspirant should indeed no longer desecrate the universality of the Overself by transposing its greatness and grandeur to earthly mortals, nor sully its pure spiritual nature by their anthropomorphic worship. Guru-less, he must stand alone before God. For God's deputy, the Overself, is a real being whose presence can be felt, whose understanding and consciousness do exist and who possesses the power to respond. Hence his call will be heard, his prayer for help will not be uttered in vain if it is uttered sincerely.

If however spirituality cannot be carried from one man to another as we carry a suitcase, those who are sensitive may feel its presence and power. It is quite possible for an attained master to give a devoted disciple a temporary glimpse of reality by imparting to him a momentary glimpse of the *first* stage of insight. This he does by telepathically quietening the disciple's thought processes and by deepening his emotional movement.

The philosophic goal cannot be achieved by mass production methods, although the religious goal may. Every individual must find his own peculiar path to it. He may find it with the help of another, of a teacher, but still it will and must be his own.

9

Self-Reliance or Discipleship

How many questionable visions have been suggested to a meditator by his so-called spiritual guide? How many mystical experiences would never have occurred to him if this guide had not told him to expect them? How much near-mesmeric phenomena masquerades as mystical experience? Consider those who are so fascinated by the ancient tenets and methods that they surrender themselves wholly to them and live in the past, wasting precious time relearning lessons which they had already learnt in those former epochs. They are victimized by the dead. They ignore the lessons of Western civilization. Why were they reborn in the West if not to learn new lessons? Should they not be sufficiently flexible to adapt themselves to the demands made by the present era? Uninspired, unenlightened teachers who do not perceive this continue to teach the old methods alone, phonographically handing down what they have received by tradition. If they could realize the vivid inner spirit of their inheritance rather than its musty outer form, they would become free of the past. For then they would stand *alone* in the great Aloneness. And out of such a spirit they would instinctively give what is needed today, not what was needed by former centuries.

The disciple who places himself abjectly under the thumb of a supposed master, or turns even a good man into the object of a superstitious idolatry, becomes a mere robot. Whoever has not the courage to think, speak and act independently of his teacher, will never have the chance to realize truth for himself. Whoever overweights the value of a master's services to his disciple is ruled by emotion, not reason, when he studies no other system than the one promulgated by his master; when, in short, he has completely surrendered himself in every way to the master, then it is right to say that such a man will never know truth, never attain realization, never become a sage himself. The slavish mentality which so-called teachers and pseudo-gurus create and perpetuate in their unfortunate disciples leads to their moral degeneration. For losing faith in their ability to attain truth by their own efforts, they do not try and consequently attain nothing.

As soon as men yield up their souls in blind belief to any dictatorial exploiting guide, the light of conscience goes out and the voice of common sense is stilled; they begin to walk in darkness; they cannot see whither they are being dragged. Those who follow such a teacher will in the end, if they are fortunate and sincere, be driven by disappointment to the necessity of retracing their steps. Those who surrender themselves wholly and blindly to him surrender the very opportunity for which they have taken birth in a human body. He who hands them a ready-made teaching so that they have nothing more to do than to believe, blocks their real path of progress and hinders their true development. Thus, instead of making his enslaved disciples conscious of their inner power, he puts a wholly exaggerated valuation on his own service and tries to make them forget their self-reliance altogether. They become more weak-willed and more negative than they were before.

The priest played a dominant part in former epochs and assumed on his own shoulders the burden of truth seeking. But his work misdirected itself when it brought men to believe that without the mediation of other men, without the intercession of salaried sacerdotal hierarchies, it would be impossible for them to achieve a spiritual status. It is unfortunately a historic fact that in ancient and medieval times especially, almost every priesthood tended to arrogate to itself social, political and economic privileges upon the alleged sanction of its title to deputize for God on earth. In time, exploiting these privileges came to occupy the minds of many priests more than the advancement of humanity. It is not genuine religion but selfish priestcraft that, in the name of God, has so harmed and hindered man's progress. This is why we see that an important part of the mission of such great souls as Jesus, Buddha and Muhammed was to curb the unhealthy power and erase the superstition-fostering influence of the orthodox priests of their times.

It was always easy enough for the credulous, uneducated, underprivileged masses to fall victim to the promises and threats of priestcraft, but a parallel if more refined system of exploitation developed where it might be least expected. It appeared in a different stratum where it tried to hold its grip through the medium of exaggerated guru-worship on those who had evolved beyond the orthodox religious state into mysticism. The spiritual teacher originally represented one who gave guidance and assistance to the seeker, but misguided belief came in time to make him represent God incarnate to him. In the Orient particularly, the ignorant deification of living men – with the consequent slavish obedience and renunciation of intellect which this often entailed – once went and still goes to the most fantastic lengths. It has fostered widespread superstition, despoiled self-reliance and destroyed independent thinking, opening easy gates to many charlatans.

The custom of getting men to regard some other man as the incarnation of God may have been helpful in ancient times when the masses were simpler-minded than they are today, but it has certainly led to unfortunate results in modern times. At best, its value was on the practical and not the philosophic side, to the untutored masses and not to the cultured classes. To ask a modern votary of mysticism to follow the same custom is to give an unhealthy direction to his inner life and a misleading one to his intellectual life. To call any guru by the Deity's name and to ascribe deific power to him is sheer blasphemy.

Philosophy is devoted to teaching principles, not to aggrandizing, glorifying or exploiting personalities. It holds that the authority of the messengers is not of such primary importance as the truth of the message, that priority belongs to what is permanent rather than what is transient and that men need a reorientation of thought and renovation of practice much more than reverence for particular individuals. It worships divine ideals, not human idols. It substitutes the veneration of verities for the adoration of persons. It declares that whoever persists in worshipping dead persons, like Jesus, is throwing thoughts into the vanishing void, but that whoever worships the immortal principles *taught by Jesus* is laying up treasure in heaven. It seeks to inculcate great truths rather than to idolize great men. It is not concerned with what A or B has said or done, so much as with whether A's or B's words are true and his deeds right.

We have often heard in recent times of this or that nation wishing to establish its political independence. We do not often hear of this or that man wishing to establish his mental independence. Yet such individualization of the human being, which is the present evolutionary goal, cannot be reached without it. That which was accomplished in former centuries by an appeal to blind faith must now be accomplished by an appeal to scientific rationality. No man and no group has a prescriptive right to own another man's or another group's mind for ever. No teacher is ethical who prevents his students from discovering and developing their own latent and inexhaustible resources today, however permissible it was in primitive times. The belief that there must, however, be somebody to walk beside him all the time, to guide his thoughts and acts continually, a leader to whom he must always be looking up, is not a belief that philosophy can entertain.

Within the very broad limits of faithfulness to the path, the teacher should allow plenty of freedom to the student to choose his own steps upon it, to develop along his own personal lines, and should encourage him to think and feel as a free individual.

All the religions of the past sought to enfold men within groups; the tribal or racial outlook still clung to them. This was right under the external conditions which previously governed men's social existence. Only a thousand years ago the inhabitants of America, for example, were completely cut off from those of Europe. Consequently, the religion useful to the one people was not useful to the other; their habits and heredity were quite different. But today these conditions have been astonishingly changed. The planet's face has been transformed by human handicraft. Man has now the possibility and power to think universally, to choose for himself the ideas he wants to accept and the ideals he wants to follow. He is becoming mentally individualized. He can begin to re-assess the values of life and the ideas of existence, not as a mere unit in a tribal or national group but as a self-respecting individual. This, indeed, is simply democracy at work in religion. But in taking this step, he has taken the first step towards mysticism. For mysticism itself is the culmination of all sincere religion. Some instructive details about the second evolutionary movement may be found in the ninth and tenth chapters of *The Wisdom of the Overself*.

The Way of Organized Groups

What has here been said of personal leaders and individual teachers applies equally to authoritarian, hierarachical institutions and public or secret dogma-bound organizations. Stereotyped religio-mystical institutionalism is forever suspicious of the member who would seek for truth with a free and independent mind. If he perseveres in the search, sooner or later he is sure to collide with it. When that happens, and he finds it neither politic to compromise nor wise to submit, he will be thrown out as a rebel, excommunicated as a heretic.

When he perceives how frequently these organizations have become the traditional enemies of man's inner progress – as in the cases of Buddha and Jesus – the prudent seeker will keep away from them, giving them his good wishes rather than his memberly presence. When he learns from biography and history how inevitably formal bodies tend to drive out what is most important and manage to keep what is least important, he will learn how dangerous to truth is gregariousness.

Most organizational forms are too illiberal and are committed by their very forms to the maintenance of past narrowness. They quickly become new cages for aspirants to enter. The religionist is now so tight-bound a prisoner in the structure he has erected that he may not utter these truths even if he knows them, whereas the philosopher is now so impressed by the dangers which confront mankind that he must utter them.

If the student of philosophy is to join any group, it should not be an external one. It should be bound together by no visible ties but only by a common mental austerity of attitude, a common devotion to the quest for truth. He should not wear a label and could not bear an organization. For the one would separate him instantly from every other spiritual group and the other would force him to entertain thoughts of rivalry and struggle for worldly prestige or power at the expense of competing organizations. It is one of the beauties of philosophy that it is the only world-view which seeks no proselytes, makes no propaganda and possesses no vested interests. It is the only one which grants a true and total freedom; all others thrust their followers into cages.

Men admire a popular movement largely because it is so large. They worship brazen idols while dust collects on the golden ones. It is unlikely that a teaching which sets itself the most exacting standards will have a popular appeal. Philosophy is cheerfully prepared for that handicap. It clearly sees that it is intended for the discriminating few and its sphere of operation inevitably provides it with well-defined limitations. It cannot hope to affect or awaken the multitude immediately and directly, hence does not seek to win their favour. Therefore, the fact that its followers may be no more than a mere handful will not disturb the peace of its custodians. If they can become an instrument of esoteric enlightenment and individual regeneration for these men and women, if they in their turn can thus be inspired to serve others in their own way, it shall surely be enough. They do not strive for the suffrages of the masses. The success they aim at does not consist in the larger number, the great recognition, the wide approbation; it consists in reaching the waiting few who are ready to listen, to appreciate and to understand.

Philosophy is encircled by a little audience of devoted followers and will not be so unwise as to stray beyond it. It has deliberately sought to limit our field of influence. It wants the friendship of its followers but it does not want this on a false basis. If pleasing their prejudices, catering to their sentiments, confirming their wrong notions and supporting their illusions are to constitute this basis and not the quest for truth, then such friendship would not be authentic. Rather than concern as to whether or not people are prepared to listen, it is a duty to place before those who seek it – and to make accessible to them – the highest counsel and the wisest guidance we are able to give. Philosophy is an educational and not a propagandist movement. Therefore, it does not seek to compete with any other for the simple reason that it cannot. It is forced to restrict itself to the few whose interest in its special teaching is deep and devoted, whose minds are sufficiently ripened to be naturally sympathetic towards it.

It may now be better understood why there is no sense of disparagement in our statement that philosophy is set apart from the motley crowd of other teachings by reason of its uniqueness. That is merely a matter of character-making destiny. The others have their place, but not one will be able to fill that of philosophy. It must be boldly emphasized that it breaks exclusive ground in reflection about, and penetration into, life. Once *understood*, even by a handful of competent persons, this knowledge makes its own way in the world. Its dissemination is not to be secured by noise and shouting but by understanding and living it. These are the reasons why it modestly voices its subtle message and does not play the part of raucous loudspeaking propagandist, why it exemplifies in its calmness and dignity its own injunction on how to meet the ups and downs of contemporary events. It will not shout with the crowd but always pursues its own policy.

The advanced aspirant is a bad 'joiner'. Philosophy is sufficient for him. He will never again feel the need to adopt a new faith or follow a new leader. He is not eager to follow his flightier sisters and brethren every few years into the latest cult. He will always show a prudent reserve towards new prophets and coteries, teachers and doctrines, and refuse to commit himself to them headlong. He will not agree to shut his mind and quest in a closed system. He will not accept anything that restricts his views and narrows his perspective. Hence, he will not, for the sake of his own spiritual advancement, join any sect or organization, any institutional religion or mystical cult. The man who is captured by philosophic truth is captured forever, for it has set him free. Once a philosopher always a philosopher. We shall never hear of men dropping their allegiance to philosophy. If such a hitherto unheard-of event ever did happen, it would be only because the renegades had never really accepted true philosophy. For it alone deals with reality, not with fluctuating emotionalist feelings or intellectualist opinions about reality. Once anyone has dug his way to the rock-bottom foundations of the higher teachings' architectural structure, be sure that he will never desert it but will become more loyal to it with every year that passes. Yet it would be foolish to expect that more than a microscopic minority – those born with a burning desire to understand the innermost significance of life – will ever take the trouble to dig so deeply. Therefore, only a few of those who merely *read about* it will ever be completely loyal to it.

Throughout its long history mankind may be conveniently divided into these two groups: those who consciously dedicate themselves to the search after truth, and those who do not. The quest is only for the man who is willing and able to step out of the herd; for the sufferer who has had enough of blind living and for the thinker who is more attracted by the lonely path of an austere individualism than by the over-trodden road of a self-deceptive orthodoxy.

How many promising souls have had their integrity violated and have been forced to abandon the path along which intuition was correctly leading them to lofty attainment, only to be placed by their organization, group or personal guide, upon a path that led in the end to disillusionment or disaster. He who attaches himself to a teacher shares not only ignorance and errors. Such a possibility might not have mattered much in ancient times when teachers who had *realized* truth could be found without excessive difficulty, but it matters greatly in modern times when one may comb an entire continent and fail to find such a one.

The Way of Discipleship

There are many aspirants in the West who have spent the best and longest part of their lives in the expectation of meeting, or in the search for, a spiritual guide of the rank of a Mahatma or an Adept. They have done so because Theosophy – especially Neo-theosophy of the post-Blavatsky period – and Indian Vedantism have told them that the initiation, assistance and continuous guidance of such an exalted personage is absolutely indispensable to the spiritual quest and that without initiation the quest can only end in failure. But their search has usually been a vain one.

Now we fully admit, and do not deny, the assistance which may be had from a true teacher. But a trustworthy guide through the dark maze of mysticism is not easily found today. Where they believe that they have found such a master, quite often their search has been worse than vain – for it has also been self-deluded. They actually endanger their inner life when they join it to a dubious inspiration and an undue subservience. We are here not passing judgement but merely stating facts. The difficulty of finding competent, pure, authentic and unselfish instruction is today so great, and only a little less so in the East than in the West, that it seems to us wiser to emphasize publicly the possibilities of making progress by a self-effort, of unfolding latent resources without over-anxiously seeking here and there to obtain a teacher. For so many aspirants are wasting precious time and energy in futile search and disappointing experiment, when they could be making progress and reaching maturity by availing themselves of their own inner guidance.

When we mention this rarity of qualified reliable teachers, the retort is often made that the mystical tradition contains a saying, 'When the pupil is ready, the master appears.' We would not contradict the truth of this saying, but we would complement it with another truth – that the master here referred to is not necessarily an embodied or an external one. He may be out of the flesh or he may be inside the pupil's own heart. In both these cases the instruction will come and assistance be rendered from within through the intuitive faculty, or the master may

be a printed book left for the guidance of posterity by one who had
successfully finished the quest himself. There are many excellent books
obtainable nowadays in which most aspirants can find sufficient reliable
instruction to suit their immediate practical purpose. But in the end,
that which brings together the seeking man and the sought-for truth,
whether the latter be found within himself, a book or another man, is
the direct agency of his own Overself.

Owing to suggestions implanted from without, the heart's yearning for the Spirit is easily mistaken by beginners for a yearning for a
master. Those who are mesmerized by past traditions – especially
Oriental ones – or misled by present cults into accepting the suggestion that it is impossible to advance without a guide, merely transfer to
the search for a human being what should be a search for their own
soul. In their ignorance they superimpose his name upon it and honour
him with the worship which should be given to the soul alone. Instead
of setting out in quest of their own soul, they set out in quest of a man.
The one being within themselves and the other without, the directions
are totally opposite. Consequently, the two quests must lead to two
different results.

When the Christ-self, speaking through Jesus, said, 'I am the door,'
it gave counsel which is still fresh today. It meant 'Do not look for
other people's doors; do not turn to other men for that which your
own higher self is waiting to give you.' The solemn proclamation of
this Christ-self in each man is: '*I am The Way, The Truth and The Life.*'
In himself he can find the guidance needed, the knowledge desired and
the goal sought. But to do this he must have full faith in the Christ-soul
within him and not go wandering from one man to another. Either
this soul exists within him or it does not. If it does, it is necessarily a
living and active force behind the scenes of his visible life. It is surely as
competent to guide him on the spiritual path as any embodied human
being. If it is not true that his own soul can directly guide him, that it
can by itself lead him into self-realization, then there is no truth in the
claim that it exists nor in the records of its power. But the fact is that
the voice which is calling him is the soul's, even though he ignorantly
gives it some man's name. If this quest is nothing less than a search for
his own deepest self, then the clinging to another human self, to
external masters, can only prevent and not promote attainment.

Just as the seeker has to learn through disappointment and suffering
to cast off sole dependence on any human being for happiness, so he has

to learn through the same means to cast off sole reliance on any human being for guidance. The higher self alone can give him durable happiness and it is the higher self alone which can give him perfect guidance. In the end he is brought back by the tragic events of life to the essential solitariness of every human soul. And it is only when he is courageous enough to face those events and this solitariness in all its fullness, looking to no embodied man for assistance, that he has the unique chance to discover its secret inhabitant, the divine soul. When he has come to realize through such disappointments and disillusionments that he must entrust himself to the guidance which comes from within, not only because it alone perceives the needs peculiar to himself but also because it emanates from that very second self which he is trying to discover, he has come to the true entrance of the mystical path. He has fulfilled one of the conditions to authentic enlightenment – he has turned away from other things to the direction of the soul itself. If he has to pass from the elementary into the higher grades, he can do so only by awakening to this advanced truth – that his own soul is the rightful God-given guide. When the novice has travelled sufficiently far to be able to understand this situation, he will start to form himself and not wait uselessly for some master to do it. He will begin to shape his ideas and direct his meditations for himself and not lie supine and helpless until he can receive them from outside. He will exercise his will and not let it lie flabby, inert or even paralysed.

It is the pupil, and the pupil alone, who has to crush all evil passions, reject all evil thoughts, overcome all evil emotions. For they are his and unless he himself deals with them, the weaknesses of character which gave birth to them will still remain. It is not only absurd but also self-deceptive to count on a master doing this for him. No external agency can assure him externally what he must assure for himself internally. The knowledge which is born by his own thinking, the strength which is drawn from his own self, the compassion which comes out of his own heart, are immensely superior to the second-hand products of exterior suggestion. He who acts on this truth will need no one else to teach him. His divine self is there, ever present and will do it better.

Even Sri Ramakrishna, the saint whom many of the swamis themselves follow, adoring him as an incarnation of God – even he has admitted, 'He who can himself approach God with sincerity, earnest prayer and deep longing, needs no guru.' It also is true that the saint qualified his statement by adding, 'But such deep yearning of the soul is rare; hence the necessity of a guru.' If the yearning is strong enough and deep enough, it will find what it truly needs without much help from outside. But if it is not, then it may become the circle-wandering slave of a dozen narrow and unsuitable techniques, the enfeebled victim of a dozen exploiting teachers, before it becomes aware in the end that it has to find the path which conforms to its own individual characteristics, before it receives the liberating teaching which comes from the purity of its own Overself.

For each is an individual and therefore unique. To imitate always the thinking, speech and action of a particular teacher, to accept always the suggestive influence which he seeks to exert upon mesmerized followers, to practise only the method which suits such a teacher – this is not to travel the path to the wider freedom.

Therefore, let nobody be led away into self-betrayal by the stereotyped formulae of any teacher or the mechanical laws of any technique. This does not mean that he will brusquely or foolishly reject whatever he can derive from other men, but it means that whilst accepting such aid he will not assign it a primary place, will not make the success or failure of his quest rest unduly on it. If he understands this situation correctly, this will not mean dependence merely upon the limited resources of his personality but upon the unlimited resources of that which dwells behind the personality. He will look, in short, with unshakeable faith to the Overself to lead him finally into that realization of divinity which is his sublime goal.

'I am forced to draw my philosophy from my own head,' remarked Socrates, who learnt his teaching from no one. His own wisdom was dug out of the hidden depths of being. No teacher set his feet upon the path, no school transmitted it to him; it was self-obtained. Therefore, it was natural that he himself should not care to unload a pack of ready-made doctrines upon a man's shoulders but rather endeavour to bring him to self-thought. A teacher's instruction at best leads to mediate knowledge, whereas the realization of truth must be immediate. The former is necessary as a preliminary step leading to the latter, but it cannot of itself give realization. The student must therefore make his own efforts to realize what he has been taught. He cannot escape this duty if he wants reality and not merely words or thoughts about it. As in Socrates' time, the seeker of today finds himself in the same position where self-effort is called for. It may be a fact that the old

Sanskrit texts anticipated many of his eventual conclusions but he has to travel towards them by a different route. For he has now to walk alone with unaided thought and by pioneer experience. When he is compelled to stand on his own feet, he is compelled to study his own problems; what he thus gains is his own and cannot be lost.

After all, it is of little use looking to others to provide that which, in the end, he has to provide for himself. He may flee to the imagined security of a master, a method, a creed, a church, an ashram, a group or an organization, but he flees in vain. In the end, life demands that he discover his *own* resources. At best, as Socrates has shrewdly pointed out, the teacher can but work like a midwife, helping students to deliver themselves of their own truths. Each should understand that mostly he must work out his own salvation. All insidious suggestions intended to enhance their dependence, weakness and enslavement must be resolutely resisted by those who would be philosophic students. The first task of a true guide, therefore, is to create this necessary self-reliance within them, to help them become conscious of their own latent power, to encourage them to nurture their own understanding by recommending reflection upon their own experiences. Intellectual integrity demands this of them – that they do not wholly subordinate liberty of action to another individual, that they do not become wholly subservient to his will and that they do not wholly forfeit their free will. If it is true that it is unethical to tyrannize over weaker men, it is equally unethical to yield to the tyranny of stronger men.

It is the student who must liberate himself from his own illusions, for no master can do it for him. He may momentarily and occasionally see the truth through the eyes of his master, but he cannot enduringly and unbrokenly see it through any other eyes than his own. If he really wants to help the student, the healthy way is for the master to get him to use his own understanding independently, to give him enough confidence to develop his own powers of comprehension and to promote his concentrative power and stimulate his thinking power. Thus, he learns to trust increasingly his own inner resources and to convert aspiration into action.

In opposition to the orthodox views selfishly held by the heads or blindly followed by the advocates of other and older Indian schools which declared enlightenment to be quite impossible without a teacher, the Buddha plainly if heretically declared that there are two ways whereby one can arrive at right insight – either by learning it from others or by self-reflection. The same point has been differently explained in detail in *Yoga Vasishta*, an old Sanskrit text, thus: 'There are two kinds of paths leading to truth's freedom. Now hearken to them. If one should without the least failure follow the path laid down by a teacher, delusion will wear away from him little by little and emancipation will result, either in the very birth of his initiation by his guru or in some succeeding birth. The other path is where the mind, being slightly fortified with a stainless spontaneous knowledge, ceaselessly meditates upon it; and then there alights true enlightenment in it, like a fruit falling from above unexpectedly.' This second path is the one which we have advocated. It is based on rationally thinking over and mystically meditating upon the remembrance of a glimpse, intuition or fleeting illumination which may have once been experienced or, alternatively, upon the description of such an experience as given in books.

There is a plain inference to be drawn from these facts. It is that because everybody has been thrown back upon himself by the further statement in *The Wisdom of the Overself* that the Overself is the one true teacher to be sought above all others, nobody has really been hurt. In depriving them of doubtful external guidance, we have given them back the surest internal guidance – the light and power of God within their own selves. We have endeavoured to awaken men, to bring them out of slavish dependence on others, to lift them up from being weak leaners to becoming self-reliant learners, to arouse them into the consciousness of their own powers of achievement and their own possibilities of knowledge. We have tried to help them to look at life from their own spiritual centre and draw out of themselves a wise comprehension of life, and to work by the light of their own creative ideas rather than by borrowed ones. We have sought to help individuals develop into the awareness of their own inherent divinity and thus fulfil the true purpose of their incarnation. The only redemption which philosophy proclaims is self-redemption. It believes that man must create out of his own consciousness and by his own effort the new understanding which shall transform him. For, in the end, realization of the Overself is nothing else than a shift of emphasis within his own being and, therefore, no outside force can effect it.

'Hold fast as a refuge to the truth. Look not for a refuge to anyone besides yourselves,' exclaimed the dying Buddha to his attendant-disciple Ananda, when giving a parting message for all disciples. What

145

he further said is also very instructive with regard to our subject. 'Be ye lights unto yourselves' is one acceptable translation, but 'Be ye islands to yourselves' is another. Whether we accept the one or the other, the meaning in both cases is ultimately the same. It is a message of self-reliance, of seeking within and not without for guidance and strength. It is, finally, a warning not to depend unduly on human teachers but mostly on the illuminative element within oneself. 'Work out your own salvation with diligence,' were the last words of this wonderful man, whose reposed form, smiling mouth and peaceful countenance evidenced his own sublime self-reliance.

The Choice Before the Seeker

Nevertheless, only the unbalanced extremist can wish to dispense with wise instruction of the right kind, *if it be available*. For without it men must experience trials and must make many mistakes and suffer much in consequence, too. Yes, the need of a reliable master is great. But he must be not only a man of knowledge but also of power and pity – power, because those who come to the quest are so weak themselves, and pity because there is no other inducement for him to help them. So if they are incapable of working out their hard problems by themselves, they should seek and accept the guidance of someone else. To obtain friendly guidance from someone who knows the farther stretches of the road is as sensible a procedure as it is senseless to become the debilitated mental slave of someone who exudes pontifical infallibility and discourages scientific rationality. It is the primary function of a competent teacher to show a sure, safe road to his pupils and thus shorten the effort needed, as it is his secondary function to impart a propulsive impulse towards the goal.

Most aspirants find that the Overself is not a thing they can aspire towards or meditate upon so long as it remains inconceivable, unimaginable and ungraspable by their ordinary mind. It is a formless, characterless and featureless void with no point of reference for them. It is too intangible, too vague and too indefinite for their consciousness to feel elevated by or for their attention to become concentrated upon. They are left by this concept suspended in mid-air, as it were. Their need, therefore, is for something or someone to provide a visible focus for aspiration towards reality, an imaginable centre for meditation upon it. That is to say, they need an attractive *symbol* of the Real.

They can find such a symbol in a historic scriptural personality known to them by tradition; in a living master known to them by personal acquaintance; in a book, ancient or modern, whose sentences purport to be inspired by the knowledge of reality; in the musical, pictorial, sculptural and other artistic productions of human genius; or in the beauty, grandeur, immensity and serenity of Nature herself. A few flowers resting in a simple vase may also convey, to some refined mentalities, an adequate symbol of divine graciousness. But whatever it is, it is indispensable that it should appeal to their personal predilections if it is to become effective. Even the accessories, instruments, ceremonies, rites and sacraments of religion can also be utilized for the same purposes, provided this condition is fulfilled and provided they are regarded, not in the light of the extravagant claims usually made on their behalf, but as tokens of the Intangible and as reminders of the Quest. The statuette of a Buddha plunged in contemplation can thus become fraught with significance in the eyes of a Buddhist mystic every time he beholds it, both as a hopeful message from the silence of Nirvana to desire-bound man and as a stimulant to the further practice of meditational exercises. The little crucifix carried underneath his shirt may become alive with meaning to the mind of the Christian mystic every time he touches it, both as a sign of the presence of the hidden spirit 'crucified' in a manifested universe and as a remembrance of the need of dying to the lower ego.

The aspirants who have found a trustworthy contemporary guide, an ideal teacher who has united with his own soul and is willing to help others seeking to attain the same state, may conveniently regard him as their finite Symbol of the infinite Overself. To accept him as a spiritual guide will not then be a blunder. On the contrary, it will be an act of wisdom, for it will help them greatly to go forward. It will give the mind something definite with which to occupy its field of attention, something that can be not only taken hold of by both thought and feeling during the aspirational hour, but also retained by them outside it. Hence, for those who have not reached the stage of fully operative mysticism – which is not an easily reached stage because it is such an advanced one – it would be foolish to underrate the value of such external helps, unwise to lack appreciation of the usefulness of such a symbol.

There are certain other advantages, over the more impersonal kinds, of utilizing a master's name and person as a focus for this kind of meditation. It is easier for many people to work imaginatively with the familiar physical senses than creatively with the much less-used faculties of abstract reflection. For the aspirant can quickly create the mental image; can rapidly remember the sense of elevation yielded by the impact of his aura; can set up an activity wherein greater strength to concentrate and apter skill to turn inward are drawn telepathically from his living presence; and can thus find a visible object for pent-up feelings of devotion, an object to whose likeness he can try to conform his own strivings. During such meditation, there will be a satisfying feeling that there is no longer a compulsory confinement to the aspirant's own limited resources.

'When one pupil is ready, the master appears.' But this need not mean his physical appearance; it really means his mental appearance. When the pupil is to some extent purified and self-disciplined by his own effort, rendered more sensitive by meditation and instructed by study, then the Overself may direct his thought to some developed man as a focus for his further meditations, prayers and aspirations. We say 'may' here because this does not always happen. It depends on the individual's history, circumstances, inclination, capacity and character. Spiritual ties created in former births may be so strong as to necessitate a teacher-disciple relation again for a time. The need for a devotional outlet of a personal and tangible character may be so overwhelming as to make it imperative to find a worthy one in order to facilitate further progress. The natural weakness of most human beings may foster depressive moods which paralyse endeavour so that encouragements and stimulants from stronger human beings become needful.

On the other hand, a man may have cultivated self-reliance, independence and balance to such an extent that he is untroubled by all these considerations. In that case, no master need or will appear to him. His own Overself will provide direct guidance from within instead of from without as in the above cases.

Where he is brought by his own wish and fate's design into touch with a master, even then it is not necessary that he stay permanently with this man. It is enough to be with him for a few minutes. But even if he has not met the master, the establishment of contact internally through correspondence is sufficient. And even if he has never corresponded with him, the absorption of thought from a book he has written will lead to some result of this kind.

To imagine that he actually is the saint who is his ideal, to picture *himself* as being suddenly transformed into the Guru he follows is indeed the shortest and the quickest method of *mystical* attainment. But it is given to a disciple only towards the end of his adventures in meditation. For he has to be sufficiently purified in character, expert in concentration and contemplation, metaphysical in separating formless being from its external appearance and detachable from the personal ego to be able first, to use such an effectual method and second, to use it in safety and without incurring harm.

In this exercise he must *act* the teacher, pretend he is him and call up all histrionic ability to imitate his ways. The initial acceleration of his lapse into contemplation will begin when he thinks of the teacher's form in this way, but the final consummation of it will come when he unites with his essence, his mind alone.

When imaging the teacher, he should think mostly of the *Spirit* which is using the teacher's body. It is more effective – and hence the more advanced part of this exercise – to think of him as a *medium* for the higher power, as a vehicle for the divine presence, than merely as a self-sufficient person. It is not of the flesh-and-blood guide that he is to think so much as of the mind which is inspiring him. It is not personality in its ordinary state that he is to imagine but in its extra-ordinary state of absorption. It is his inner consciousness, when plunged in the same deep meditation which the pupil seeks to attain, that the latter is to contemplate and identify himself with. He is not to worship the man but rather the Spirit which has taken possession of him. He is not to concentrate thought on the fleshly frame so much as on the presence within it. It is not the name of the dead prophet or living guide which is to receive his homage and devotion, his reverence and prayer, but rather the Nameless being which overshadows him. Thus the aspirant passes from appearance to reality, and thus he prepares to become a vehicle of the same divine life.

When a guide, who is still frail and fallible because he is still human, is taken as divinity, when he is credulously draped in deific titles and reverentially enshrined by his disciples far beyond the profane reach of common reason, the philosophically minded can do nothing else than gently smile and silently withdraw. To be worshipped by others is, in their view, not a privilege but a nuisance. To call any guru by the Deity's name and to ascribe deific power to him is sheer blasphemy. The truth about this has been plainly and tersely set down by St Paul: 'I have planted, Apollo's watered, but God gave the growth.' (1 Cor. 3:6)

We should not worship any man. We should venerate his embodiment of the ideal, of the heart and mind in a perfect condition. It is the idea he represents that is to be worshipped, not his person. Philosophy ardently advocates the necessity of veneration but does not advocate a blind and credulous veneration devoid of wisdom. We should venerate the master not because we want to turn a man into God, as the superstitious often do, but because we want to turn *ourself* into a master, as the philosophic try to do.

There are many stories which seem to show that even if they have not given enduring realization, the gurus have at least given transforming occult experiences to their disciples. What is the hidden truth about this matter? Where these experiences occur in the teacher's presence and lead to a state of half or full inward absorption, they are of a hypnotic character. If the teacher is really of a superior kind and has really gone deeper into his own soul than ordinary people, he will be able to communicate something of this depth to the student if the latter falls into such a self-absorbed state. This is very useful, in its own place, to picture before him what the next stage in mystical meditation is like. From the philosophic standpoint its value is limited because of its transient nature, because the psychic revelations which often accompany it may be merely hypnotic suggestions of a dubious kind, because it cannot yield permanent results and because the student will still have to work out his own development to this stage. The character and worth of this experience have often been grossly exaggerated in India, in ignorance of the historic fact that the annals of Western mesmerism record many cases of similar experiences where the mesmerizer was not necessarily a spiritual man at all.

Where, however, a disciple experiences the psychic presence of his teacher although both are in different cities or widely-separated lands, when under such conditions he perceives the vision of his teacher's face and form confronting him, and when he holds daily thought-conversations with this living presence and form, it is natural that he should come to the conclusion that the teacher is actually with him in some 'astral' body and that the meetings have been deliberately willed by the teacher and successfully brought about by his yogic power. But these conclusions may be erroneous. The facts on which they are based may exist only in the student's imagination. The teacher will most probably be quite oblivious of what has happened to the student and quite unconscious of these daily visitations and telepathic conversations. What has really happened then? The answer is that the form taken by his experiences and the ideas it yielded him were entirely self-suggested. The student's own concentration on the idea of the teacher, his tremendous faith in the power of the teacher, his great devotion towards him, have unlocked the latent capacities of his own mind and turned them temporarily into kinetic forces. Thus, instead of disproving the existence of yogic powers, this interpretation of his experiences actually proves it. Only it is not the teacher's but the student's powers which are really in question.

This explains most cases but not all. Where the teacher is a man of genuine Overself-consciousness, a further force is brought into play. There is a spontaneous reaction to the student's thought about the teacher, but this comes from the Overself direct to the student and over the head, as it were, of the teacher himself. It is, moreover, not necessary for the adept to think of each of his disciples separately and individually. It is enough if he retires daily from contact with the world for a half hour or hour and turns his attention towards the Divine alone and opens himself as a gate through which it shall pass for the enlightenment of others. During that same period, *all* those who are mentally devoted to him will then automatically receive the transmitted impulse without their even being consciously in the adept's mind at the time. But such a guide is rare and such cases are consequently exceptional.

The disciple of such a qualified master who lives at a far-off distance, or in a foreign land, and is consequently able to meet him only at long intervals if at all, may nevertheless benefit by the mystical link which exists between them. If he has developed sufficient sensitivity through meditation practice, he will feel at critical times, or after periods of intellectual perplexity, that he is mentally in the presence of his absent master and either receiving spiritual help from him or conversing with him upon the subject about which enlightenment is needed. In this way, his drooping spirits may be revived and his silent questions answered satisfactorily through a genuine telepathic process. The impact of such a teacher's power on the disciple's mind cannot but be beneficial to him.

Therefore, a fifteen-hundred-year-old Chinese text, the Chisto Tao Lun, says that a beginner on this quest should search and inquire for a man who possesses insight. If he is unable to find such a man, then he should search and inquire for one who is well-versed in meditation and well-advanced in knowledge. Having found a suitable teacher – even if younger than himself – he should, the text continues, respectfully express his desire for enlightenment and assistance.

The help which can be given by such a guide is to be admitted but, because there are few philosophers in the world and comparatively many more mystics and metaphysicians, the difficulty of finding it unentangled must also be admitted. For a man may have made some mystical or metaphysical progress and be willing to assist others to do so too, yet his attainment may not be sufficiently perfect to free him from adulterating this willingness with other motives. He may be swayed by the desire for financial gain, by an unconscious yielding to the sex impulse, by the wish to exercise power in the world, by the complex of being worshipped by many followers, or by unseen powers which are tempting him to his own destruction. The progressing mystic, betrayed by his own ambition or spurred by his own arrogance, may take to the teaching path before he is fit to do so. One result is that he becomes an exploiter, not a teacher. He dominates the souls of his disciples, deliberately prevents them from finding out for themselves anything that is hostile to the teacher's interests or doctrines, issues arbitrary orders and expects unthinking obedience, hinders and does not help the true growth. When he wants them slavishly to echo all his teachings under pain of denunciation as heretics if they do not, when he ritually treats every manifestation of independent thought as sin – then he does not really teach them. He merely extends his egotism to include them, enlarges his 'I' to overflow into them.

It is not difficult to find such a guru possessed of mixed motives or of the desire to exploit others, who simultaneously possesses the desire to enlighten them. Where the instrument is itself impure, the inspiring power cannot but be equally impure. It will be an intermittent shuttling between the Overself at some times, and the egoistic illusion at other times, with bewildering results for the unfortunate disciples – for they cannot be expected to understand what is happening behind the scenes of their guru's mentality. We say 'unfortunate', for they may be led aright on some points but will surely be misled on others. It is most desirable, therefore, that if a seeker feels he must find a guide, he should find one who is personally in such a position that he need not be affected by these temptations. That is to say, he should be karmically fortunate as well as spiritually competent – either he should have independent financial means of his own or should have achieved financial success through the exercise of a profession or business; he should be happily married; he should possess, through the accident of birth, a respected position in the world or have attained it through his professional, business or social services. These, of course, constitute ideal surface qualifications but it is next to impossible to find them all combined in the person of a single man. Nevertheless, it is well to know them and, hence, to seek for someone with as many of them as possible.

The ancient ideal of a completely ascetic teacher who had entirely renounced the world cannot externally exist in modern Western civilization today, outside of sectarian monasteries, but it can exist internally in the heart of a man who has absolutely mastered his thoughts and emotions, even though he does wear the best clothes and sport a jewelled tie pin. Five hundred and fifty years have passed away since Shaikh Sharfuddin, a Sufi sage, wrote a letter in Persian which contained this clarification for a seeker: 'A spiritual teacher is not the body, the head, or the beard visible to man. He is, in reality, the inner being in the region of Truth.' The wisdom of these words is needed today and will always be needed. The aspirant should not be influenced by the slave mentality of monkish teachers who will regard with shivering horror the picture of a modern guide such as we have here pointed out, but should use his God-given capacity to think for himself and comprehend that the form under which instruction is imparted must adapt itself to the needs and conditions of the times if it is to be genuinely useful. An honest teacher must be something more than a benevolent onlooker. Such sincere, genuine spiritual guidance as seeks to make the aspirant eventually able to dispense with the services of a guide altogether is healthy and helpful; but such selfish, bogus or incompetent guidance as depletes the aspirant's own powers and intelligence is unhealthy and harmful. The first places a key in his hands and bids him use it, whereas the second neither possesses a key nor, possessing, would be willing to give it away. Instead of increasing the student's feeling of weakness, the true teacher endeavours to instil in him the heightened confidence and deeper conviction which come with the personal exercise of his own powers. For his ever-present aim is to lead the aspirant towards attaining his own proper maturity. While the right kind of teacher, like the right kind of book, will not save students from doing their own thinking, he will certainly help them to do it well. He cannot pursue the quest for them, but he can help them to pursue it in the right direction. The right kind of teacher must be able to convince his pupils of the truth of his teaching – not all at once, of course, but within a reasonable time. For muddled thinking and vague perception, insufficient experience and incomplete development inevitably disclose themselves in dark obscure expression and imperfect unconvincing exposition.

We who write this piece sometimes think of the ancient wisdom as a giant statue, magnificent and beautiful to behold when it was made, but now, alas, fallen into the desert sand, half-buried, prostrate, slowly crumbling, waiting perhaps for some Napoleon of insight to arise one day and lift it. We sometimes even play with the thought that the disincarnate voice of a custodian of this half-lost wisdom may suddenly issue forth from the world's radio sets and speak those authentic words which many students would so gladly welcome. For is it not the sages' business to preserve the teachings of the philosophy of truth, to keep them from fading out of humanity's memory and to guide men into the ways of realizing the Overself in their own experience?

But alas, it is no use being befooled, whether by others or by oneself. The fact remains that sages, in the old integral sense of the term, are now a vanished race. Let us not waste our time looking for such perfect men. We are unlikely to find them. Let us not expect to meet gods walking upon this earth. Let us not ask where such sages exist and where they can be found. Who is there who knows? All that has been written on the subject is really a composite picture of different advanced types to be encountered and of the ideal master of whom to dream. So, let us take good guidance wherever we get it and be glad that we do receive it, whether from someone who has gone some way or from an inspired text written by a sage himself, whether ancient, modern, oriental or occidental.

This situation being what it is, students must keep a clear sense of the realities which compose it. If historic change has largely brought about the disappearance of teaching sages and thus hindered the opportunities for the progress of present-day aspirants, it has also brought about the appearance of new opportunities which have helped it. In two points, at least, they are better off than their earlier brothers. They have available today the written or printed memorials of the thoughts and conclusions, the labours and victories, the methods and results of a host of seekers, yogis, mystics, sages and philosophers who lived in different centuries and in different lands throughout the whole world. The knowledge developed during some thousands of years can now be added to their own store. If a guide is most valuable for beginners to chalk out their path, to advise them in perplexity, to explain difficult doctrines and to protect them against pitfalls and snares, it is equally true that such guidance can also be obtained from available books. They have also available easier living conditions which free them from the absorbing manual toil and drudgery which swallowed up so much of the effort and energy of those earlier men. In the end, the seeker arrives – and must arrive if he is going to advance at all – at a stage where he must learn to walk by himself, must learn to extract from within all that is needful. The student who walks alone may make some mistakes, but he will also gain useful experience and develop his own responsibility. He will become a learner instead of remaining a leaner. And, in the end, another man can only teach him what he needs to know and do, but he cannot set him free from the ego, from the limitations of the consciousness evolved to its present point throughout so many ages of evolution. The belief that true teaching can come only from outside is an erroneous one. Indeed, sooner or later it becomes essential for the aspirant to learn the loftiest kind of self-reliance, that wherein he will look more and more to the Overself for guidance, and nowhere else.

It is true that were he to adopt a wholly independent attitude prematurely – that is to say, before he was ready for it – he would commit a grave error; but when he reaches the study of philosophy, the ripe and right moment to begin to adopt it has arrived. Thus, the paradox arises that just as the stage of long search for a guide is itself overpassed when a guide is found, so the stage of discipleship must, in its own turn, be overpassed if the Overself is to be found. The embodied master must be given up for the disembodied Overself. Just as the developing mind grows out of the belief in an external and personal God, replacing it by the belief in an inward and impersonal God, so little by little it grows out of dependence on an external and personal teacher and replaces it by dependence on the inward impersonal soul. The disciple can now see that all means – from elementary ceremonial rites, the following of scriptural injunctions and the study of metaphysical or mystical books, up to personal discipleship itself – have been merely temporary and successive pointers to the real means, which is to renounce everything and everyone else for an utter surrender to the Overself alone. They were needful and helpful to him in his spiritual childhood because they could be seen, touched and read, because they existed as sense-perceptible forms in space and time. But because the Overself exists in the invisible, intangible, nameless, timeless and spaceless void, he who seeks it must at last step out of such sensual limitations and seek it there alone in all its pure transcendence.

Only after he ceases to search for any human teacher, because the usefulness of such a search has been exhausted, does he begin to receive the inner counsel which shows why all enfleshed teachers have to drop out of his life. The persevering seeker learns, in short, that he must surrender the false independence of his little isolated finite life, not to this man or that one but to the indwelling ever-present universal being within his heart; that there is no use going any longer to human beings; the last step is to go directly to the Ultimate Mind itself. The grace he needs and seeks must come from God. No institution can grant it. Any claim to the contrary is merely an act of human exploitation, not an affirmation of divine instrumentality.

This explains why no divine man ever appoints a direct successor. That usually occurs only in the institutions which arise around or after him, and whenever this has happened the successor is invariably not up to the stature of his predecessor. In fact, the degeneration of all spiritual institutions is due to the belief that historical succession is really possible as an inward and authentic fact rather than as a merely outward and apparent one. Spiritual genius is individual and unique. It can no more be delegated by such external methods as spoken or written appointment than artistic genius can be delegated. Shakespeare could not by such an easy method appoint a successor capable of writing plays as perfect as his own. Indeed, if this were really possible, divine men like Jesus and Buddha would have saved all mankind by the simple process of transforming all mankind overnight. Mankind would have been immensely superior and gloriously different from what it now sadly is. But they did not do so because they could not do so. The work that they did was good but always unfinished. The condition of spiritual genius must be attained by diligent effort and protracted striving through many a lifetime. No guru can abruptly give away his higher consciousness as a permanent gift, though he can and does give temporary glimpses of it. No guru can lastingly effect an enchantment wherein his disciple's entire past evolution and present characteristics can disappear entirely and abruptly. In the superstitious adherence to the doctrines of pontifical, apostolic, episcopal, hierarchical and lamaic succession, often with an accompanying pretense of infallibility which arises out of this single error, we may discover the genesis and evolution of most religious imposture, degeneration, hypocrisy and materialism. All such doctrines are philosopically untenable and intellectually unhealthy. The only true line of valid succession, however, is that every avatar predicts, before he passes away, the coming of the next avatar. Thus his words give hope to those who, living later and in a period of degeneration, become concerned about the future of mankind, just as they guarantee to others that the World-Mind will not forget its mortal progeny.

Now that we who write can look back, with a better balance and a surer judgement than ever before, upon a varied life of more than thirty years' spiritual seeking through service, aspiration, meditation, reflection, study, travel and personal contacts with holy men, if anyone were to ask from what source we derived the greatest help and made the quickest and farthest progress, we would be forced to answer – in contradiction to traditional Indian belief in this matter – that it was not from the holy men but our own manifold striving and humble prayer. Indeed, we would add the further conclusion that the importance attached to persons in both religion and mysticism is nearly always a most exaggerated one. It arises out of the human weakness which regards the formal symbol as more attractive than the formless spirit, the tortuous allegory more convincing than the clean-cut concept and the sensuous image more real than the abstract idea. Yet it is the teaching that always outlives the prophet – the truth that is the essence of its messenger and the principle that is above the personality. This is why, in our published writings, we have tried to lead seekers away from mere personalities to sublime principles.

Nothing in the foregoing pages should be taken to mean that we are opposed to organizations and institutions as such. We recognize that they have a proper purpose, which is to conserve spiritual gains and prevent spiritual teachings or literature from being lost. If they have the right men at the top; if they are worthily conducted; if they are vigilant against falling into the vices of exploitation, selfishness and materialism; if they sincerely keep always in view the inner purpose of their coming into being – then, indeed, they may play a useful, helping and honourable part. But if they are turned into machines for dominating minds, tyrannizing consciences, serving private interests and conserving superstitions – then we are opposed to them.

Those who have so far followed us with adequate understanding

157

will now understand also that we have made no attack on the institution of discipleship itself. We have tried only to reveal its proper function and mark out its proper limits.

The physically blind man will not hesitate to ask for and obey the leading of a guide. The spiritually blind man, however, does not even do this much, for he suffers from delusions and imagines that he is seeing his way when he is doing nothing of the kind. Although the Buddha taught spiritual self-reliance, opposed priestcraft and exposed guruship, he did this only because he found himself in a land where these things had been so abused and pushed to such extremes that they did more evil than good. The Buddha did not intend his teachings on these points to be universally held and eternally valid. No sage ever adopts such an attitude exclusively. He is always a practical man and therefore always gives out what will best help his period and place. Only the student himself, by his own experience in trying this and testing that, can develop the capacity to solve his own problems, can ripen the power to discriminate between the real and the apparent, the true and the false, the good and the evil. It is indispensable to his progress that he discover his weaknesses, errors and ignorance, and then seek to correct them. But this is not to say that he must always experiment blindly and move from one mistake to another. He can utilize the knowledge of those who, in the past, have gone before him on the road of life and of others who, in the present, have gone ahead of him on the same road. Anyone can reach the highest goal by his own power – that is perfectly true. But if he has a teacher to remove his doubts and correct his errors, to strengthen his capacity for meditation, inspire his efforts and explain his duties, he will reach it more quickly and safely. There are times when everyone feels the need for something or someone to rest on, to whom he can appeal for help, encouragement, instruction, inspiration and direction, to assist him through the dark corridors of hopelessness and doubt. Certainly, it is common sense to look for the man who can provide these things. Without being too cautious on the one hand or too rash on the other, he may seek a teacher. It is only by such an ideal balance that his efforts will achieve the best result possible under given conditions.

But it is hard to find such a person, hard to find anyone who unites in himself wisdom, compassion, experience, strength and the willingness to serve others without reward. The average seeker will have to look long and warily before he can find a competent or even an honest guide. What, then, is he to do? Shall he be so foolish as to entrust himself to an incompetent, a dishonest or an insane teacher? If he refuses to do so, and is too discriminating to accept a sham substitute, is he to fall deeper into depression, sink more and more into despair? Or shall he trust the plain words of Jesus: 'Seek and ye shall find. Knock and it shall be opened unto you.' That is to say, shall he seek guidance from the ray of Godhead within his own breast and mind?

Why should I seek a teacher? Why should I want an intermediary to discover God? Is there not all truth within me? Is the desire for a teacher the last desire to be surrendered? Is the running hither and thither in quest of a guide the last step in the wrong direction? Do we not thereby confess that we are seeking within, in our own internal and spiritual being? This is the suspicion that sooner or later will throw a shadow across the road and call us to 'Halt'. If we fare further, we do but seek outside that guidance the truth, help and inspiration which, in the ultimate, must come from the divine self alone. For is not the teacher's work but to lead one to the knowledge of one's own true self? Such are some of the inwardly prompted questions which naturally arise in an age when the human species is increasingly individualizing its mentality.

Amid this conflict of thoughts, each apparently true, the mind may well reel. But after war comes peace, and the troubled soul can find an honourable solution. It is this: Let him pray daily to the divinity within him, and pray as though it were for life itself when in great danger, choosing some words like these: 'O, Thou Divinity within this body. Unto thee Love and Obedience. None else does this self know to whom to turn save Thee. Yet art Thou shrouded in impenetrable darkness. Thou art the object of this search, yet how art Thou to be found? If only through Thy Light in some other human form, some teacher, grant that this being may meet him soon, and know him as soon as met. But if Thou wish that this self know Thee directly, without another's aid, then must Thou open by Thy grace the gate which leads within, for I am helpless to do so.'

A very earnest Western seeker once travelled to an Oriental country in quest of a guru. She selected the monastery of best repute and rented a cottage up on a hill. She sought for tuition from the abbot but her requests were ignored. After six months, as it seemed useless to stay longer, she began arranging to depart and return home. Just then the comprehension struck her, as in a sudden flash, that no one outside herself could do for her the work resulting in self-realization. This seemed to clear her mind and show her a path of self-improvement. She was now ready to depart in peace. But that was the very moment when the abbot unexpectedly came at last to visit her and to tell her she was now ready for his help. So she remained and, thus, began her discipleship. It is significant that the country where this happened was not India.

Every real master ardently wishes his disciples to attain the state where they can dispense with his own services. He knows that he will help his disciples more by giving them the strength to escape from him than by leading them to depend on him. Every true master delights when his disciples begin to walk alone. If he does not have this wish and this delight, then he is no master but an exploiter. It is a fact, which vested interests and selfish exploitation have hidden from many for thousands of years, that divine guidance, inspiration and help can also come to the aspirant who deliberately walks alone. For his own Overself is the unfailing witness of all his efforts and aspirations and is everready to befriend them. The inner light which is always there for such a man is a safe and reliable light by which he can walk. When he begins to walk by the light of his own unveiled understanding and not by the borrowed lamp of another's, he begins to walk with sure steps. Such a sublime self-reliance is in every way better than the abject dependence on another human being which passes so often for discipleship. The few who will gaze on these lines with confidence rather than with contempt; who in default of finding the right teacher and whilst refusing to accept the wrong one will make the experiment of working with their own natural intelligence, enkindled by their own heartfelt yearning, prayer and warm devotion towards the Overself, shall find that the divine guidance can unquestionably become a living dynamic within their hearts – wise enough to give them all needful new instruction and strong enough to shape their whole lives. The inward teacher will lead them upward to the realization of their diviner possibilities as well as any outward teacher, or else it will lead them to such a man if he be available.

After the student has taken the decisive step of depending on nobody but his own Overself, he makes a strange discovery and one of peculiar importance today when authentic sages are – so far as we know – perhaps a vanished race. The silence begins to speak to him with a new and profounder voice. We refer to the mystical phenomenon known as 'the Interior Word'. He learns that Truth has never departed from mankind. It is around every man; it is within him, too. It is his hidden nature. But is he willing to receive it? Is he ready to recognize and to trust it? When he can answer these questions affirmatively, he shall perceive that he needs no other teacher than the Overself. Once he awakens to this light, he need henceforth search in no other place than that occupied by his own heart.

Ramakrishna's words, quoted earlier, are supported by a passage in the Arabic writings of Ibn Ul Farid, the thirteenth-century mystical adept of Cairo: 'I saw that he who brought me to behold and led me to my spiritual self was I. . . . Even so my prayer was to myself. . . . Here I reached a point from which the intellect recoils before gaining it, where from myself I was being joined and united to myself. . . . And since I was seeking myself from myself, I directed myself to myself, and my soul showed me the way by means of me. Thinkst thou it was another, not thyself, that conversed with thee in the drowsiness of sleep touching various kinds of exalted wisdom?'

10
Cleansing of the Emotions

It is not enough for a student to utter the petition or make the demand that his soul shall reveal itself. This is necessary – and moreover in a sustained form – but he has also to provide the requisite conditions for such a revelation. Having accepted the philosophic way of soul-realization as the higher purpose of his earthly life, he should next consider what he must do to fulfil it. That will depend on both his inward state and outward circumstances. If he has mastered the few basic principles and accepted the chief ethical ideals, he must learn to apply philosophy to his own particular personal requirements. Something more than a mere intellectual interest in its teachings is needed if he wishes to honour them. He ought not to expect to receive enlightenment from the higher self, much less be possessed by it, before he has established within himself proper conditions for such a divine visitation.

Such a condition will not arise of itself. To prepare it, he must impose some moral and mystical discipline upon himself. The initial weak desire for self-betterment and character-building must grow into a strong, mastering passion. The aspirant must exceed his own best, go beyond his own past. He may not loll in indolent complacency but should begin to strengthen his moral impulses, to build up his character and to train his thinking. Leaving behind all dilettantism, he must strive vigorously and persistently toward clearer self-understanding and emotional detachment. A strict endeavour after self-improvement, a continuous effort after self-purification must also be made. It is most necessary for the philosophic aspirant to aim at such moral self-improvement, to develop the exercise of his character and to cultivate the chief virtues preached by the great prophets of all religions. A well-balanced equipment is as valuable on this quest as is a well-balanced effort, which is neither too feeble nor too violent. The higher will is latent within him and is developed only by recognition, submission and exercise. He ought to feel ashamed if a single day has passed without its proper share of mystical meditation, devotional prayer and moral endeavour, disciplining the mind and cleansing the heart.

His first duty is to get rid of the last traces of animality. Hence mystical tradition has called this early phase of his spiritual career the phase of purification. Yes! the Higher self will eventually come and enter his consciousness if only he will prepare the requisite conditions of a still mind and a pure heart. But this he will not be able to do successfully unless he loves It more than he loves the world. For the first condition calls upon him to surrender his thoughts in meditation and the second, his desires in renunciation. There are two factors which are noticeably absent from modern life and which must be brought into it if it is to become spiritually worthwhile. They are contemplation and renunciation. While the senses completely rule the mind, ignorance is its necessary companion. While the heart is totally given up to outward things, suffering is its intermittent visitor. Only by disciplining the one and introverting the other can the light of understanding dawn and the calm of balance prevail.

Yet it is needful here to beware of extreme views. There are fanatics for virtue who say that no one should sit down to meditate until his character has been thoroughly purified. There are fanatics for meditation who assert that virtue is itself only an effect, of which meditation is the cause. Philosophy is more reasonable because it is more balanced. It requires the side-by-side parallel endeavour of both these ways. It says, practise meditation but purify and ennoble character still more at the same time. For the aspirant's work begins and ends with moral re-education even more than with mysticism. He must eliminate weaknesses and acquire virtues.

For most beginners it is often more important to better the character than to practise meditation. This is because, firstly, the results of meditation may be good or bad according as the character is good or bad. Secondly, the success obtained with meditation will be less or more, according to the presence or absence of virtues or weaknesses. Thirdly, that which stands in the way of union with the Overself is the ego-self, which has to be weakened and thinned, little by little, through the purification of character until the great final battle with it can take place in the inner mystically developed stillness.

This ego-self is made up of two parts. The first includes the emotional desires and mental attachments for things or people in the outside world. The second includes those elements which we share through the body with the animals. Thus the first part is human and the second is animal. The two together constitute the lower ego-istic self.

His first disciplinary act cannot escape being a painful one. It is to take out of the heart all those instincts and passions which bind him to the animal self. He may mitigate the pain by extending the time of the operation. If he is young in years, probably he will. But if he is middle-aged, still more if he is old, he cannot afford to delay. In particular, all the malevolent emotions and aggressive attitudes have to be thoroughly cleared out from his nature; he will have to perform some drastic surgery upon them.

But that is only the beginning of his work. His aim at the next stage is to discover and rid himself of the evil qualities and secret attachments that bar the way to his soul. There are several great tempters of man which must be overcome if he is to achieve inward freedom. Amongst them are the ambition to gain power, the desire to increase possessions, the craving to become famous and the lust to gratify sex. 'Give up desires,' is the essence of the discipline enjoined by the Bhagavad Gita, the New Testament and the Buddhist Tripitaka scriptures. Why? There are two reasons. First, the mind must be made free to seek the Truth. Second, the will must be set free to express it. A man who is controlled by any desire and who cannot himself control it, has a warped outlook. He unconsciously demands that Truth should con-form with his desires. He cannot 'see straight', cannot apply himself wholeheartedly to inquiring into Truth. Philosophic discipline is the best method of freeing a human being from such distortions in mind and feeling and rendering him truly fit to ascertain Truth. It detaches a man from worldly ties, gives him an independent outlook and trains him to view things without personal passion or suggested bias.

A hard precept is *Light on the Path*'s instruction to 'kill out desire'. There is no harm in recognizing our needs and calculating how to provide for them. What we have to do is to distinguish between the lower and the higher desires, between ignoble and noble ones, between those that harm our fellow creatures and those that help them. We must oppose the one, accept the other. There are various ways which, combined, will help us rule our lower desires and bring them to the service of this quest of the Overself. On the physical side, we should foster willpower, practise self-denial, discipline our bodies by occasional short fasts, cease from frivolities which stimulate desires and nourish passion. On the intellectual side, we should study the metaphysics and ethics of philosophy and lift ourselves regularly above the very realm in which desires operate. There is inspiration and power – not merely information and argument – in the study of true metaphysics. These intellectual endeavours, this reading and study, these reflections and musings, are necessary and useful and will in time begin to have their effect not only upon his knowledge but also upon his character. Not only are they uplifting, but they are also purifying. Not only do they explain the presence of lower desires and animal passions in man, but they also contribute towards checking them. Not only do they give the reasons why he should make his character better, but they constantly give powerful suggestions to realize this betterment. Thus, if his doubts and misconceptions will be slowly cleared, his morals and motives will be slowly bettered.

Another well-known precept of the ethics of mysticism which is dangerously open to misunderstanding or easily liable to nonacceptance is the Bhagavad Gita's injunction not to look for the results and fruits of our actions. The correct meaning is that we are not to be personally so attached to the results that our mind's peace, our heart's happiness utterly depends on them. We must appraise our needs correctly and use our forces worthily. The Gita teaching does not absolve us from this duty. This will certainly lead to results, and we shall certainly be responsible for them. The teaching does not mean that we are to stand aside and do nothing and so avoid personal entanglements; indeed, the whole keynote of the book opposes such a futile conception, such glorifying of complete inertia. It means that we are to stand aside from attachments and clingings.

The practical side of this quest begins by a slow turning away from the old unconsidered life, a deliberate rearranging of unsatisfactory habits, a voluntary cutting-out of desires that weaken or degrade the character and a constant analytic self-examination to detect faults in thought, feeling and conduct. This effort has not only to be started in real earnest but also carried to a certain point before authentic spiritual, as distinct from psychical, experience may be expected. Any system of ethics which is based on spiritual fact must always discipline, and sometimes oppose, the natural desires of man. For a time the animal in him must be crucified, the human mortified.

The full if distant goal is to liberate himself from entire submission to the calls of the flesh and the turmoils of the mind, from animalistic urges and humanistic graspings. He has to pass from the common state of willingness to accept the flesh as his master to the uncommon state of rebellion against it. The process of self-cleansing necessarily involves the acceptance of discipline, the practice of penance or asceticism and even the showing of moral courage. He has to deny this or that thing to the body for a time, in some cases even for all time. He has to curb the vehemence of deep-rooted long-lived feelings. He has to set about the reversal of ancient mental habits. He has to abandon emotions which are instinctive in human nature. It would be almost impossible to continue in these endeavours were it not for the stimulus he receives from glimpses of the ideal, the longing he feels to transform it into a reality, and the reality of grace.

For these controls, the exercise of modified asceticism – the practice of a certain austerity – is indispensable. It must be sincere and sane, however, which means it must be first, imposed from within himself by intuitive promptings and second, temporary and limited. He himself must determine of what kind it shall be and how much. He himself must impose it and not anyone else. For the discipline must be demanded from within by his own soul, which best knows what he needs at the time. Sacrifice in some form is demanded of him, but it is not demanded before he is ready for it. Animal instinct and human greed will have to submit themselves to spiritual intuition, but they need not submit prematurely. Thus philosophy pursues neither an impossible perfection on the one hand nor an impracticable asceticism on the other.

Desire is necessary to human life and the spiritual desires do not extinguish desire, but only give it another and higher direction. If there were no desire there could be no universe, for God could not make this universe if He did not desire to do so.

Everything that hinders the Divine will's passage through his heart and life must eventually be cast out. What these hindrances are will be made known to him from time to time by both inward promptings and external events. He has to affiliate his lower will with his higher one; the two must be brought to work in unison. All his thoughts and feelings are to be permeated with this diviner motive. A steady self-discipline, a constant obedience to ideals, a faithful carrying-out of spiritual duties – these are demands upon the will. To meet them he will have to harden and strengthen it. The task of making himself strong enough to ride turbulent passions and restless thoughts is not a weakling's one. When his passions and desires and instincts conflict with his ideals, there is no way out except to fight and overcome them. He cannot afford to leave his inner life at their mercy.

The purification of his sense-life, the training of his thought-life and the bridling of his emotional life constitute the great preliminary cycle of the quest. Consequently, it involves and cannot escape being a cycle of irritation, tension, conflict and suffering. It is true to say that the consciousness of a man engaged in this quest swings like the pendulum of a clock, to and fro, in the struggle between earthly passion and spiritual aspiration, between egoistic pettiness and ethical grandeur, and between contrary moods. This cannot be helped. He has become a field of struggle for powerful antagonists, with nothing less than his soul for the prize. The animal and the angel are both in himself. He discovers that the lower emotions are more easily aroused than stilled; subduing them will be accomplished only at the end of a long period of time. Most people find it too much trouble to engage in self-improvement or too fatiguing to do more than talk about it. They are hardly to be blamed. This arduous enterprise, once started, never really comes to an end. How long it will last cannot be predicted in a general statement, for it will differ with different individuals. Sometimes it is a matter of a couple of years, more often of several, not seldom of a whole lifetime. The achievement of a reasonably desireless state is necessarily the travail of many lives on earth.

The process of detaching himself from the lower nature is also comparable to the process of extracting teeth. But there is no spiritual anaesthetic here to mitigate its painfulness. Nevertheless it may help him to endure the pain to remember first, that quite a number of Orientals and Occidentals have demonstrated that it *is* possible to spiritualize mental energies, reorient disturbing passions and elevate strong emotions; and second, that if the search for man's soul begins in agony, the finding ends in joy. The emotional chill which the teaching of renunciation always gives the trembling beginner will one day be succeeded by the emotional freedom which the same teaching gives the maturer disciple. It is misery for the ego to renounce its desires. The feeling of unbearable sacrifice weighs heavily upon it. Yet it is happiness for that some ego when, at long last and by the Overself's grace, desires renounce it, for the feeling of liberation from their burden will uplift it.

To enable man to free himself from these lower emotional hindrances

167

and attain this objective of ruling animal appetites, a systematic training must be employed, a course of discipline must be passed through.
The power of unruled desire in man is strong and terrible but it can be
negated by a twofold process: observing and analysing constantly those
harmful deeper consequences which most people ignore, and dwelling
constantly on the benefits and attractions of its opposite state. He will
need to use the service of both analytic reflection and creative imagination in his meditation exercises; of contrite penitence, humble prayer
and lofty aspiration in his devotional ones; of short occasional fasts and
a meatless diet in his physical regime.

It is not easy for anyone to disentangle himself from animal tendencies. But anyone may discipline the will by degrees – out of weakness
into strength and out of animal subjugation into holy governance.
Therefore ascetic disciplines, practised for short limited periods and
repeated at convenient intervals, are prescribed by philosophy to assist
and quicken the process. But they are never prescribed alone. Suitable
meditations are coupled with them, for the real battle occurs within the
mind. Through constant thought and repeated aspiration, he must
make himself so familiar with the higher ideals that obedience to them
becomes second nature. He has to learn by severe discipline how to
follow higher intuitions rather than lower instincts, how to greet the
tempting images that enter his mind, how to dissect them at once and
separate the warm emotional temptations from the cold thought-out
facts. If his animal tendencies and egoistic fixations prevent a full
surrender to the higher self and even disturb his faith in the possibility
of ever achieving such a surrender, this is still no reason to fall into
despondency. By prayer he may invoke grace. By grace he may conquer
self.

It is plainly not the ego's own will that is either willing to turn
upon, or capable of subjugating, itself. From what source then is the
power drawn to execute the Overself's commands? There is indeed a
higher will that transcends the ordinary one. It is a necessary though
painful experience of this quest for a man to arrive at the humiliating
discovery that, do what he will, the ultimate conquest of the animal
part of his nature is beyond his control. He may have periods when it
would seem that this conquest has been effected, but an unexpected
happening or a sudden incursion of thoughts will disillusion him. This
self-discovery will be most valuable in the end, however, if it leads him
to avow his inability and to acknowledge his imperfections, if it makes

his ego utterly humble. For then, in his anguish, he will have to seek help from a higher power, be it the Overself or someone who has learnt to live in the Overself. He will, in short, have to seek and pray for grace. And this, when it comes, will be truly amazing. For he will feel himself being lifted above animal instincts and physical passions to a higher level of his being. And it will be accomplished without any struggle on his part – indeed, with wonderful ease. He no longer weakly accepts the negative suggestions of undeveloped men and evil spirits, of his own past tendencies or low environment, but the higher will, of its own accord, rises up inside him and rebuts or rejects them. He who could not extirpate the passions by his own effort will find them extirpated for him by the Overself. The attainment of this sublimer consciousness automatically delivers him from their chains.

He will know when he is progressing by the sharpened recognition of his own yieldings to the lower self and by the deepened insight into their characteristic degrees, operations, and origins. Thus on this philosophic path the seeker is not called on formally and peremptorily to renounce any desire; for, little by little, the desires will themselves renounce him! The power of the evil principle over him becomes weaker and weaker, the power of the divine self stronger and stronger. As this self takes more and more possession of his character, his passions become subdued, his earthly desires become less and less troublesome. When he feels himself sufficiently advanced to make the test, he may even deliberately imagine alluring stiutations and attractive forms and note how he reacts to them. But to attempt this at too early a stage would be an error. He may mentally work out a temptation in advance and pursue it to its inevitable consequences. Thus by purely rational and imaginative processes, he may obtain the benefit of such an experience without receiving the troubles and sufferings which, in many cases, develop from it.

The True Meaning of Desirelessness

We feel our insufficiency and incompleteness. All our ventures in friendship and love, marriage and association, are really strivings to remove this feeling. We never succeed fully or for long, however. This is so and must be so, because what we are and what we are seeking outside of ourselves exists only inside ourselves. The missing factor is none other than our own living soul.

169

Man is chained to earth by a score of desires. When he engages in the quest, he sees then that all these sweet desires end in sorry captivities and that if he is to escape from the misery of a divided self, he must disengage himself from them. Hence the strength of all his desire-being is to be withdrawn from its former objects and reoriented inwards to the divine soul. Even the body is to become a mere instrument for his wisest thought and best will, not for his lowest nature. This is the great contest to which he is called.

If we have to worry constantly about the sustenance and shelter of the body, we become preoccupied with it just as much as if we have too much, too many possessions and become preoccupied with them. So the ideal is to find the middle ground between too much and too little in order to liberate the mind from continual concern with the body and its possessions.

Let both the physical body and the things it owns be given their rightful place – no more, no less – so that they may be made to subserve the higher purpose of life, which is to fulfil the Quest of the Overself.

Yet man lives in a highly acquisitive world. That is why there have been and still are so many nominal but so few real Buddhists and Christians. For both Buddha and Jesus insisted that the way to the goal to which they called men lay through giving up the hungers for possessions, position, sex and self-assertion. There is no durable happiness in these things but only the illusion of it. Nobody can put a term to the acquisition of better status, more wealth, increased fame, greater glory, extra possessions. It is a game easier to start than to stop. Because desires grow as they are fed, he will never have enough. Today a thing is a luxury; tomorrow it becomes a necessity. Today that is superfluous; tomorrow it is indispensable. He must ration his desires if he wants inner peace. The more he increases them, the more he has to struggle to satisfy them. Until he gets this clear in his mind, he shall not get peace in his heart. There is spiritual realization only for him in whom the grasping hands of the ego are forever withdrawn and the fires of passion have subsided into the ashes of renunciation. What he counts his best possessions are in the highest region of his mind and the deepest region of his heart.

These truths hit a man hardest, perhaps, in the personal love which he seeks to give to or get from a girl, a wife or a friend. For he will have to acquire the power to trample resolutely on his own emotions, if and whenever the Overself calls upon him to do so. Indeed, the entire course of the preliminary ascetic discipline is one long sacrifice. Coolly to stand aside from emotions like personal love and sexual affection, ruthlessly to dissect their nature and unyieldingly to repel their invasion is the hardest of all its ordeals. The application of mentalism to such dissection may help him a little. All desire is really mental. Were it not for the images which it forms in the mind, no desired object would attract him. When a young man falls deeply in love with a particular young woman, he is really deeply in love with his idea of her. In the moment that he yields the mind's calm to any disturbing passion, be it jealousy, sex or anger, he yields it to an *idea*. He must learn to control his ideas if he is to control his conduct. And by learning to check imagination, he learns to control desire.

'All dependence on another is misery, dependence on oneself is happiness,' declared the Indian lawgiver Manu several thousand years ago. To the extent that a man depends on others for his happiness, to that extent he is likely to lose it one day through death, desertion or disease. And because normal sexual passion is entirely dependent, it is also entirely deceptive. If a man seeks a happiness which will stay with him under all circumstances, then he must not seek it from another man or woman, else he invites disappointment. He must seek it at its enduring source – the Overself. He who depends on others for his happiness will never enjoy its enduring reality but only its ephemeral appearance. Human love may be withdrawn from him after a time but the divine love never. He must learn how to live without feeling the absolute need of someone else in and to his own existence. Where there is such dependence, there can be no durable happiness. The moment he makes another person his chief basis for happiness, he has opened a door to possible unhappiness. He should look for supreme happiness to no embodied creature. For such a happiness, in its truest sense, cannot be found unless it be found in and from oneself. This is because it is to be got only from the divine, which is pure spirit, and because it is attainable only through the gateway of one's own heart, not through another's. Man's quest of ideal love, let alone perfect companionship, can never be satisfied by any woman but only by the soul hidden within himself. She indeed is the true Beloved who, ever patient and ever faithful, waits for the time when he shall discover and woo her. The love which he can find in the soul will not depend on a changeable human mood for its existence, will not be affected by the conditions or accident of human flesh, but will be perfectly trustworthy and serenely sure. More, it will always be there, always be more faithful to him than any human love could ever be. If he passes from this world into another, or even fifty other worlds, still it will remain his loyal companion. It must be. For it comes not from a different, a separate entity; it comes from his own inmost self and is an eternal attribute of his eternal soul. The truth brings with it great serenity and also great independence. He is no longer at the mercy of others for his happiness.

The growing disciple will learn to live a strange paradoxical existence. Events will so occur, the course of his external life will so flow, men and women will so behave towards him that in the end he will be driven away from externals and forced to find reality, truth, love, friendships, possessions, beauty, satisfactions and even spiritual guidance within himself – in the worlds of imagination, of thought and of that which transcends both. In the end he will have to accept the fact that human solitude is inescapable, that the human soul is inviolable, that the separation between one human being and another cannot be overcome in reality but only in appearance. He who has found the Beloved within is not afraid to be alone. He is always gratefully ready to accept the company and friendship, the affection and devotion which others may wish to give him, but he can live without them if fate bids it be so. He has attained to practical wisdom who has attained to inward self-sufficiency, who does his best for all men yet expects nothing from any of them, whose work contributes its utmost to life but whose heart expects little from it. Because he expects little from others, whatever does come will be thankfully accepted as a bonus – but not as anything more. He looks only to himself for happiness and relies only on himself for achievement. 'What one gets without any expectation is like nectar,' wrote Swami Sahajananda, a Kathiwar master, in a letter to his disciples more than a century ago.

The divine self asks for nothing less than the whole of his heart for a sacrifice utter and complete. In return it will give him the consciousness of its presence, the awareness of its love and the blessedness of its time-free state. If he is to attain and feel intensely its heavenly peace, he can do so only by buying it with a heavenly desirelessness. Nature gives everything at a price. Much that he believes to be a part of himself must go. This process of divesting himself of the lower desires and emotions is agonizing yet indispensable. He must come to this point that he shall desire to be possessed by the divine soul above all other desires.

Such a hard counsel is not for the many who feel no hunger for truth, no readiness for a higher life. The enslavement by body, senses, passions, and thoughts is supposed by them to be the natural state of man – so weak have they become. Yet he alone is really natural and perfectly at ease who has gained his self-freedom and self-mastery. They have become so strong in earthly habits and so weak in spiritual longing that the disciplinary requirements of the quest seem too forbidding and too unrealizable. To such people, the quest's ideal seems as cold and as implacable as the snowy heights of the Himalyayas. No! this counsel is tendered to disciples only, that is, to those who have voluntarily put themselves under a discipline for the sake of finding the soul. It is tendered to the person who has made the great decisions; who negatively has renounced animal appetite and put aside human desires; who positively has accepted the Intangible Reality as the chief Good in his life and the Overself as the true ego of his being. An ethos of desirelessness first baffles and then repels the modern mind. Its disparagement of wants which are natural, ambitions which are legitimate and possessions which are civilizing does not seems to deserve discussion because it does not seem to make sense. There is a short step only from the intellectual position that such an ethos is insane to the emotional position that it is inhuman.

What is the practical value of such an ethos? How far is it requisite to the needs of modern man? These questions can be properly answered only if he looks to his terms. First, he should not confuse necessities with wants. He should come to a clearer understanding of what is and is not essential to his life, so that he can simplify and elevate it. Secondly, let it be specially noted that the call is to a renunciation that is essentially of an inward character. He may keep his possessions outwardly if he forsakes them inwardly. If he is called upon to abandon everything, it is only sometimes that this is to be done externally, although always to be done internally.

The declaration that entry into the kingdom of heaven can be effected only by the man unweighted with possessions, is a true one. But the possessions referred to are not external ones; they are wholly interior, intangible, and invisible. He is secretly dead to the world even whilst apparently moving, working, enjoying and suffering in the midst of it. Such is the true desireless state. He has to learn the paradoxical art of having natural desires like other men and yet being as if he did not really have them. That is to say, he may possess them insofar as he is a human being with human needs – although with him they will be simplified, disciplined and elevated – but at his heart's core he is ready at every moment to desert them instantly. Thus he establishes a sane equilibrium between the wish to possess and the will to renounce.

The most satisfactory attitude to adopt is the one which the Buddha had to adopt after experiencing both extremes of the princely life in a palace and the Spartan life of an ascetic. In the end he taught that the middle way was best. Thus, he makes use of things without becoming entangled in them. 'When thou hast surrendered all this, then thou mayst enjoy,' says the Isha Upanishad. Renunciation need not prevent him from loving his friends, need not deter him from valuing his comforts, need not deny him the use of clever inventions, luxurious homes and artistic creations. But it will permit all this only when and to the extent that it does not trespass upon his time with the Divine, his devotion to it and his choice of it. Philosophic discipline is not ascetic discipline: it does not ask him to renounce all ties of friendship, family and marriage, all affection for other human beings. He may keep the ties and the affections. It asks only that he shall free them from possessiveness, that he shall care deeply for others along with, and not in denial of, the Divine, that he shall maintain all lesser loves inside its larger love and not be imprisoned inside them. He is not required to abandon his worldly life but to spiritualize it, not called upon to renounce his personal relationships but to approach them from a new point of view. It would be a sad error to think that this passage from attachments to detachment, from earthly entanglements to heavenly ones, is made by destroying human relationships and chilling human affections. The actuality is that the man becomes more loving in his behaviour to family or friends and not less. But it is a love of higher quality than before, purer, less selfish and more benign.

Purity of heart means in philosophy the forsaking of all possessions and all persons, not before the world's gaze but before God's. There is peace for those who have entered the desireless state. So long as they are inwardly dead to the world, they may outwardly remain active in it. Neither an external asceticism nor an external abandonment of worldly life is what matters or is called for so much as an internal detachment. When ascetic renunciation has fulfilled its inner purpose, when it has helped to bring the animal self to subjugation and the personal self to submission, it may itself be renounced if he chooses to do so. For it is not an end, only a means to an end. Once his thoughts and feelings are sufficiently pure, the value of external sacrificial discipline drops to little. The needs of the human body and the human entity tenanting it may be satisfied on two conditions: first, that they are disciplined by reason; second, that they are not allowed to obscure the needs of human life's spiritual and ultimate goal. These conditions he has fulfilled.

When he has truly entered into the desireless state, when he no longer feels the need for anyone or anything, when the feeling that wells up continuously from his inmost heart is self-completion and self-contentment, he will perceive how pitiable is the tragic state of those who, still earthbound, walk with fettered hands and clanking feet but know it not and even glory in their bondage. The twelve labours of Hercules are an allegorical description of the aspirant's struggle with his lower nature and adverse forces.

Beyond the clinging to possessions and the yielding to passions, the quester must travel still further. Even the overcoming of his ego's desires in these directions will not bring him to the goal, though it will advance him far beyond the captive multitudes.

He still needs to penetrate to the depths of contemplation, where all is emptiness profound, where personal identity is dissolved and where God alone is.

He then needs to learn the art of bringing all this into relation with his common everyday existence, with his activities in the world. He further needs to make a fresh orientation toward the intellect, replacing his contempt for and detachment from it by a constructive, positive and integrative attitude.

When this period of self-training is at an end, he will possess the capacity to attend adequately to whatever duty, work, matter or pleasure his faculties are called upon to attend to, and yet the moment it is finished to dismiss it so utterly from his mind that it is as if it had never been. With that he will return to unflagging spontaneous concentration upon, and abidance in, the inner self.

When so far as is humanly possible he has achieved this independence of externals, when he lives from and is true to his own inmost being, he discovers a plausible and perennial satisfaction the earthly man never knows.

Whoever fights and succeeds in overcoming the lower nature becomes filled with the serenity and wonder of the higher. The period of tormenting stress and internal division will come to a sudden end, to be followed by a period of satisfying calm and internal unity. The intermittent or personal conflict which goes on in so many hearts will be abolished in his own. He would be foolish indeed to sacrifice for a lower satisfaction the insight, calm and power he has gained at such great cost and after so many hard conflicts. The sacrifices which in his novitiate seemed so enormous to make are now, in his proficiency, quite effortless to accomplish.

When the struggle with his passions and thoughts is brought to a triumphant end, a great tranquillity settles in the heart. The animalistic life has gone out of him. The angelic life has entered into him. The intellectualist tumult has been silenced. The impulses no longer war within him. Indescribable is the serenity of being so self-contained. When the individual consciousness is thus separate from the passions, desires, emotions and ideas that agitate it, serenity comes to pervade it. And then he will discover the great paradox, that for one who can inwardly, willingly and secretly renounce the world before the grave forces him to renounce it outwardly, unwillingly and openly, the world is truly his and will lie at his feet. This has been pithily stated by Patanjali in his *Yoga Aphorisms* [1.37, 1.40] which provides the first recorded textbook on yoga:

Or the mind-stuff reaches the stable state by having as its object a mind-stuff freed from passion.

His mastery extends from the smallest atom to the greatest magnitude.

We may match these words with the mystical statement of Jesus: 'He who loseth his life shall gain it.' In a different way, this yet has somewhat the same meaning as Patajanali's remarks. For in the mystic's highest experience, that of the nihilistic Void, he is divested of his entire personal ego, of every thought, thing and desire. He possesses nothing and is nothing. Nevertheless he has put himself in a position where, because the Void is the source of everything, everything may be granted him. Thus paradoxically, by giving up all, he gains all.

Swami Vivekananda has said:

'When the world is given up, what remains? What is meant? You can have your wife; you certainly do not have to abandon her; but you are to see God in your wife. Give up your children – what does that mean? To turn them out of doors? Certainly not. But see God in your children. . . . This is what

Vedanta teaches: Give up the world which you have conjectured, a false world of our own creation. Open your eyes, it was a dream, a maya. What existed was the Lord himself.

"What is meant by giving up desires? How will life go on? The solution is this: not that you should not have property, not that you should not have things which are necessary and even things which are luxuries – have all that you want; only know the truth about property: that it does not belong to anybody. Have no idea of proprietorship, possession. All belong to the Lord.

"If we understand the giving up of the world in its old crude sense then it would come to this: that we must not work – that we must be idle, sitting like lumps of earth, neither thinking nor doing anything. But that is not what is meant. We must work. So do your work, says Vedanta, putting God into everything and knowing Him to be in everything. When desires are thus purified, through God, they bring no evil, they bring no misery.'

In the foregoing pages the subject has been considered from the standpoint of students and aspirants. Let them note that the ethical problems and mental conflicts which it touches do not arise for the sage. For at the very moment when the student attains supreme enlightenment, whatever desires and passions may be left fall away from him of their own accord. Whatever he does in his external conduct thenceforth cannot alter this inward state of sublime if secret detachment in which he perpetually rests. He may play the total ascetic if he chooses or he may play the complete worldling, but his own exalted status remains unaffected by either role. In renouncing the ego, he has renounced everything. He has reached a point where there is nothing else left for him to renounce. His desire to achieve desirelessness has been fulfilled. A wonderful feeling of liberation floods his heart, a vast serenity stills his mind. An intense and enduring satisfaction with the Overself is present. Nothing else in the world seems so worth having, for having this he feels he has what is most worthwhile in life.

11

Ethical Qualifications of the Seeker

He who possesses the name and bears the form of man is to be respected only when reason rises to the ascendant over the animal in his nature. The danger of passions like lust, anger and animal violence is proverbial, but the blindness of the emotions like attraction and repulsion in often unrecognized. Passion is brought down to defeat by the combined labours of reason and will from his own side and Grace and suffering from beyond himself. He has to quell the periodical turbulence of passion until it tires of revolting and gives up the struggle, and he must refuse to be victimized by his emotions. The battle against the animal nature is fought inside himself. Especially must he learn to fight his own emotions. He must give battle at some times to his pleasurable feelings, at other times to his painful ones. His lusts and cupidities war against his worthier ideals. Continually must he strive to be as truthful in his feelings and as accurate in his emotions as he should already seek to be in his ideas. It is during these periods of emotional strain that he is likely to make faulty decisions and take wrong action.

The exercise of calmness under all circumstances is a definite aid to the student's progress on the path. Out of this unruffled calmness there will come naturally an accurate discernment of values and a balanced judgement.

There are moments of great tribulation or of great temptation when a man's controls may be shattered. The student must never permit himself to get so angry about anything that he loses self-control.

His judgements should be dispassionate and disinterested, not conditioned by his desires. His appraisals of the most hotly disputed issues will then be balanced and fair, correct and reasonable. He will not make a negative criticism without at the same time making a positive suggestion.

One of the targets of the philosophic aspirant in his endeavours for self-improvement is liberation from all those emotional prejudices of a personal and communal nature which divide and antagonize mankind and retard its progress. Philosophy makes for a more charitable attitude towards all men. Malevolence must yield to goodwill unwarped by prejudices. Such goodwill acts as a solvent of the prejudices, dislikes, frictions, envies and hatreds which darken social life.

It is not that we should reject emotion from our attitudes (as if we could) but that we should not form them solely in terms of emotion. The emotional appeal is not absent from philosophy, but it is an appeal to our higher and not to our baser emotions. Philosophy does not sterilize emotion but spiritualizes it.

If our thoughts were deprived of all feeling, they would make little positive impression on our minds. Each idea would then carry the same weight, the same importance as another. The thought of a teapot would be in the same category as the thought of truth. So it is not that we are to eliminate feeling from life. It is that we are to control and discipline it, to keep it in its proper place. For a consciousness in which passion or emotion has got the upper hand and from which reason is absent, is like an unsubstantial cinema screen world whose objects can be distinguished by sight but not felt by touch. Hence in this quest for truth, the metaphysical facts must be related together by reason but they must also be made actual by feeling.

As mystics, we must educate our hearts as effectively as we have already educated our intuition. When the workings of emotion get the approval of reason and the sanction of intuition, then are they safe and healthy. Only when passion is bridled and emotion is curbed do we become reconciled with life and discover the meaning of serenity.

The emotion which in various grades of keenness we call satisfaction, pleasure, joy, felicity, bliss or happiness reaches its fullest volume and loftiest quality when it deserts the lower self altogether and expresses only the higher one. Our thoughts about these higher things must be blended with feelings about them. But the feeling must be in consonance with the ideas. These noble moods are not to be put in the same category as the sloppy emotionalistic ones which merely disfigure rather than express the mystical life.

The seeker must learn the art of being his own master under every kind of circumstance. The way of self-overcoming is an upward one, a difficult one, but it is as essential to the quest as the smoother way of giving himself up to emotional ecstasies in meditation. What must be

179

done is to assert dominion over the thoughts which would drag him down, the feelings which would tear him and the many foolish selves which would misrepresent him. It is not enough to try to deal with the manifestations of the lower self by creative thought alone. It is also necessary to make a parallel effort of the will, a self-denying endeavour to lift action onto a higher level, an active tearing struggle to resist what seems to be a veritable part of his own being. Not only must he control the actions which seek to satisfy desires against his better judgement, but even the day-dreaming which seeks the same objective. He should beware of the first onset of merely negative and viciously destructive or shamefully egoistic emotions. It is easier to stop the life of tender shoots than of maturer ones. This is especially true of emotions like jealousy, pique, wounded pride, bitter resentment and hot anger.

The seeker must discipline himself to face the vagaries of fortune and surmount the vicissitudes of life. Such a self-discipline will provide his youthful years with more security, his aged ones with more dignity. Whoso will not arrive at this self-discipline from within, peaceably and voluntarily, will have it imposed upon him from without compulsorily and violently.

Prolonged association with certain people may deeply alter an individual's character and powerfully divert him from his general direction. It depends upon him either to accept or to resist their influence. He must be on his guard against the misdirection of his forces and the deflection of his aspirations. They can be correctly led only if he follows the counsels of philosophy. Just as the best when corrupted becomes the worst, so strength when misdirected becomes weakness. He must seek and find the proper balancing and safeguarding factors.

To the habit of orderly thinking which education may have given him, he must add the habit of disinterested thinking, which in its perfect form philosophy alone can give him.

He will neither take refuge in complacent escapism nor give himself up to helpless despair. He will look the situation in the face, calmly and steadily. He will approach men and events, ideas and problems, not as one belonging to any of the conventional orthodoxies but as a detached truth-seeker. He must see things in their true light without the deceptions or distortions provided by greed, hatred, lust, prejudice and the like. His personal reaction to world events must be brought into line with the rest of his truth-seeking endeavour.

Those who can use their thinking power in the purest way – that is to say, unbiased, undeflected, unweighted, unegoistic – are extremely rare. Yet the philosophic training seeks to lead men to do just this.

It should be the seeker's aim to retain and sustain his ideals whatever the surroundings in which he happens to find himself. In a society animated by narrow prejudices and unworthy selfishnesses, he must steadfastly keep his moral integrity. He must strive to maintain a strict integrity of character henceforth, as being a vital part of the path towards the Overself. Thus the quest is not easy and not always pleasant. He must defend the integrity of his mental life against all physical foes, human or environmental.

We do not progress by yielding to weakness that masquerades as virtue, but by nurturing strength even though it bears a disagreeable face.

It is not enough only to discover the principles which secretly control human life. It is also necessary for the student not to contravene the precepts which arise from them, nor to act at variance with them in his daily conduct. These principles are not to be obstinately supported at one time only to be suddenly sacrificed at another.

As his character matures and his intuition develops, the soundness of the ideals for which he works becomes plainer than ever. When a man is really in earnest about this quest, there will come a time when he will have to make a heroic stand for its moral principles, when he must refuse to sacrifice them for the sake of a shifting passing advantage. He will reach a stage where he will not only refuse to violate this code of ethics but will refuse even though he could gain greatly thereby, or even though his violation could never be discovered by others.

The aspirant should know that if he has been true to the injunctions of the teaching, he will sooner or later receive deliverance from his difficulties. His steps may still be halting, his mind still unsure of itself, yet with the passage of time he will find that definite progress has been made.

He will reach a bodily age and mental ripeness when certain truths will be clearer to his view and less repulsive to his feelings. Of these he should consider three: the illusory value of sex; the need to subordinate emotion to reason; and the reality of the invisible, intangible Overself. He should meditate again and again upon these things if he wants inner peace.

His success in life can no longer be measured adequately by externals alone but must be measured also by how far he has succeeded in purifying his heart, developing his intelligence, unfolding his intuition and attaining balance.

12

Surrender of the Ego

Philosophy is uninterested in flattering a man or in pandering to his vanity. Therefore it begins the practical side of its discipline by pointing out his defects, faults and shortcomings, and by opening his eyes at last to the weaknesses, incapacities and complexes which hitherto have been unconscious or disguised. To go forward safely on the path, a man needs to be cured of fanatical obsessions and irrationalities. He may think that eradication of personal faults has little to do with finding the true self, but this is not correct. These very faults arise out of the false conception of the 'I'. Moreover the eradication is suggested not only to help him to overcome such false conceptions but also to help him become a better servant of humanity.

It is true that a man cannot help being what he is, that outward circumstances and inward nature, karmic tendencies and past experiences have combined to shape his character. But only if he is honest with himself, if he ceases hiding his ugly faults and starts bringing them into the full light, has he a chance to make solid progress on the quest.

He will do well to know what his ego is really like before he attempts to know what his Overself is like. The ruthless searching into his complexes and trends, his hidden vanities and desires, is a valuable preparation. It is those of which he has been hitherto quite unaware for which he should probe.

While this constant scrutiny of motives, this searching analysis of character is shirked or feared, egotism is able to disguise itself, subtly turning the most altruistic situations to its own advantage and unsuspectedly satisfying its desires even when seeming not to do so. When allowed to intrude into a man's observations of life, it makes them fallible, doubtful, distorted or wrong. The ego must be flattened and even, if necessary, punctured!

That which matters is inspiration and motive. Is the deed prompted by the ego? Or is it prompted by the Overself? Does it seek personal gain? Or does it seek to render altruistic service? The pattern of duty may sometimes be unclear, but the prompting of egotism may always be unmasked. It is easier to overcome the bias of temperament which, after all, is only a surface thing, than the bias of egotism which, too often, is so deeply concealed as to be quite invisible. These unconscious purposes operate quite effectively in their own way, and much of the conscious activity shows their influence to the trained observer.

The student must begin with the lowest opinion of himself if he is to end one day with the highest. On no account should he fall into the common blunder of deeming himself more advanced than he really is, for this will lead to failure. Let him not too soon regard himself as one of the privileged elect, lest he become spiritually proud or morally conceited. In this matter he should heed the counsel of an old Indian proverb:

'Extend your feet according to the length of your sheet.'
——Hindustani

To wear such rose-coloured glasses as will magnify the good into the best serves no other purpose than self-deception. Lapses from the path as well as achievements on it should be reviewed; the self-humiliation thus caused must be accepted and not avoided by a retreat into cynicism or by side-stepping into hypocrisy. The student must have the humility to acknowledge these faults and the willingness to drive them out of himself.

If, for instance, the student will only have the moral strength, the little-prized power of renunciation, to desert the lower ego in all his unfriendly differences, disputes, irritations and troubled relationships with others, he will be compensated by spiritual satisfaction, by a quickened growth of inward being that will far outweigh the initial cost to personal feeling. When he learns, painfully, slowly, and falteringly, to put the lower ego aside in all his considerations, reflections and decisions, he learns one of the greatest lessons that life has to teach him. And if he has the strength to oppose his own ego and the greatness to deny his own ambition, he has crossed the threshold of renunciation.

The unillumined man has no greater enemy than his own lower ego, as the illumined man has no greater friend than his own higher self. Not only is the lower nature his greatest enemy, it is also his subtlest one. It will pretend and deceive, mask and disguise, twist and turn in so cunning a way that quite often he will not know it from his greatest friend, which is also within himself.

The aspirant must take the greatest care about his motives and watch them well. The ego is the real enemy on the path, the mountain that cannot be moved by faith but only by agonizing surrender. But the agony is diminished when, through appropriate instruction, he comes to understand how illusory the 'I' really is. Without vigilance it is easy to go astray in such matters. The dividing line is often fine. He must be aware of the undeniable dangers, the tremendous temptations and the pitfalls around him. How hard it seems for a man to give himself to his own guardian angel, how easy to give himself to his besetting demon.

The student must beware of the cunning disguises of the retreating ego. He must beware of its self-flattery pretending to be the Overself's flattery. He must beware of any 'mission' to which he is appointed. If the inner voice promises him a remarkable future, whether a spiritual attainment or a worldly triumph, disbelieve it. Only if it makes him humbler and meeker should he believe it.

The ego will resist repeatedly in a long-drawn struggle. It must be brought back into the heart and pinned down there. It will struggle violently against capture and will be driven to defend itself by cunning rationalizations. But if the aspirant's own patience matches the ego's robust antagonism and if grace is sought and found, victory will come at last. So subtle an enemy on the path is the ego that even when the Overself's grace is leading him onward through his mystical practices to moments of sacred exaltation, the ego surreptitiously steals the credit for these results.

All the way from the quest's start to its finish the aspirant will need and must have the capacity for self-extinguishing humbleness and self-abasing reverence. The first is needed not in the presence of men, but of God; the second not in the bustle of the world, but in the secrecy of the heart. The lower ego must surrender to the higher individuality, not to another ego.

The need for a self-humbling before the Overself (which is not the same as self-humbling before other men) is greatest of all with the aspirant of an intellectual type. The veil of egotism must be lifted and with his own hand pride must be humbled to the dust. So long as he believes he is wise and meritorious for entertaining spiritual aspiration, so long will the higher self withhold the final means for realizing that aspiration. As soon as he believes he is foolish and sinful, the higher self will begin by its grace to help him overcome these faults. Then when his humility extends until it becomes a realization of utter helplessness, the moment has come to couple it with intense prayer and ardent yearning for divine grace. And this humility towards the higher self must become as abiding an attitude as firmness towards the lower one. It must persist partly because he must continually realize that he needs and will forever need its grace, and partly because he must continuously acknowledge his ignorance, folly and sinfulness. Thus the ego becomes convinced of its own unwisdom, and when it bends penitently before the feet of the Overself, it begins to manifest the wisdom which hitherto it lacked. Instead of wasting its time criticizing others, it capitalizes its time in criticizing itself. In old-fashioned theological language, he must consider himself an unworthy sinner; then only does he become able to receive grace. He should measure his spiritual stature not by the lower standards of the conventional multitude, but by the loftier standards of the Ideal. The one may make him feel smug, but the other will make him feel small.

At some moments he may feel the animal within him, at other moments the criminal, and at rarer moments the angel. He must convict himself of sin, must become deeply aware of his wretched state in clinging so hard and so long to vanity, animality, selfishness and materiality.

He may become anxious about his progress, disappointed about its slowness or confused about its nature. But his striving must be patient and sustained, always faithful to its far-off goal, and he should not become blinded to the necessity for maintaining a balanced personality. Nor should he become so obsessed with himself that every trivial fluctuation of his feelings is regarded with exaggerated importance and studied with morbid analysis. In short, he must not become an over-anxious neurotic. The repeated dwelling upon his faults, the constant analysis of his deficiencies, the self-exposure of his mis-steps and mistakes should humble, chasten and purify him.

The keeping of a diary devoted to confessing and noting faults in conduct and feeling as they appear may also be a help in the work of self-improvement.

Because he must first recognize and correct his errors and sins, critical self-examination must not depend on itself alone but must also take guidance from the consequences of his actions and the criticisms of his enemies. Where the ordinary man sees only enmity, the earnest aspirant sees a chance to hasten his own growth. Where the one deplores opposition, the other uses it for his own development.

The ego is ever eager to defend itself by deceiving itself, ever gratified to cover its own shortcomings by pointing out those of other people, and seizing upon the wrong example set by others to rationalize its own wrong conduct.

The disciple cannot take the easy course of always blaming someone else's misdemeanors and never his own. What he knows of his own self, with its defects and frailities and sinfulness, should teach him a little caution about others, a little carefulness in his dealings with them. He should be as silent about the faults of others as he should be eager to correct his own. Only where public or private duty make it imperative to speak out, or where he is actually asked for such criticism by the person concerned, need he break this rule.

He must liberate himself from emotional pride and intellectual self-conceit. The confession of his personal powerlessness is the first step to the discovery of his impersonal strength, and grace will begin to operate when he feels that he himself can no longer operate, no longer direct his own life without falling into further sinfulness and further foolishness.

A man's ego is naturally unwilling to put itself obediently under the behest of the Overself. Only when it breaks down through the miserable results of its own mistakes and turns despairingly contrite through the sense of its own failures, does it begin to renounce this unwillingness.

To the extent that a man empties himself of himself, to that extent the Overself may enter into his ordinary consciousness. But the displacement of the ego will not and cannot happen through any act of his own will. It will be produced in his emotional and intellectual consciousness by an act of the divine will.

He who has the humility, strength and wisdom to give his personal will back to his higher self thereby gives the chance for forces greater than his own to bless, inspire and use him. Let him have the courage to perform this one dynamic act of self-abnegation. He will never regret it. For whatever it takes from him, it will return more.

The simple meaning of those common mystical expressions 'self-annihilation', 'giving up the ego' or 'losing the I' is to put aside the thoughts, emotions and personal affairs which ordinarily occupy the mind and to let the latter sink unhindered into a state of complete absorption in a felt higher power. It is a self-offering to the sublime entity within him.

The aspirant is told to displace the egotistic life only because he may thereby find a deeper and superior life. He is not to deny his existence, but to change its quality for the better. And the ego itself must prepare the way for this phenomenal change by forsaking its self-pride and by supplicating the Overself to possess it thoroughly.

The advice to look within would be idiotic if it meant only looking at the student's human frailty and mortal foolishness. But it really means looking further and deeper. It means an introspective examining operation much longer in time, much more exigent in patience, much more sustained in character than a mere first glance. It means intensity of the first order, concentration of the strongest kind, spiritual longing of the most fervent sort. He will need to look into his heart more deeply than ever before, and search its darker labyrinths for the motives and desires hiding there from his conscious aspiration. He is called upon to make the most searching criticism of himself and to make it with emotional urgency and profound remorse.

So long as he is enslaved by his lower nature, so long will he be subject to confusions and misunderstandings, so long will he cherish delusions and deceptions during this period of his search for truth. Hence the need for an effort to transcend the lower nature through self-discipline. He starts this inner work best with the firm understanding that he is sinful, faulty and ignorant, and with humble realization of his personal unworthiness, his great need of self-improvement, purification and ennoblement.

The aspirant should guard against allowing over-strong emotions or undisciplined passions to break down the maintenance of moral and mental balance. Even personal bitterness over a great injustice may harm it.

We do not say that the philosophic student, as distinct from the philosophical sage, should be entirely without passion. We only say these two things about it. First, he should strive to create a central core within where his passions cannot touch him, and whereby they are themselves controlled and disciplined – a level of profound remembrance where they suddenly lie still. Second, he should rescue them from being exclusively animal in character and redirect them to human channels also. Intellectual and artistic passion should be cultivated as a complement to those of a lower level.

If a man's inner life is repeatedly wasted by passion, he will know no assured peace and attain no enduring goal. He must govern himself, rule his passions and discipline his emotions. He must strengthen his higher will at the expense of his lower one. For the first promotes his spiritual evolution whereas the second inflames his animal nature. He must present an imperturbable front to the inescapable ups and downs of life, and he must guard his heart against becoming the sport of tumultuous emotions and riotous passions. His emotional attitude towards others must be watched lest he betray his deeply hidden invulnerable independence and suffer its loss in consequence.

The hardest task anyone can ever undertake is to align his lower ego with his higher self. This objective cannot be reached by feeble means. It demands all a man's powers and faculties and it demands them at peak level. It demands a wholesale and wholehearted reorientation of thought, ideal and will. The enterprise of patching up the old way of life under the belief that he is setting up a new one is self-deceptive. If it is to have any karmic value, repentance must not end with emotion alone. The final proof of a changed heart is a changed life.

The result of this self-critical effort to remake his personality will be self-punishment. He will see the acute need to make reparation for former wrongdoing and, as he tries to make it, this reparation will take two different forms. The first is where it involves others, and he will make his peace with them. The second is where it involves himself alone, and here he will perform penance and impose an ascetic discipline.

The aspirant must train himself to view his thoughts in the proper perspective, refusing to regard their insistent attractions and repulsions as his own. He must cultivate the habit of being an observer of his own thoughts and activities in the same objective way as he observes strangers in the street. He must regard himself with detachment and his experiences with calm, if he is to arrive at the truth of the one and learn the lessons of the other. While he clings to the possessive little ego, he clings also to fears and anxieties, discords and despair. He gets too emotionally involved in his personal problems and so obscures true issues, or distorts or magnifies them.

If the student has continued faithfully with his meditations and disciplines, his studies and aspirations, the time will come when he will approach a cyclic turn in his inner life, when he will review the pages of both his remote and recent past. During this turning point he will be tormented by grievous thoughts of his unworthy past and by the consequent self-reproach. He will pass through a period of intense self-criticism. These sharp pains of conscience and bitter remorse are inevitable during this purificatory period when his past assumes an uglier configuration in the light which falls upon it, when he is first made aware of the dark places in his character and the weak parts of his nature.

Such memories will enter his mind unbidden. They will concern themselves only with the darker side, however, only with his sins, mistakes, errors of thought, judgement and conduct, with wrongs done unwittingly or wilfully to others. With these broodings will be linked poignant memories of and bitter regrets for the unnecessary sufferings brought upon himself as a consequence, as well as remorse for his lapses from the path of goodness and wisdom. Such reflections and feelings will spread themselves out intermittently and fragmentarily over a period of several months or even a couple of years, but at the proper time the period will be brought to a sudden, unexpected and abrupt end with a tremendous emotional upheaval. This is the second 'mystical crisis' (the first being that which set his feet on the path's entrance). It continues for three days. During this time, many of the chief episodes, happenings and decisions stretching back to childhood, involving remorse and regret, are re-lived in a kind of cinema-film review in which he is both spectator and actor. At no time in this review should ill-will or angry resentment against other people concerned in it arise. If it does, and he permits it to remain, the crisis may end abruptly in failure to yield its benefits. These remembrances should fill his heart to overflowing with despair at his own wickedness, his weakness and foolishness. He will be driven by his inner conscience to impugn both his character and intelligence as they manifested during internal struggles and external problems. Towards or at the end of this three-day experience, he may even feel it is better to die than to continue such a worthless life. He will perceive quite clearly how different, how much better for himself and others, how much happier, how much more fruitful its course would have been had he decided and acted more wisely. This perception will bring him immense anguish through the comparison of what was with what might have been. But with the coming of the fourth day all this self-reproach will leave him. A strong and clear intuition will now address itself to him in more or less the following words: 'Take to heart and keep in remembrance the lessons of the past, but let go of the past itself. Avoid these sins, get these weaknesses out of your character, improve your judgement, make what amends you can. But be done with the past, and be at peace about it henceforth. Today you begin a new and higher life.' Thereupon a vast feeling of relief uprises within him and a welcome mood of peace enfolds him for some days. Students will note that the second mystical crisis is strikingly similar to the after-death review of earth life described in *The Wisdom of the Overself*.

The pursuit of this spiritual self is not to be undertaken as a hobby, nor as an adjunct to eating and working. The task of changing himself is the greatest one any man can undertake. It is a lifetime's work. This improving of himself and advancing of humanity, of elevating his character and increasing his understanding, will keep him busy until the very end of his term on earth. The philosophical life is neither easy nor lazy, and perhaps it is only the exceptional persons who will engage in the adventure. It is hard work altering many habit-patterns that, in the light of philosophic teaching, now seem unsatisfactory. But inasmuch as he has accepted this teaching, the student cannot help but wish to conform his whole life to it. The task is tremendous but not impossible. It is not only theoretically conceivable but practically achievable, and it is to be made the student's primary activity whence all others take root and draw life.

The quest must become the centre of his thinking and hence of his living. He must be quest-conscious and surrender completely to the philosophic ideal, becoming thereby a seeker after truth. He feels now the inward completion and full possession of himself must be sought and found if life is to be endurable; he knows now that hitherto he has been groping blindly after it. Henceforth the quest must be a conscious and deliberate one. He must now pass from dream to reality, from the wish to find his soul to its fulfilment. These truths must be proven within the student's own experience and not remain merely a concept in his mind. He must believe more in his own activity for salvation and less in reliance on some individual teacher.

Philosophy teaches a sublime moral code to be followed for the disciple's own good as well as the good of his fellow men. Whatever differences in metaphysical outlook and external practices there may be between him and others, the philosopher abhors quarrels and loves amity. He observes tolerance towards all others. Although there is no moral code which can be called an absolute one, all moral codes must condemn hatred if they are to be worth the name at all.

As a consequence of all these strivings and meditations, disciplines and reflections, certain changes will take place in the disciple. Little by little the mental images born of his lowest self fade out of consciousness and he may come to see the whole of his past life as a dream. The sense of the soul's nearness becomes real, and will become for him a daily presence and a continuous reality.

There comes with the travelling of this path a subordination of personal identity, a diminution of those egoistic limits which keep man from attaining his best in life, an abstraction from the entire set of mundane desires which normally compose life.

Such people are set apart from the mass by their aspirations and fine sincerity.

If mankind have not attained, it is because they have not sought.

13

The Probations and Tests of the Aspirant

To master his desires, to overcome his passions and to ennoble his emotions: self-reform and self-purification are the first practical fruits of philosophy. Thus an interval of long probation must inevitably pass before the results of this effort can become apparent in his thought and action. The task before him is really a tremendous one, requiring his whole nature and his best mind. Anything less will bring him so much nearer to failure. And its significance is so vast that failure will, in turn, bring a like measure of mental suffering. He may believe that he has already achieved certain things, but he should remember: first, the French proverb that the better is the enemy of the good; second, that whether his progress is genuine or whether, being so, it can maintain itself, is a matter which still needs to be ascertained. His fidelity to the higher values and how far his spirituality is real or supposed, are sure to be put to appropriate tests at intervals of his mystical career. All his earlier experiences and preceding struggles, victories and defeats have been a training for them. Hence he may expect temptations to accompany him at one period and tribulations at another. He himself hardly knows what weaknesses are waiting beneath the surface of his conscious life, ready to rise above it when opportunity offers.

In some great mystery schools of antiquity, it was the task of the Grand Master to administer the necessary tests and arrange the fateful ordeals which determined the fitness of a candidate for entry into any of the successive degrees of initiation. The Egyptian hierophants applied their tests of the worthiness of candidates *before* granting them the enlightenment of initiation. The ordeals were divided into five ascending grades. Each corresponded to a different element – earth, water, air, fire and spirit. The candidate for initiation into esoteric degrees was made by the hierophants to enter places which tried his nerve and to undergo ordeals which tested his courage. They also brought him into surroundings and amongst individuals where powerful temptations to his sensual desires had to be overcome. But those schools have perished and their methods have perished with them. They would not indeed suit the conditions of the modern world.

The farther he advances, the more formidable and less recognizable will be the obstacles, trials and temptations he will have to overcome. Men and women, circumstances and situations, will be used as bait to tempt him from the quest's moral ideals or disciplinary phases, from its intellectual goals and ideological truths. One of the strange methods used by the powers to test him will be to arrange coincidences in his external life-cycle. Thus, within a short time – sometimes within a single day – of his solemn renunciation of a certain thing, it will be offered to him! Such coincidences may be evil or good. In the very moment when he is powerfully attracted by some desirable thing or person, he is to renounce it deliberately and heroically. In the very midst of a situation where the ego has but to stretch forth its hand and take, he is to practise self-abnegation discriminatingly and relentlessly. At such times, he may remember well the warning of Awhadi, a medieval Persian mystic: 'When Fortune's cup into your hands doth pass, think of the headache as you raise the glass!'

These experiences are designed to make him conscious of the weaknesses in his character and to show him how far he has really withdrawn from vanity, passion, ambition and possessiveness. What he is in his deepest impulses will betray itself during his probation. These ordeals will be the final proving-ground for his character and will forcibly reveal its weaknesses and deficiencies. No concealment will be possible. Although the same opportunities, the same trials and the same temptations cannot repeat themselves in precisely identical circumstances, nevertheless they may do so on levels of a different kind. For sins and faults seldom entirely disappear, but often recapitulate themselves in subtler ways or more refined forms. The chief latent weaknesses will be stimulated until they show themselves. This happens largely because the outer circumstances, in which they can express themselves freely, are now provided by fate. If he proves too weak to resist them, then the tragedy of a fall in consciousness will be enacted alongside his moral fall.

Some of these seeming opportunities present the most attractive appearances, behind which it will not be easy to discern what the reality really is. Satan sets traps at intervals along the path. They are so cunningly disguised that they look like pleasant parlours instead, and those who fall into them may spend years under the delusion that they are actually in a parlour. If the adverse forces cannot entrap him by blatant seductions, they will try to do so by subtle ones.

Refinement of feelings and elevation of ideas attained in his religious and mystical experiences have to be remembered whenever such temptations find lodgement. They will take the forms which they have always taken in mankind's long passage from enslavement by the flesh to exaltation by the soul – the forms of sex and money, power and position, property and self-regard and so on. But, in addition to these, there are some special forms peculiar to the mystical quest. They are ways of exploiting it for personal power, vanity or profit. But the result of such action is continual self-contradiction. If he uses the soul as a lever to gain personal ends, he loses it. For it will not abide with anyone who loves it for less than itself. If he invites the higher forces to use him, he must not expect them to share him with the lower ones.

For instance, the notion of selling his spiritual help for financial gain should, at any stage, be unthinkable. If he does so, then he will surely lose both knowledge and power through being cast down into the abyss. When he is sufficiently advanced, even the notion of accepting voluntarily-offered contributions will become equally repellent. He may not know, at first, why this feeling comes to him however, for it will come as a vague inner prompting. It is indeed a lead given by his higher self. If he fails to obey this prompting, then the higher self will, for a certain period, fail to reveal itself. He is to desire the Divine and assist its seekers for its own sake alone, not even for the mixed motives of securing both its inner presence and its outer rewards.

If spiritual help is to be given in the way it ought to be given – as an altruistic service – no payment should be taken, not even in the least obvious and most disguised form. No money gifts should be accepted, whether as remuneration for work done or as contribution to the work's cost. Indeed he must not only put students and seekers in his spiritual but also in his material debt. For if he undertakes to go out and teach others, as far as he can he should himself pay the very travelling expenses incurred as a result of making the journey to reach them. It is highly undesirable to let either the mention of reward by the disciple, or the thought of it by the teacher, enter and sully the pure relationship between them. The only thing that he may rightly accept, should it be voluntarily offered and should he choose to do so, is hospitality while away from home – that is, shelter and food as a temporary guest.

These prohibitions may seem unduly rigorous, but if we consider what is likely to be gained by them they will then seem worthwhile. First, the students will receive a vivid demonstration and inspiring example of perfectly selfless service. Second, where the teacher has himself not yet completely crushed his ego, he will avoid the risk of his motive losing its purity, his heart its non-attachment and his life its independence. Any service which really helps others but which keeps up the server's ego may be good for them but is bad for him. For the second object of rendering service is to lessen the ego's strength. The spiritual teacher, above all others, is expected by God and man to be the first person to follow his own teachings and to practise the virtue which he inculcates. This is why it is a grave responsibility' to appear before the world as such a one. His doctrine must come out of his own experience as well as thought, out of his own noble actions as well as elevated beliefs. Only the egoless adept has the right to receive money, for he alone can be trusted to use it for impersonal ends. But even he will rarely be willing to do so. Thus, two serious tests connected with money will have to be passed.

The Glamour of Occultism

At some stage, the practiser of meditation is likely to have extraordinary experiences or develop powers of visionary, mediumistic or hypnotic character within himself. His developed concentration will energize all his thoughts. As they increase in power, so should he increase in carefulness over them. Danger to others as well as to himself lurks here, but beneficence too. Whoever falls victim to the lure of occult forces and lets himself become obsessed by thirst for their permanent possession, first gets mentally confused, then loses his way altogether and deserts the higher path and finally falls into sheer black magic. If the worst happens, he will bring ethical ruin and material disaster upon himself and those who become associated with him. The earnest aspirant should prefer to follow a lonely path rather than to follow the crowd which foolishly runs after the sensational, the occult, the psychic and the fanatic, the pseudo-mystical, or joins esoteric cults.

One way in which the opposing power works to bring about the downfall of a promising student is to influence him to believe, prematurely and incorrectly, that he stands in a highly-advanced position.

He is told flattering things about himself to test his vanity. He is thus rendered over-confident and soon deceives first himself and then others.

While he is dominated by the ego and its desires, he courts the greatest dangers of, first, intellectually misunderstanding his experiences and second, ethically misusing the powers in order to attain selfish ends at the cost, or even to the injury of other persons. In most cases, however, the Overself in its wisdom lets these occult powers lie in reserve until such time as the strength of egoism has sufficiently slackened, until moral power and philosophic knowledge have sufficiently manifested themselves within him to render their use safe to both the student and those with whom he has dealings. Only when it is no longer possible for him voluntarily to injure another person in any way for some selfish consideration, does the higher self deem him ready to possess such powers permanently.

There is however an unpredictable element in the pattern of human life, which increases rather than decreases as the quality of that life rises above the average. We see it markedly in the case of a maturing aspirant who has to undergo tests and endure ordeals which have no karmic origin but which are put across his path by his own higher self for the purpose of a swifter forward-movement. They are intended to promote and not delay his growth, to accelerate and not impede his development. But they will achieve this purpose only if he recognizes their true aim. Such recognition is impossible if he persists in clinging to the lower ego's standpoint or if, sensing the unearned character of his suffering, he treats them with resentment rather than with comprehension, with bitterness rather than with resignation. Thus human life is not wholly confined within the rigid bounds of karmic law. The Overself, which is after all its real essence, is free. He who has entered his name in this high enterprise of the quest, must be prepared to trust his whole existence into its sacred hands, must be ready to accept and eager to understand the tribulations and afflictions which its deeper wisdom may see fit to impose upon him.

By a series of successive losses, troubles or disappointments, or of so-called good fortune ending in these painful things, the seeker will be successively parted from those attachments which he had not the strength to part from willingly. He has entered a stage where he is being assayed from within and without, where his yearnings and attachments, his virtues and vices, will be forced to show their real strength.

197

Let no one engage in the quest with the false hopes of a perpetual good time. For he has also engaged in a struggle. Once an aspirant takes to his quest, peace – in the sense of inward idleness or outward eventlessness – will never again be his. The relation between his lower and higher natures will always be one of tension and, at certain crises, this will be terrible and unbearable. His preliminary struggles will deny him any smug rest or complacent satisfaction. Depressive moods will inevitably come again and again as he becomes poignantly aware of faults and shortcomings or filled with memories of lapses and failures. He has to overcome prejudices and conquer passions, to abandon the lower emotions and discipline the lower mind.

Hostile forces, open or disguised, will challenge him or will wait in ambush for him along the path. He will have to make his way between them. For they will employ baits to lure him from the quest, devise snares to entrap him and use people to hurt him in various ways in fulfilment of maleficent designs. Suggestions will come to him which, if persistently traced to their source, despite their appearance of correctness, virtue or wisdom will be found to originate in such forces. The danger of losing his way besets him at every stage until he has emerged from completion of his novitiate. This situation exists equally for the aspirant who walks guideless and the one who walks with a trustworthy guide. No master can exempt him from the necessity of facing ordeals, experiencing temptations, undergoing trials, and being beset by the harassment of adverse forces.

The very last sentence uttered by the dying Buddha to his disciples contained the warning words: 'Be on your guard.' The farther the seeker advances, the more he must be on his guard against the wiles of evil forces, whose operations to lead him astray grow subtler and subtler as he himself grows wiser and stronger. The harder he works, the more he provokes opposition; the swifter his travel, the more often he meets with temptations, snares and traps. As a novice, he will have to fight the promptings of such forces inside himself. As an adept, they will be driven out of lodgement in his mind and heart only to find lodgement in the minds and hearts of other men or women, who will thereupon become suddenly antagonistic to him. These persons may, in a few cases, belong to his personal environment; in some cases they will be brought to cross his path and in others they will only have heard of him. But each will manifest some negative quality in response to demonistic suggestions and direct it against him. There will be a mesmeric character about each suggestion. It may be doubt, suggestion, lying, anger, fear, envy or hatred. There will be attempts to embitter feelings, inflame passion and arouse hatred. This adverse power seeks to hinder or even destroy the aspirant's personal progress as it seeks to hinder or destroy the adept's altruistic endeavours to promote the progress of mankind. The latter, especially, may suffer criticism, endure unearned vilification or experience spiteful opposition too. Thus when his inner troubles are at last overcome, outer troubles begin to rear their heads. He may avoid the first by avoiding the quest. He may escape the second by renouncing altruism and becoming a self-centered mystic. This is why philosophy is for the strong and compassionate only, not for cowards, egotists or idlers. Nevertheless adeptship has it compensations. If others here stumble in the night or grope through the dusk, the adept walks surefootedly in clear noonday light. And where they must struggle alone, he on the contrary is ever conscious of a blessed presence at his side.

Persons expressing negative forces are nothing less than mental highwaymen and will one day suffer the karmic penalty for such wrongdoing. It is easy for the discerning to recognize the unmistakable marks of false or unscrupulous pretension when they appear as extreme and exaggerated personal claims – as the cloven hoof of commercialistic exploitation, as the incitement to sexual looseness, as the suave encouragement of political hate and social destructiveness – but it is difficult for the unsophisticated to recognize them when they are masked by lofty teachings or fine phrases.

The Danger of Obsession

The next danger which the disciple has either to foresee and avoid or to meet and overcome, is that of becoming partially influenced or intermittently obsessed by an evil spirit who has emerged from the darkness of tellurian depths. This danger arises from his ingorance of the psychic forces and their mode of operation, from the moral impurities and emotional indisciplines of his character and, above all, from his increased sensitivity, from his inescapable necessity of cultivating a passive, surrendered attitude, and from wrong meditation causing mystical development to degenerate into a merely mediumistic development. Just as there are divine invasions of a man's inner psychological being when grace sheds its light upon him, so there may also be demonic invasions when he goes astray from the path. That the will of a disincarnate being may control the body of an incarnate one is one of those abnormal possibilities which we must admit into our scheme of things. That this will is more often evil than good is, unfortunately, quite true. That demonistic possession is in short a psychological fact, and not merely an exploded superstition, is a warning whose utterance is necessary.

The possibility of evil spirits usurping the human ego's rightful place is real. It is a possibility which was recognized by antique races throughout the world and still is recognized in most Eastern lands. It is satisfying to know that, in the kingdoms of Nature, this race of invisible demons is kept apart from the race of human beings by a strong psychic wall. But it is disturbing to learn that under abnormal conditions they may break through this wall. The unhappy sufferer's willpower may be completely overcome, his bodily organs completely used and his mental faculties completely overshadowed by the supplanting entity at certain times – mostly during the hours of darkness. When a malevolent entity possesses a man, when an unseen evil influence overshadows his mind, he feels that he is performing actions not dictated by his own personality. The unfortunate victim may or may not be conscious of what he is doing during the hours of obsession. If he is, his movements will be merely mechanical. If he is not, this will not prevent his from carrying on conversations with other persons.

It is a common trick with these invisible evil entities to secure the faith and trust of a man by cunning flattery, fulfilled predictions or lofty teachings and this done to lead his unsuspecting feet over a precipice into material disaster, mental despair and sometimes moral ruin. They conceal their real character at first, and may pretend to have the same moral ideals and religious beliefs as the man they are seeking to enslave. He may rightly suspect their presence when he feels the urge to make vital decisions in great external haste and under great internal pressure.

Anyone who has fallen into this danger of obsession will best be liberated from it by the help of a mystical adept or a true priest. Sometimes a single interview will suffice to effect the liberation. The exorciser will probably have to perform a short external rite in addition to his internal mental work. Where such help is not procurable, the sufferer may attempt to perform the rite of exorcism for himself. It begins with kneeling down in humble prayer for help, protection or salvation to whatever higher power or inspired master he has most faith in. It ends with the firm utterance: 'I command you in the name, by the power and compassion of X –, to come out of this body,' combined with the sign of the cross made positively and slowly with the right forefinger. On a deep inhaled breath, the same sign is to be made again, simultaneously with the same utterance repeated silently and mentally only. X – represents the name of any higher power or personage in whom there is full faith. This rite should be performed each morning and each night before retiring to bed.

Falls on the Path

His way is not a smooth, untroubled movement from one satisfying position to another. It is a to-and-fro struggle, an incessant fight, a mixture of victories and defeats. Therefore it should not be a matter for surprise that so many candidates fail to pass these tests and abandon the quest in its early or intermediate stages. But even after sucessfully passing them, there arises the further danger of falling from whatever height has been attained, which is another peril to be guarded against by novices, intermediates and even proficients – in fact by all who have not yet reached the final degree. Until this degree is reached it is always possible for the aspirant to slip from his position and fall back. The risk is even greater for the proficient than for the neophyte for, in the degree before the last one, the occult opposition to his progress rises to its crescendo; the temptations become more subtle, more numerous and more complex than ever before. In this grade, he has arrived close to success; but that is the very reason why he must guard his gains with the utmost vigilance or through the machinations of evil forces he may unwittingly cast them all away. Having reached this penultimate stage, he has reached the position of a man who, though in sight of the harbour, may still be shipwrecked. It is then, more than ever before, that the adverse forces will make their last desperate attempts to detain, overcome or destroy him, to plunge him into unutterable despair or moral ruin. He must beware of diabolically inspired efforts to deprive him of all that he has gained and will need to take the utmost care to protect and conserve it. During this phase, he must test his foothold at every step as he takes it, moving with the utmost care and ensuring the fullest safeguard. All his shrewdness and sincerity, all his discrimination and patience must be drawn upon to surmount this ordeal triumphantly.

Other tests will come, both to the intermediate and the proficient, through the egoistic emotions being awakened as a subsequent reaction to ecstatic mystical experience or by the discovery that subtle mental powers are developing within him as a fruit of that experience. His path will be staged by pseudo-attainments, which may bear some but never all the marks of the true, final attainment. If the experience is of the right kind, he will feel no inflated pride in having had it; rather, he will feel a greater humility than before, knowing how dependent it is on the Overself's grace. Indeed it is better that he should not communicate it to others, but remain silent about what is happening to his inner life. And this is sound counsel for other reasons, too. For if through ardent longing or mere vanity he allows himself to fall into deception about his true spiritual status, and especially if the experience be used as justification for setting up as a public teacher or cult-founder, then the 'dark night of the soul' will descend on him, too.

He should wait patiently until the divine assurance clearly and unmistakably comes that it is within his competence to engage in such activity. Until then he should beware lest his emotions be carried away, not by the divine impulsion but by his own egotism. He should not interfere with the self-chosen spiritual paths of others. Yet what may be wrong for him, at his present stage, may in later years be permissible if he reaches a higher one. For then he will speak out of wisdom and not out of foolishness; he will act out of impersonality and not out of the limited ego.

To remain faithful to the teaching when passing through a test or an ordeal becomes easier when he realizes that this is what the experience really is. He will be tested not only for sincere loyalty to ideals but also for adequate comprehension of ideas. If in the result he finds himself confused and unclear, this will be a pointer to new channels for his study. Should he desert the quest, circumstances will so shape themselves and repentances will so persistingly intrude themselves that, whether within a few years or half a lifetime, he will have to yield to the call or else suffer the penalty, which is to be struck down in premature death or life-wasting madness by his higher self.

He needs to be intellectually prepared and emotionally purified before the higher self will descend to enlighten intellect and ennoble emotion. Hence, before it sheds the sunshine of grace upon his way, it will test his perseverance in this effort and try his faith to a point of anguish which at times seems beyond endurance. In the moods of black despair which will inevitably follow each failure, he may dwell again and again on the thought of abandoning the quest altogether. Yet if he holds on an end will come and rich reward with it. If always he returns to the right path in a humble, chastened and repentant mood, he will be given the needful help to redeem his past and safeguard his future. Grace is ever ready to mantle its shekinah, in protection, over the truly penitent.

All these and other tests are in the end calls to greater and greater self-purification. When his yearning for the Spirit is thoroughly permeated with ardour and passion and when these qualities are deep and sustained, it will greatly help to achieve hard renunciations and surmount temptations. But it comes to this in the end – that all lesser loves have necessarily to be thrust out of the heart to make room for the supreme love which it inexorably demands from him. There is little virtue in surrendering what means nothing to him, only in surrendering what means everything to him. Consequently the test will touch his heart at the tenderest points. Will he step out of his little ringed-in circle of personal loves, desires and attachments, into the infinite, unbounded ocean of impersonal love, self-sufficiency, satisfaction and utter freedom?

The choice is a hard one only so long as he keeps his gaze fastened on the first alternative and remains ignorant of all that the second one really means. For whatever delight the first can possibly yield him, that delight is already contained in the second. But it is contained merely as a watery dilution of the grandly ineffable consciousness which the Real offers him. He should be wise or experienced enough to comprehend now that if each attachment gives the pleasure of possession, it also gives the disappointment of limitation. The one cannot be had without the other. Every egoistic feeling which stands in the way of his utter self-giving to the Spirit, every personal bond which inhibits his fullest self-surrender to it, must go. But the agony of his loss is soon overwhelmed by the joy of his gain. The sacrifice that is asked from him turns out to be compensated for on a higher level with immensely richer treasure.

This does not mean that he need abandon the lesser loves altogether or crush them completely. It means that he is to give them second place, that they are to be guided and governed by the Soul.

Tests are a necessary part of the spiritual growth of a man. When he can be placed among desirable possessions or foods or women and feel no temptation to reach out for what is not proper or right or intemperate for him, he can be regarded as being master of himself.

He is seeking truth. The opposite of truth is falsehood. Therefore, these forces seek to divert him into thoughts, feelings and deeds which will falsify his quest. Hence the warning given in Plato's precepts to Aristotle, 'Be always on the alert, for malignancy works in manifold disguises.'

There are snares cruelly laid to entrap him, deceptions cunningly fashioned to lead him astray and pitfalls callously dug to destroy him. Nor are these all to be met with in his external fortunes only. They occur inside his own fortress also. His own intellect, his own emotions, his own impulses and his own character may betray him into the hands of these adverse forces. If a disciple falls victim to a temptation, makes a wrong decision, becomes deluded by a false teacher or is misled by a false doctrine, this can happen only if there exists some inner weakness in his character or intelligence which responds to these outer causes. If he may lay blame upon them for the unfortunate result, he must lay much more blame upon himself. The 'dark night of the soul' which may then follow is a warning from his higher self to practise penetrative self-scrutiny, to ferret out this weakness and to set about its gradual elimination.

Thus the aspirant will find himself engaged in a war against evil forces. Their metaphysical existence being granted, their practical helpfulness in discovering and exposing his weaknesses must also be granted. Nevertheless the need to defend himself against them still arises. It is for him to see that he so conducts himself in thought and deed as to frustrate their dangerous machinations. But the first protection against them is, as already mentioned, always to regard the lower ego as his worst enemy. For it is the smug repository of all his failings, weaknesses and wickednesses – the unguarded door through which those who dislike, oppose or hate him may really cause him harm. It is highly important, for this and several other reasons, for every serious student of philosophy to make the sacrifice of the self-love and self-worship which bolster up these weaknesses and which defend them against all accusations. So long as he persists in maintaining an inner acceptance of their right to exist, so long will he be unable to climb out of the pit of darkness where he dwells with the rest of mankind, and also to keep these unseen forces in permanent defeat.

Purity of motive in his dealings with others and loftiness of character in his thoughts of them, are further requisites. These too will protect him from some of the perils to which he is exposed, but not from all.

If the aspirant is to escape from this twilight realm of empty fancies and distorted realities, he must devote himself to purifying the body, emotions and mind, to developing the reason and strengthening the will. This will provide him with the needed means of obliterating vain illusions and correcting disordered perceptions.

Psychic manifestations may be vouchsafed to him, but the question of their degree of authenticity will remain, whether or not he likes to look it in the face. Until he has reached the firm ground of sufficient knowledge, purity, balance and critical judgement, he would be wiser not to seek and pursue such manifestations.

Too many are carried away by a current of sensational psychic messages and experiences that makes its begining nowhere but in the fantasies of their own subconscious mind. Here the imagination is released and left without control, as in the dream-state, so that anything may happen and anyone may be encountered. The wish to be personally honoured by the association and guidance of a famous or exotic Master finds here its imaginative realization. In this way, self-hallucination easily starts to rule their lives.

Those who become preoccupied with such messages, whose belief in them and their importance is unlimited, tend to stray from the real quest – which should be for the Overself alone and not for the occult phenomena incidental to it. If the messages are falsely imagined, they fall into the danger of attributing to a higher being what is actually their own subconscious creation.

He will be brought into brief contact or long association with the persons or ideas, with the examples or atmospheres of other men who may unwittingly be used to bring out more fully the latent or half-expressed traits of his character. According to their own natures, they will either provoke the evil or influence the good to manifest itself. A man, once humble, may begin to become arrogant. Another, once clean-living, may begin to become dissolute.

When the aspirant is about to take a wrong course the result of which will be suffering, he will receive warning either from within by intuition or from without through some other person. In both cases, its source will be his higher self.

Vanity pursues both the fledgling aspirant and the matured profi-cient with its flattering whisper. Even at the threshold of the divinest attainments, there comes the ambition to found a new religion where he will be held in superstitious reverence, start his own sect of easily led followers or acquire an adoring flock of disciples within a school or ashram. Of course, the temptation disguises itself as an act of altruistic service. But such service can safely and rightly begin only when the ego's dominance has utterly and permanently gone and his personal inadequacies have been remedied. A premature yielding to this masked temptation will inevitably bring down the misery of a 'dark night' upon him. Personal ambitions very easily dress themselves in the pea-cock feathers of service to humanity. If he wishes to serve his genera-tion, he must equip and prepare himself for such service, must purify, enlighten and develop his inner being. Only as he becomes strong in himself can he inspire strength in those who come within range of his personal influence. His ego must first become an instrument in its holy hands, a servant of its sacred commands.

There is one special value of these experiences, tests or ordeals which often makes them of front-rank importance. What the disciple cannot achieve through mental self-training, except after several years of time, he may achieve in a few days of reacting in an unwonted but right way to such tests. Because a decision or an action called for may be momentous in its nature and far-reaching in its consequences, if he leaps bravely from a lower to a higher standpoint, from a selfish or desire-filled one to an altruistic or purer one, his spiritual advancement may be tremendously accelerated.

Whatever happens during the quest's long and varied course, it is always required of the aspirant that he should never abandon faith in the divine power. It has brought men out of the gravest danger to perfect safety, out of hopeless situations to happier ones, out of dis-heartening stagnation to encouraging advancement. Setbacks will occur. They may weaken his efforts to find reality, but he should never let them weaken his faith in reality. During the tremendous and sometimes terrible vicissitudes of the years devoted to the mystical researches, what will sustain him throughout and, in the end, probably save him from utter destruction will be faith and hope. Yet a faith that is unchecked and uncritical, a hope that is vain and deceptive can just as easily lead him straight into the dark fate. No! It is a faith in the Spirit rather than in men, a hope that places its value above all else, which will prove so effectual. He must hold its realization ever before him as a master aim to be patiently and perseveringly sought.

There cannot be an effective substitute for keenness of discernment. As he advances in the quest, he will need to develop the capacity to discern friends from foes, to peer under masks and to strip events of their appearances; otherwise, he will be entrapped, waylaid or ambushed by evil forces whose pernicious business is often to disguise their maleficent operations under virtuous masks. Consequently it must be part of his business to be on his guard to penetrate behind their appearances. If it is the task of these forces to seduce him from the straight and narrow path, it is his task to discern their hand behind each attempt and to resist it. If he is to overcome them, it will not be enough to depend on his self-criticism, sincerity and prayers, his nobility and goodness. He needs to be informed about the existence of these forces, the signs whereby they may be recognized, the subtlety of their operations, the deceitfulness of their character and the way they attack and lay ambushes. It is not only faith and hope which sustain him during these hard trials, but also intelligence and will, shrewdness, critical judgment, reasoning power and prudence in dealing with these probationary tests and evil oppositions.

When Jesus said, 'Except ye become a little child, ye shall not enter the kingdom of heaven,' he did not invite his hearers to become childish, foolish or fanciful. Indeed, a warning is needful here. The mystic who forgets the complementary warning, 'Be ye as shrewd as serpents,' and who persists in misinterpreting Jesus' words as being an instruction to become irresponsible, gullible and utterly uncritical, who believes that such qualities can bring a man nearer to divine wisdom is welcome to do so. His very belief unfits him to grasp the truth about the matter. But those who can fathom the philosophic meaning of the quotation, know it to be an utterance of the highest importance. The student of philosophy who has trained himself to look beneath the surface of things and to understand words with his head as well as his heart, regards it as being significant on three levels. First it is an invitation to note that, just as a child surrenders its own self-reliance to what it regards as a higher being – its mother – so should the disciple surrender his egoism to God and adopt that surrendered attitude which is true humility. Second it is a call to seek truth with a fresh mind, an unselfish mood and a freedom from conventional preconceptions. Third it is a warning that the natural goodness and purity which make children so contrasting to adults, must be attained before the mystical consciousness can be attained. There is abundant evidence to corroborate this interpretation of Jesus' saying.

14
What Can we Do for Philosophy?

We are told from time to time about men changing their religion or passing from one psychical outlook to another. We hear also of those who change a particular sectarian belief for a different one or of those who go over from one religious fold to another. It is easy to understand that this is sure to happen in time, because most people and especially most women tend to be swept away by the popularity of an organization or institution, the glamour of a romantic personality and the forcefulness of their own emotion. Hence they usually enter and stay within the religious or religio-mystical folds alone. Let us rejoice thereat, for this evidences that religion or mysticism is indeed amply nourishing them.

But life's upward movement does not and cannot stop there. One day it will also have to show some of the intellectual loftiness, the impersonal grandeur and compassionate altruism of the philosophic goal. And although this higher path includes emotion it does not depend solely on it. Emotion is fickle and naturally sways over to whatever happens to please it at a particular time. When the belief gradually shows up its deficiencies and the fold betrays its defects, the followers become ripe for change. But if they misplaced their faith once, they may misplace it twice and even thrice. If they yesterday think something to be true which today they think to be false, where is the certitude that tomorrow they will not again reject this also and have a fresh idea of what is true? And if they can bring themselves to remember the strength with which they held those views which are now just as strongly rejected, how can they continue to trust their own judgement?

Time and experience may bring doubts and misgivings of this character to the mystically minded, but they can never bring them to the philosophically minded. For it is part of the duty of a philosophic student to apply internal and external tests to his ideas. He must not only know that a thing is true but also know that the basis of his own knowledge is sound and irrefutable. Hence, the impression which philosophic truth makes on those who have comprehended it is so deep that it cannot be other than an enduring one, whereas the impression which any religious organization or mystical belief makes on the emotions of those who are attracted to it may fade and pass altogether when a different organization or another belief rises and supplants it.

Philosophy is not a different conception of life facing and opposing other conceptions. It is too wide and too deep for that. None of the existing labels really suit it, none of the ready-made classifications really fit. The intellectual or the mystic, the devotee or the doer who is exclusively absorbed in his own special path of life, permitting only those faculties which are engaged in it to function and repressing the others, is defective and inadequate as a truthseeker and consequently can obtain only defective and inadequate results. Philosophy alone avoids such one-sidedness and achieves the greatest and finest results. It cannot, by its very nature, reduce itself to party rivalry with any other teaching or worship. Its inmost heart is too loving, its practical attitude too generous and its intellectual understanding too great for that to happen. Whereas each organization, group or sect closes the door of heaven to every other one, philosophy leaves it open to all.

If we contrast the nature of true philosophy with the character of present-day mankind, we shall realize that the path of propagandizing is not the right one for us. We may drag the horse to the trough but we cannot make it drink what it regards as unpalatable. It is natural and inevitable that those who have an imperfect intelligence, impure intuition, faulty character and selfish limitations should possess a world view that is itself imperfect, faulty and limited. Therefore the philosophic world-view, being the outcome of a deliberate discipline of thought, feeling and action, refuses to oppose itself to any of the others – just as the philosopher himself refrains from interfering with the spiritual path of the unripe. The portal of religion is open to all men irrespective of their qualifications, whereas the portal of philosophy is open only to those who possess a certain required degree of qualification. Anyone can become an accepted member of a religious body, whatever kind of character or intelligence, desires or aspirations he possesses; but there exists no philosophical body to admit him into its ranks. Anyone afflicted with the wildest hysteria, the most unbalanced neuroticism, can join a conventional church or even a mystical society; but such a person could not obtain acceptance by a philosophic teacher before he sufficiently restores his balance. Before philosophy can serve him fruitfully, he must bring his whole psyche into a healthier balance or at least stop his emotions from running wild, his egotism from being dominant. He should not ask for spiritual illumination when his real need is for psychological treatment.

The aspirant to philosophy first has to fit himself with the needful qualifications. It is he who has to refine and elevate his character, cultivate his intuitions and conduct himself in a worthy manner. It is he who has to learn to study and think for himself. Thus, nobody is deliberately shut out from entry into philosophy. Let him gain the requisite qualifications and he will soon find himself inside; but because few are willing to pay this price, most people are to be found limited to the merely religious point of view and ignorant of the philosophical one. Hence nobody can convert anybody else to philosophy any more than he can convert a child into an adult overnight. Everybody must grow into it of his own accord, by the growth of his own character into readiness for it, by his own experience of life and practice of intuitive reflection.

Although so few are consciously seeking philosophic truth, the sage is not dissatisfied with the fact. He knows it cannot be otherwise. He knows that the uncomprehending dullness of the unevolved will give way only with the lapse of centuries, but it will surely give way to the unfoldment of the higher possibilities which even now lie latent in the multitude. Those who have had an opportunity to acquire the teachings of philosophy have had good fortune. But if they reject it because they are not ready, no blame can be attached to them.

It is a great fallacy, prevalent in religious and religio-mystical circles, to believe that men may change their characters overnight by some miracle-working spiritual means. What really happens in such cases is that a temporary vein of evil tendencies runs out and exhausts itself abruptly at the same time that a more durable vein of good ones shows itself. The belief that people can be changed overnight in moral character, motives, goals and habits is naive. The fact is, they will embrace any -ism which appeals to their psychological make-up and temperament and their intellectual level, and which offers a medium for bringing about the change. But if they are not ready, then the so-called change will be on or near the surface, not really deep. It will be merely emotionalist and subject to a counter-change as soon as a new wave of opposing emotion sets in. The philosophic way also seeks to change men. But it sets up such an aim as an ultimate, not an immediate goal. For it guides itself by knowledge and wisdom; it walks by sight rather than by wishful thinking. Hence it is satisfied to do whatever it can to help men seek their higher selves, to gain a better understanding of the same and to aspire towards nobler characters than their present ones.

If all this is grasped, it will then be easy to grasp why ordinary religionists and mystical cultists eagerly set out to make converts whereas philosophy quietly sets out only to make its knowledge available to those who have become ripened to appreciate it – which are two entirely different activities. Philosophy recognizes the inexorable fact that men can be saved only individually, one by one, man by man. It has never expected many votaries. How could this be otherwise, when it expects so much of a man before it will accept him? For it expects humility, the consciousness of his own ignorance; repentance, the consciousness of his own sinfulness; deep aspiration, the consciousness of his duty to attain the highest standards; hard intellectual work; constant meditation; and rigid moral conduct. Because philosophy offers what is more precious still, it demands a higher price from us. Even though World War II awakened many sleeping minds, it would still be foolish to expect a whirlwind growth of genuine interest in the quest of ultimate truth. A quantitative development is always possible, given some sensational and catchy turn of events; but as philosophic students we know that only a qualitative development is worthwhile, because it alone is deep enough to affect men's lives.

We must practise a wise reserve in such matters as the advocacy of truth, the conversion of foolish ignorant men into wise ones and the spreading of these glorious truths in an inglorious world. We may be tempted, by the deplorable failure of religion in so many countries today to control the ethical conduct of mankind, to offer our philosophy as a universal panacea which will succeed in restoring everyone to ethical good health; we may like to play with utopian dreams of bringing heaven to earth overnight; we may even hope that the human race, more literate and better educated than ever before in its history, will rise eagerly to the offer of philosophy and accept it as the only faith fit for the twentieth century.

But to entertain such optimistic hopes is merely to deceive ourselves, and to act upon them is to invite failure. Philosophy demands keen, subtle intellectual acumen quite above the average even before its outlines can be understood, and mankind has an immense distance to travel before such full growth of intelligence is discernible. It requires a determined pursuit of truth *for its own sake*, which is little evidenced anywhere today. It makes no such blatant appeal as those religious and mystical systems which seek to bribe people with offers of emotional satisfaction for material gain. It is therefore and must remain a teaching for the few, not for the masses. Dreams of suddenly changing the social and economic structure of the world to a moral basis are faced with the unpalatable fact that human character cannot change *en masse* so suddenly and that until it is so changed all systems must inevitably be defective and unsatisfactory.

It is the teaching of philosophy that men are not to blame for rejecting it. A shallow mind, a weakened will and a pampered body cannot let them do otherwise. Therefore, it desires to leave every man free to choose his own concept of truth; to interfere with him by any attempt at proselytization would be to interfere with his real progress. If later through the test of riper experience he discovers that his concept is unsuited to him or is a false one, the accompanying disappointment will enable him to finish with it once and for all and set him free to search elsewhere. Our duty is to make our knowledge available to him so that he need not grope or hunger one unnecessary day once the critical moment arrives when he is mature enough to perceive that here indeed is his bread of life.

These facts being comprehended, the futility of seeking a widespread reception of these ideas will also be comprehended. There is no need for dejection because we have perforce to walk alone or almost alone, however. Does this mean that we are to do nothing at all? No, it does not. We still have a duty. What is possible and practicable, is gradual improvement. Competence must precede conversion and education must walk in front of propagation – in this field no other way is open. That is to say, we must train teachers in each of the populated continents of the world. We must use the printed word and make this knowledge available in the form of periodical publications which will gradually educate their readers. We must have a centre of instruction by correspondence in each of these continents, too. We may even have to use the radio for simple and elementary talks on our teaching – but here we shall have to be most careful to keep out the propagandist note and to retain the educative one. The best way to preach your doctrines – meaning the most effective and lasting way – is first, to promote your own virtues and second, to increase your own direct knowledge. Personal example and private teaching will be more effective in the end than aggressive public progaganda. Men are still like sheep and walk obediently after the leader. It is our grand privilege as pioneers to hold tomorrow's ideas today. These teachings have appeared in the world in their present form and at the present time because they correspond to the genuine need of a portion of humanity. They have appeared because certain seekers of the West must now enter on a new phase in their evolution. Philosophy's objective will be to give such guidance on vital subjects as can be obtained nowhere else. It is not that the religious or mystical are asked to become philosophical, but that the potentially or actually philo- sophical should not limit themselves to religion or mysticism. Hence although philosophy is utterly uninterested in converting anybody, it is conscientiously interested in stimulating those whose moral outlook, mystical intuition and mental capacity could be put on a wider stretch without much difficulty. Only it does so quietly and unobtrusively.

Both novice and sage may present the same truths to a man with the intention of helping him. But whereas the first will be emotionally eager to convert the other's mind to acceptance, the second will be calmly indifferent to the result. And whereas the novice will betray all his eager missionary fervour, the sage will not. He serves the gospel with a manner that is so quiet and restrained, so hidden and subdued, that only those who are ripe for its influence will be able to detect it. His effort will be primarily to expound the truth rather than to dis- seminate it. For his attitude is that of Confucius, who confessed: 'I do not expound my teaching to any who are not eager to learn it.' He knows that propagation should be done with wisdom. For some it should not be obvious, almost undetectable even; for others it may be very open and frank. He considers well beforehand his own position and capacity, as well as those of the people he wishes to influence, and then does only what the circumstances call for and permit. Loud and ostentatious propaganda is not for him. Silent and unobtrusive education is. He follows the wisest course in spreading such abstruse ideas and works intensively, not extensively, deeply amongst the few who are loyally 'truth's own' and not superficially amongst the many who are lukewarmly here today, gone tomorrow. His students live their own autonomous lives. They arise spontaneously, and come to him or his writings out of their own desperate need for inner guidance. Thus their energies are channelled into purely spiritual lines instead of being wasted in merely physical ones. He will indirectly impart this knowledge through writings to some and directly coach others to carry on the work after he has gone. If he can create a loose, scattered and unorganized group of individual students separated and spread out far and wide, in whom the finest ethical values, the loftiest intellectual standard and the soundest mystical experiences will live on after he has vanished from the scene, even if each of its members strives and works in isolation, he will have done no less in the end for humanity than if he created a formal organization. And to the eyes of those who can look on life from the inside, he may have done more.

If it be true that the world cannot be converted to acceptance of such superior values, such lofty religious, mystical and philosophic principles, and if it be likewise true that the world must be redeemed one day, what is to be the duty in the matter of those students who are the present-day bearers of these principles and values? Are they to stand helplessly by and let the impetus of evolution do everything? Or are they to propagate their ideas frantically and everywhere? The truth is that to indulge in over-pessimism is as fallacious as to indulge in over-optimism. They are to accept neither of these alternatives. They will rise to the level of their obligation by making a gesture towards their fellow men which will not only combine what is best in both but also reject what is foolish in both. And this is to make available to mankind those ideas which have helped them, to let it be widely but quietly known that they do exist, to live faithfully up to them in actual practice so as to exemplify them as best they can, remembering that people will discover in their personal conduct the best account of their beliefs and the best echo of their knowledge.

This done, it should be left entirely to others whether or not they wish to accept. Students are not to waste their lives in forcing unpalatable food into the unwilling mouths of millions who are content merely to exist in mental apathy and emotional indifference, bereft of an inner life. Nevertheless, the opportunity to get this food must be presented, and in that our compassionate duty consists. It is true that truth needs no boosting. It can live on its own worth. Nevertheless, the fact of its existence needs to be made known. It needs its John-the-Baptists, for it sits remote and apart, silent and voiceless. It is not enough that the world sufferings have awakened the minds of many people and that the war, which has badly shaken men's feelings, has also quickly sharpened their wits. This awakening must also be directed into proper channels. Admittedly the higher teaching is, in its philosophic fullness, above the heads of the masses in their present state of evolution, although in the remote future it will certainly percolate through into their understanding. Most people are disinclined to struggle with doctrines that claim to give an insight into the mysteries of man, God and nature if these are too profound. But it is not above the heads of the intelligent or intuitive few among them, whilst its religious portion is well within the intellectual grasp of all and its mystical portion within the grasp of most.

There is a new hope. In the past, philosophy could not directly reach the popular mind. Popular unpreparedness blocked the way. But today there has been such a development that some of it can directly filter down to the people. The unrelenting pressure of this crisis and the harrowing distress of recent war have abruptly aroused a number of people from their spiritual sleep. Mysticism, which they had – in common with most moderns – ignored as an empty abstraction, began to acquire vivid meaning and to assume personal reference. They started to take an interest in it, to seek information and to read books about it, to ask questions of or to discuss it with their friends. Mystical truths and practices have certainly carried some serenity to where it was most needed – to lands and homes which have endured the noise and tumult, the horrors and fears of scientifically waged war. There is now something which did not exist in pre-war days, an entirely new public for these teachings drawn from classes which have been brought by wartime experience into the ranks of seekers.

Under normal conditions, philosophic truth should be administered to a sick world in small doses, if on the one hand the patient is to be persuaded to swallow it and if on the other it is to be administered successfully at all. But today we are living under very abnormal conditions. If it was sinful to disclose the philosophic teaching in former times to the simple, illiterate masses and thus break their faith in the only spiritual standby they could comprehend, it is equally sinful not to disclose it today, when inherent sufferings and democratic educational developments have rendered them ripe for its consolation and instruction. Consequently the moment has come when it is the sacred duty of progressed students to disclose cautiously what will help their fellow men in the present crisis and to quietly, unostentatiously, make these teachings available to all seekers; for the past eras of secrecy have served their purpose and come to an end. They need not expect to enlighten all mankind and would be mad to do so. But they may reasonably expect to enlighten a small nucleus around which the future will form steadily expanding accumulations under evolutionary pressure.

Those students who are alive in these dramatic epoch-making times should know better than to regard the fact as accidental. Karma has put them on this planet, which means that the superior wisdom of their own Overself has put them here precisely at the present moment because it is charged with tremendous significance. That these nobler religious, mystical and philosophic ideas will inevitably and eventually assert themselves sufficiently to influence the further course of mankind's mental history, is certain. Anything they can do within their different capacities and varying opportunities to accelerate such a process, it is their sacred duty to do.

Peace to all who read these lines!